CRIMINAL EVIDENCE
AND PROCEDURE

An Introduction

THIRD EDITION

For Susan

CRIMINAL EVIDENCE AND PROCEDURE

An Introduction

THIRD EDITION

Alastair N Brown PhD
Advocate

Avizandum Publishing Ltd
Edinburgh
2010

Published by
Avizandum Publishing Ltd
25 Candlemaker Row
Edinburgh EH1 2QG

First published 1996
2nd edition 2002
3rd edition 2010

© Alastair N Brown 2010

ISBN 978-1-904968-32-0

British Library Cataloguing in Publication Data
A catalogue entry for this book is available from the British Library

Typeset by Waverley Typesetters, Warham, Norfolk
Printed and bound by Bell & Bain Ltd, Glasgow

Preface

When this book was first published, in 1996, it was intended as an introductory account for those coming new to the subjects of criminal evidence and criminal procedure, which, between them, provide the framework within which criminal courts conduct their business and take their decisions. It turned out also to be helpful to established practitioners who were interested in a practical and useable account of the essentials of the subject. With the encouragement of Margaret Cherry of Avizandum Publishing Ltd, I have tried to strengthen that dimension of the book for this edition. The aim is to provide both a readable way into the subject for those who have not previously studied it, and also to provide what the Scots Law Times reviewer of the first edition called a *vade mecum* for practitioners. This book is not, however, intended to be a comprehensive reference account of the law of criminal evidence and procedure. That already exists elsewhere; but common things occur commonly and 30 years in the criminal courts seems like a reasonable perspective from which to spot them. I hope that the book will provide at least a starting-point for most issues that arise in criminal practice.

There is a substantial degree of interpenetration between evidence and procedure. Not only can procedural irregularities have a profound effect upon the admissibility of evidence but many questions relating to evidence also have consequences for the procedure which is followed. Accordingly, so far as possible, this book sets out to describe evidence and procedure in an integrated way, rather than making the more conventional separation between them.

The law of procedure is considered in the general order in which steps occur in prosecutions. Solemn and summary procedure are dealt with together, so far as possible, since the same principles underlie both and they share many common rules. Where the two must be treated separately, solemn procedure is taken first, following the pattern of the Criminal Procedure (Scotland) Act 1995. Matters of evidence are dealt with as they become relevant to the topics considered. As a result many rules of evidence are considered primarily in the context of solemn procedure. This is because, although summary cases account for the great majority of criminal cases in terms of numbers, aspects of the law of evidence are in fact easier to understand if the perceived needs of jury trial are kept in mind.

The Criminal Procedure (Scotland) Act 1995 is the single most important source for the law of criminal evidence and procedure and a thorough familiarity with that Act is essential. It consolidated the law, and the drafting intention was to provide in it everything necessary for day-to-day work in the criminal courts. More recent criminal procedure legislation has tended to operate by making insertions into that Act. Accordingly, although at about the same time Parliament passed a number of other Acts which have a bearing on criminal practice, in this book the expression "the 1995 Act" refers exclusively to the Criminal Procedure

(Scotland) Act 1995. Other Acts are given their full titles. Moreover, any reference to a section number without an accompanying reference to a particular Act is a reference to the 1995 Act. It must be emphasised, however, that the book does not purport to be a commentary on the 1995 Act as such. The Act is not in itself a fully comprehensive code of criminal evidence and procedure and to confine consideration to material dealt with in the Act would be to fail to cover important subject-matter. Not only that, but an attempt at exhaustive consideration of the material would make the book too dense for its purpose and important themes would be submerged in the detail.

It should also be borne in mind that the law develops. Law reform is a constant and continuing activity, and if the textbook writer waited for a lull nothing would ever get published. For example, at the time of writing, the Criminal Justice and Licensing (Scotland) Act 2010, containing important provisions on disclosure, sentencing and Crown appeals (among other things), had just been passed by the Scottish Parliament; Lord Gill's recommendations (in the context of a review of the civil courts) for the creation of the office of District Judge and of a Sheriff Appeal Court, both to deal with summary criminal business, were under consideration; and Sheriff Principal Bowen was leading a review of sheriff and jury procedure. So far as possible, the likely results of such developments are taken into account in the text; but the prudent reader of this or any other textbook will note the date at which the law is stated and make his or her own enquiries about more recent developments.

In this book, the law is stated as at 1 November 2010 but on the assumption that the provisions of the Criminal Justice and Licensing (Scotland) Act 2010 will be brought into force by, or shortly after, publication.

ALASTAIR N BROWN
Edinburgh
November 2010

Contents

Table of Statutes

Table of Orders, Rules and Regulations

Table of International Materials

Table of Cases

1 Absolute Basics

THE COURTS

There are three levels of criminal court in Scotland. The High Court of Justiciary is the most senior of these. The High Court sits as a trial court, where it is made up of one judge and a jury of 15. The High Court also sits as an appeal court. In this book, the expression "the High Court" is used to refer to that court sitting as a trial court. The expression "the Appeal Court" is used to refer to a bench of two or more High Court judges sitting to hear criminal appeals.

The intermediate level court is the sheriff court. At trial, it may consist of a sheriff sitting with a jury of 15 (under "solemn procedure") or sitting alone (under "summary procedure"). The Scottish Civil Courts Review 2009 has recommended the creation of the office of district judge, to sit in the sheriff court and deal with summary criminal cases (as well as low value civil claims). That Review has also recommended that a Sheriff Appeal Court should be established to hear appeals including appeals from summary criminal cases. At the time of writing, no decision had been taken about whether those recommendations were to be implemented.

The lowest level of court is the JP court. This level of court was introduced by the Criminal Proceedings etc Reform (Scotland) Act 2007, as a replacement for the former district courts. The JP court consists of one or more lay people sitting with advice from a legal assessor. JPs are appointed for a period of five years at a time. Alternatively, a person who has been a solicitor or an advocate for at least five years may be appointed as a stipendiary magistrate and a person so appointed may exercise judicial functions in the same manner as a JP. At the time of writing, there were stipendiary magistrates in Glasgow but nowhere else.

THE PARTIES

For practical purposes, all prosecutions in Scottish courts are public prosecutions conducted in the name of the Lord Advocate (referred to in indictments as "Her Majesty's Advocate", which is abbreviated to either "HM Advocate" or "HMA") or in that of a procurator fiscal. The prosecutor is usually referred to as "the Crown". The accused person is referred to as "the accused" or, strictly, once a jury has been selected, as "the pannel". A person who says that he or she has been the victim of a crime is referred to as "the complainer".

FINDING THE LAW

The Criminal Procedure (Scotland) Act 1995

As indicated in the Preface, the 1995 Act is, by a large measure, the single most important source for the law of criminal evidence and procedure. Going into court without immediate access to a copy of the 1995 Act is courting trouble. Going into court with an out-of-date copy is almost as bad. The 1995 Act has been amended repeatedly, sometimes by substitution and often by inserting additional material. This led the Scottish Law Commission, in a report published in 2004, to observe that "[s]ince the time of its enactment the Criminal Procedure (Scotland) Act 1995 ... has been the subject of numerous amendments. As a consequence the Act has become cumbersome in form and difficult to use".[1] Unfortunately, the Scottish Parliament continues to make amendments of that sort and that makes it all too easy to overlook a provision and even easier to overlook an amendment. For example, between the original ss 271 and 272, one now finds ss 271A through the alphabet to 271M. (The additional subsections were inserted by the Vulnerable Witnesses (Scotland) Act 2004 and we shall deal with them below.) Ironically, precisely the same method has been used to implement the recommendations made by the Commission in the Report which contained the observation quoted.

The Act as amended up to date is available in published, hard-copy format and, on certain subscription websites, electronically. In due course, the up-to-date text of the Act should be available, free of charge, online at the UK Statute Law Database[2] but at the time of writing the version available there was three years out of date.

The "nuts and bolts" of procedure are set out in the Act of Adjournal (Criminal Procedure Rules) 1996.[3] The Rules are subject to amendment and updating from time to time. They make detailed provision for the manner in which various notices have to be given, what must be in various applications, procedural forms and so forth. The content of those Rules is too detailed for this basic text; but the practitioner cannot afford to ignore them in his or her day-to-day work. The other material which must be kept in mind (some of which is dealt with in the book) is the series of practice notes issued by Lords Justice-General about the way in which court business is to be conducted. In general, there is a high level of procedural co-operation between parties in the criminal courts and, indeed, one of the themes of the practice notes is that the court will expect that level of co-operation. Ultimately, however, those practice notes impose responsibilities on agents, counsel and procurators fiscal and from time to time a practitioner is required to explain publicly why he or she has failed to meet the standards expected. The experience is an uncomfortable one and best avoided.

The Justiciary Appeal Court

As we shall see below, criminal appeals are dealt with by a bench of two or more judges of the High Court of Justiciary. Their decisions are published in paper form in Justiciary Cases (in the Session Cases volumes), Scottish Criminal Case

---

1 *Report on Insanity and Diminished Responsibility* (Scot Law Com No 195) para 14.
2 www.statutelaw.gov.uk. This website is being decommissioned and will be replaced by www. legislation.gov.uk.
3 SI 1996/513 (S 47).

Reports ("SCCR"), Scots Law Times and online at the Scottish Courts website,[4] where there is a searchable judgments database. That database also includes decisions of single judges of the High Court and these may also be helpful. Cases on that website which have not, or not yet, been published in printed form are given the "neutral citation" which appears on the first page (for example, "[2009] HCJAC 5").

The Supreme Court

With effect from October 2009, the Supreme Court, in succession to the Judicial Committee of the Privy Council, considers and decides some devolution issues from the Scottish criminal courts. The significance of this is explained below. As well as being published in the same reports series as decisions of the Justiciary Appeal Court, Supreme Court cases are available online[5] and they also have neutral citations (for example, "[2009] UKSC 11"). Privy Council cases remain available online,[6] and, like the decisions of other courts, they too have neutral citations (for example, "[2008] UKPC 46").

The European Court of Human Rights

The guarantees accepted by the UK in terms of the European Convention on Human Rights and the decisions of the European Court of Human Rights can be important in understanding criminal evidence and procedure law. The Convention is available at the Council of Europe website[7] and the case law of the court is available in printed form in the European Human Rights Reports ("EHRR") and through the court's website,[8] where it is best referred to by the case name, application number and date of decision (for example, *Dickson v The United Kingdom*, 44362/04, 4 December 2007).

TYPES OF PROCEDURE

The first thing which has to be understood about criminal procedure is the division of cases between those dealt with under solemn procedure and those dealt with under summary procedure. Solemn procedure is the procedure under which serious cases are dealt with, whilst summary procedure relates to less serious cases. At trial, solemn procedure involves a jury and summary procedure does not. The best explanation is probably that provided by Trotter, writing in 1936:

> "Criminal jurisdiction is exercised by summary procedure when the trial takes place before a judge or judges alone, without a jury, by summary and expeditious process, and without all the formalities and solemnities requisite in solemn procedure. Hence the term 'summary' procedure."[9]

---

4 www.scotcourts.gov.uk.
5 http://www.supremecourt.gov.uk/decided-cases/index.html.
6 http://www.privy-council.org.uk/output/Page31.asp.
7 http://conventions.coe.int/Treaty/en/Treaties/Html/005.htm.
8 www.echr.coe.int.
9 T Trotter, *Summary Criminal Jurisdiction According to the Law of Scotland* (1936) p 3.

The High Court of Justiciary (as a trial court) exercises jurisdiction under solemn procedure only; the sheriff court exercises jurisdiction under both solemn and summary procedure; and the JP court exercises jurisdiction under summary procedure only. The High Court of Justiciary also exercises an appellate jurisdiction and, since the Sheriff Appeal Court is as yet no more than a recommendation, the High Court is at present the only appeal court for Scottish criminal cases other than those involving devolution issues. In a criminal procedure context, for practical purposes, devolution issues are questions, in terms of s 57 of and Schedule 6 to the Scotland Act 1998, whether the acts of the Lord Advocate are compatible with the Convention rights (that is the rights set out in Schedule 1 to the Human Rights Act 1998) or Community law (that is, EC law). In some circumstances, devolution issues go on appeal to the Supreme Court (formerly the Judicial Committee of the Privy Council) but the Supreme Court has no jurisdiction in relation to Scottish criminal cases in general.

THE ESSENTIALS OF EVIDENCE

The other foundational material relates to the basic principles of the law of evidence. In his important nineteenth-century work on the subject, Dickson suggested that the purpose of the law of evidence in Scotland is:

> "to exclude valueless and deceptive proofs, to secure regularity in the investigations and to confine within reasonable limits the duration and expense of judicial pro-ceedings".[10]

It is of some assistance in understanding this aspect of the law if these objectives are borne in mind.

Credibility and reliability

The oath which is taken by a jury at the very start of a trial includes the phrase "give a true verdict according to the evidence". Whether the trial is heard by judge and jury or, under summary procedure, by a judge sitting alone, it is upon the evidence that the verdict must be reached and the case decided. The most basic question for whoever is deciding the facts is, therefore, whether they are willing to accept any particular piece of evidence. Two concepts are relevant to that. The first is credibility, which refers to whether the witness who gives the evidence is, on that point, telling the truth. If he or she is not, then, obviously, that piece of evidence, given by that witness, must be rejected. The second is reliability, which refers to the possibility of mistake. A witness might be honest and truthful but simply mistaken about what he or she heard, saw or remembers. If the witness is not reliable on a particular piece of evidence, that piece of evidence, given by that witness, must be rejected.

This must not be taken too far. First, it is possible (though not very common in practice) that another witness will give evidence about the same thing and be both credible and reliable. In that case, the fact can be treated as established on the basis of what is said by the credible and reliable witness. Second, the evidence of a witness does not have to be rejected in whole just because he or she is not credible

---

10 W G Dickson, *A Treatise on the Law of Evidence in Scotland* (1887) preface.

or reliable on one point. The jury or judge can be selective. Parts of what a witness says can be accepted while other parts are rejected. In *Anderson v HM Advocate*,[11] the Appeal Court said:

> "[I]t is well settled that a jury may accept parts of a witness's evidence, and reject other parts. So the fact that the complainer's evidence was in parts contradicted by other witnesses does not mean that her entire testimony must be rejected, even assuming the contrary evidence to have been accepted by the jury. Thus the jury in the present case were entitled to conclude that the complainer was wrong in her evidence about the locus [ie the place of the crime]. The jury may also have rejected the complainer's evidence as to her sobriety at the time, and the circumstances in which her underwear came to be torn. But equally the jury were entitled to accept other parts of the complainer's evidence. For example, the jury were entitled to accept the evidence of the complainer and J (and thus to reject the evidence of Mr and Mrs M) on the question whether there had been any intimate behaviour such as kissing and cuddling between the complainer and the appellant before the intercourse complained of."

Third, the fact that a piece of evidence is rejected does not prove the opposite. If the jury or judge rejects a piece of evidence on the basis of the credibility or reliability of the witness, that piece of evidence should simply be set aside. It drops out of the picture.

Burden of proof

The most fundamental principle in the law of criminal evidence and procedure is that the burden of proof is at all times upon the prosecution. The prosecution is required to prove its case and the accused does not have to prove anything. Accordingly, the prosecution leads its evidence first and if, at the end of the prosecution case, there is insufficient evidence for a conviction, the accused is entitled to be acquitted in terms of the 1995 Act s 97 (solemn procedure) or s 160 (summary procedure). Insufficiency may arise because there was simply never going to be enough evidence for a conviction (in which case the Crown made a mistake when it commenced proceedings); because essential parts of the prosecution evidence have been ruled inadmissible; or because (for one reason or another) Crown witnesses have not given the evidence they were expected to give.

As a result of the principle that the burden of proof is at all times on the prosecution the hope that some investigators and some complainers express, that a case will succeed because "the accused will never be able to explain it at court", is entirely illusory. The accused does not have to explain anything at all, ever, unless the prosecution case is sufficient in itself to justify a conviction. This is the meaning of the presumption of innocence as it has long been recognised and understood in Scots law and as it is now expressed in Article 6.2 of the European Convention on Human Rights ("ECHR"). However guilty the accused may be in fact, he cannot be *found* guilty by a court unless the prosecution provides evidence to prove his guilt; and, of course, he cannot be punished by a criminal court unless he has first been found guilty. As the European Court of Human Rights put it in *Barberà, Messegué and Jabardo v Spain*[12] (speaking of Article 6.2 ECHR):

---

11 2007 SCCR 507 at 517.
12 (1989) 11 EHRR 360.

"Paragraph 2 embodies the principle of the presumption of innocence. It requires, *inter alia*, that when carrying out their duties the members of a court should not start with the preconceived idea that the accused has committed the offence charged, and any doubt should benefit the accused."

What this means is that when the accused is charged with a crime it is up to the prosecution to lead evidence which shows that the accused did in fact commit the crime charged. That evidence has to be led in the course of the trial of the accused. In *Howitt v HM Advocate*[13] it was held that the outcome of an earlier trial against other persons did not establish facts that had any validity outwith the context of that earlier trial. In that case, it was an earlier acquittal with which the court was concerned; but the principle applies equally if the earlier trial ended in a conviction. In *HM Advocate v Duffy*,[14] the Crown tried to prove that property was benefit from crime for the purposes of a money-laundering prosecution by leading evidence that the people from whom the accused got it had convictions recorded against them for misuse of drugs offences. Applying *Howitt*, the court refused to allow that approach. What one jury decided about a fact does not tell a later court, considering a different case, anything at all, even about that same fact.

There comes a point, however, at which the evidence led by the prosecution is sufficiently complete and sufficiently convincing that the accused can expect to be convicted unless he leads evidence which casts doubt on the reliability of the prosecution evidence or on the conclusions to be drawn from it. In that situation it is sometimes said that the "tactical" or "evidential" burden has passed to the accused; but to say that there is such a burden of proof on the accused is simply a way of expressing a judgment about the strength of the prosecution case which has unfolded against him. Accordingly, when it was suggested in *Lambie v HM Advocate*[15] that an accused who wished to invoke the defence of incrimination (that is, to say that the offence was committed by some particular other person) must prove that defence, the Appeal Court said that this approach was incorrect and that all that was necessary for the acquittal of the accused was that the evidence left a reasonable doubt in the minds of the jury.

An example of a case in which such a "tactical" burden did arise is *Milne v Whaley*[16] in which an accused person was acquitted by a sheriff on a charge of driving without either a licence or insurance because there was no corroboration of his admissions. (Corroboration is dealt with at the end of this chapter and, in more detail, in Chapter 9. It is essential to the proof of the overwhelming majority of crimes.) The Appeal Court held that the sheriff's approach had been incorrect, saying:

"[A]ll the Crown has to do is to demonstrate *prima facie* the absence of an entitlement to drive, and the Crown has amply done that in this case by proving the circumstances in which the charge was brought. Thereafter, if an accused person wishes to displace the *prima facie* inference ... it is for him to do so."

The expression "*prima facie*" inference encapsulates the position nicely. Since the position in that case was that Mr Whaley, when stopped by the police and asked

---

13 2000 SLT 449.
14 [2009] HCJAC 5.
15 1973 JC 53.
16 1975 SLT (Notes) 75.

to produce his licence and insurance, replied that he had neither and then gave evidence that he had not had a licence or insurance, he clearly could not meet the tactical burden. But the need to do so would never have arisen if the prosecution had not put before the court evidence sufficient to allow the court to conclude, *prima facie* and in the absence of evidence to displace the inference, that he had committed the offences.

Standard of proof

The standard to which the prosecution case must be proved in Scotland is "beyond reasonable doubt". Precisely what that expression is intended to convey is very difficult to expound, and in *McKenzie v HM Advocate*,[17] Lord Justice-Clerk Thomson counselled against attempts at reformulation. That is all very well but it is unhelpful both to the student and, one may suppose, to juries. What is generally understood is that, before an accused person can be convicted, the evidence must be such as to persuade those who have to decide the facts in the case—the jury, sheriff, stipendiary magistrate or JP—that there is no reason of any substance, no material reason, to doubt his guilt. The standard to be reached is much higher than a mere balance of probabilities (under which it would be enough if the thing sought to be proved were more probably true than not) but certainty is not required. Juries are usually told that a reasonable doubt is not a speculative or fanciful doubt but is the kind of doubt which would cause them to hesitate in some important decision in their own affairs such as a decision to marry, to take a particular job or to move house. In *CWA v HM Advocate*[18] it was held by the Appeal Court that it was incorrect, in a prosecution which depended on the evidence of the complainer and an admission by the accused, for the judge to say to the jury:

> "If you have no reasonable doubt about either of those two sources of evidence, *if you are reasonably sure* about them, then it is open to you to convict" (emphasis added).

The Appeal Court considered that:

> "[T]he use of those words added an unnecessary complication to the straightforward issue that the jury had to decide. To suggest that the idea of being reasonably sure was an alternative way of looking at the question of being satisfied beyond reasonable doubt was not correct."

A reasonable doubt may exist because the evidence is simply not cogent enough to establish the guilt of the accused to the standard required, perhaps because there are gaps in it or perhaps because important parts of it are either not believed or are regarded as unreliable. In this situation, the prosecution has failed to discharge the burden of proof and the accused must be acquitted. Alternatively, if the accused gives evidence himself, or calls witnesses who give evidence, that evidence may be sufficiently credible to create doubt about the prosecution case on one of the essentials of the charge, even though the jury or judge might not be prepared to go as far as to say that they actually believed the defence evidence. Of course, if the defence evidence *is* believed and points to the accused's innocence, that will certainly be an end of the matter.

17 1959 JC 32.
18 2003 SCCR 154.

Admissibility of evidence

It is a serious matter to charge any person with crime, and it was even more serious during the nineteenth century and earlier, when the principles which underpin the law of evidence were being developed. At that time, capital punishment was available for a wide range of offences and the death penalty was imposed with some frequency. It was (and, since miscarriages of justice remain unacceptable, even if reversible, still is) of considerable importance to ensure that the evidence laid before a court, and especially before a jury of lay people, was evidence which was of a sort which can be regarded as trustworthy. The law developed what is called an "exclusory" approach to criminal evidence. What that means is that much of the law about the admissibility of evidence in Scotland consists of a set of rules relating to the exclusion of those types of evidence which are perceived as unfair or not tending to assist a just result. If evidence is excluded as inadmissible, the jury (in a solemn case) will not hear it and that will mean that it does not influence the verdict. If it is a piece of evidence which is essential to the proof of the case, the result of it being excluded as inadmissible will be an insufficiency of evidence and the case will fail without the truth of the allegations ever being considered.

Questions of admissibility will often be cut and dried; but it should also be understood that the courts are likely to have to strike a balance in deciding some questions as to admissibility. The nature of that balance was well expressed by Lord Wheatley in *Milne v Cullen*,[19] where he said:

> "[I]t is the function of the court to seek to provide a proper balance to secure that the rights of individuals are properly preserved, while not hamstringing the police in their investigation of crime with a series of academic vetoes which ignore the realities and practicalities of the situation and discount completely the public interest."

As a result of the principle that the burden of proof is always on the prosecution, the courts will always prefer the interest of the accused if to do otherwise will involve material unfairness.

Sufficiency of evidence

We have already noted that one aspect of the importance of the concept of admissibility is that if pieces ("adminicles") of evidence essential to the proof of the case are held inadmissible the case will fail without the truth of the allegations ever being considered. The importance of the concept of sufficiency is that even if all of the evidence which is admissible is believed, the case will still fail unless there is evidence sufficient in law to entitle the court to consider that the essential allegations have been proved. Fundamentally, this means that there must be corroboration—that is, there must be two sources of evidence to prove every element of the charge which is essential to the definition of the crime. These are called the "facts in issue".

This does *not* mean that corroboration is required for absolutely everything which is narrated in the charge. There is a distinction between those matters which are essential to the constitution of the crime (referred to as *facta probanda*) and those things which are mere narrative (a point made with particular clarity by Lord McCluskey in *Fox v HM Advocate*).[20]

That may be difficult to grasp in the abstract and an example might help. Suppose a man is charged with theft (by shoplifting) of a bottle of whisky. Without going into all the possible qualifications, theft is the appropriation of corporeal moveable property belonging to another person, without consent, where the alleged thief knows that the property belongs to another and where he intends to deprive the owner of it permanently. That means that the Crown has to prove, by corroborated evidence, that (i) the particular person who is accused (ii) took an item (iii) of corporeal moveable property (iv) which belonged to someone else (v) without consent (vi) knowing the item belonged to someone else (vii) and intending never to return it.

The first element—the identification of the accused—is always essential, no matter what the crime. The other elements may look complicated; but, since the law allows inferences to be drawn from the circumstances (as is about to be explained), it is possible to prove a charge of theft by shoplifting on the evidence of two store detectives, who identify the accused and say that they saw him take the bottle from its place on the shelves, hide it in his bag and walk out with it without going to the checkout to pay for it. The accused is identified. He is seen to take a bottle, which is a corporeal moveable, in circumstances in which it plainly belongs to the shop. The store detectives can give evidence that the shop only gives consent to people taking things if they pay for them. By hiding it and walking out without paying, the accused's conduct makes it clear that he knows that the property belongs to someone else and that he intends to keep it.

Corroboration has nothing to do with admissibility of evidence and it is *not* the case that evidence which is not spoken to by two witnesses is not admissible, as is sometimes thought. But essential facts must be proved by two sources of evidence. Accordingly, for example, the identification of the accused as the person who committed the crime is not proved unless there are two separate sources of evidence to demonstrate that it was him. In an assault, the charge cannot be proved unless there are two sources of evidence to show that an attack took place. Other examples could be given very easily and we shall consider the concept of sufficiency in more detail in Chapter 9, in the context of submissions of "no case to answer". The basic principle must, however, be borne in mind as the rest of the book is read.

It is necessary at this point to notice an analytical division of evidence into direct and circumstantial. The terms describe a relationship between evidence and the facts in issue. Direct evidence consists of a witness's testimony as to direct observation of a fact in issue, whereas circumstantial evidence is testimony as to facts from which the fact in issue may be inferred. Circumstantial evidence is indirect evidence of a fact, consisting of something which is at least consistent with the fact to be proved but which might also be consistent with other possibilities. However, such evidence becomes capable of proving the fact in issue when there is an accumulation of such evidence, perhaps (but not necessarily) in combination with direct evidence of the fact in issue, such that, unless one is to resort to speculation or believe that coincidence has been heaped upon coincidence, the combined effect of the evidence is consistent only with the matter to be proved.

20 1998 SCCR 115.

The important point is that both direct and circumstantial evidence are equally valid, at least for purposes of sufficiency of evidence.

There is no limit on the ways in which adminicles of admissible evidence can interact to amount to a sufficiency. In *Howden v HM Advocate*,[21] for example, it was held that an accused charged with two offences, positively identified by several witnesses as the perpetrator of the first crime but only tentatively identified as the perpetrator of the second was properly convicted of the second where circumstantial evidence established beyond reasonable doubt that the same person committed both offences. *Little v HM Advocate*[22] is an example of a murder case proved in part by circumstantial evidence and, in considering the case, the Appeal Court pointed out that the question is not whether each of the several circumstances points by itself towards the fact in issue but whether taken together they are capable of supporting the inference that the fact in issue was so. So, for example, in that case unusual transactions on a building society account were of importance in establishing incitement to murder and were relevant even though they did not bear directly on the facts.

An admission by the accused can provide one source of evidence. Some other source or sources will be required to corroborate the facts admitted. So in *Innes v HM Advocate*,[23] on a charge of theft, the evidence to identify the accused was (i) an admission to a single police officer; (ii) possession of the stolen property, again spoken to by a single witness, not the officer in (i); and (iii) presence at the time of the theft, spoken to by yet another single witness. In upholding the conviction Lord Justice-Clerk Thomson said "[s]o long as there are separate sources, each incriminating the accused person it is unnecessary to have more than one witness to each source". *Heywood v Smith*[24] provides another illustration. In that case the evidence of one police officer who saw the accused swallow an object thought to be drugs combined with a confession to having done so heard by another officer was sufficient to convict the accused of attempting to pervert the course of justice. The argument in that case was about the admissibility of the confession but the point of the argument was to try to reduce the prosecution case to the evidence of a single witness as to seeing the swallowing of the object, which would have been insufficient.

It must be understood that all of this relates to proof by the Crown. In *Robertson v Wilson*[25] Lord Cooper said "it is not essential that the evidence tendered by the [accused] should be independently corroborated", and in *King v Lees*[26] the Crown conceded that a sheriff had been wrong to refuse to give effect to the accused's evidence that his breath alcohol was attributable to drinking after a road accident and not before it (so giving himself a defence to a drink driving charge). The sheriff's reasoning, which was in error, had been that the accused's evidence was uncorroborated.

---

21 1994 SCCR 19.
22 1983 SCCR 56.
23 1955 SLT (Notes) 70.
24 1989 SCCR 391.
25 1949 JC 73.
26 1993 SCCR 28.

2 Jurisdiction

If a crime is not within the jurisdiction of the Scottish courts then it cannot be the subject of a trial in Scotland and Scottish rules of procedure and evidence will not apply to it. The converse—that a crime within the jurisdiction of the Scottish courts will be subject *only* to Scottish rules—does not hold true. For a variety of reasons crimes can sometimes be subject to the jurisdiction of the courts of more than one country. We are concerned here only with whether or not the *Scottish* courts will have jurisdiction. Whether the courts of some other country might also take jurisdiction is, for us, immaterial.

The jurisdiction of the Scottish courts is primarily territorial in its basis. This means that if the crime is committed within the geographical area covered by the court, the court will have jurisdiction to deal with the crime. The key question is what constitutes committing the crime and much will depend on the manner in which the law defines the conduct necessary to constitute the offence. In *Gilchrist v Scott*,[1] for example, the offences related to the "publication" of material. On analysis, "publication" meant printing or distributing. Accordingly, the fact that the newspaper in question was circulated in Paisley did not suffice to give jurisdiction to Paisley Sheriff Court when printing and distribution took place elsewhere.

THE HIGH COURT OF JUSTICIARY

The High Court of Justiciary has jurisdiction as a trial court in respect of crimes committed anywhere in Scotland. The 1995 Act s 3(2) provides that "[a]ny crime or offence which is triable on indictment may be tried by the High Court sitting at any place in Scotland".

Crimes triable on indictment

All crimes may be tried on indictment except those for which an Act of Parliament prescribes prosecution under summary procedure only. The 1995 Act s 292 contains detailed rules for determining when an offence is triable only summarily but in practice such restriction to summary prosecution is usually by implication, where the legislation provides for a penalty only on summary conviction. Many such offences are listed in Schedule 2 to the Criminal Procedure (Consequential Provisions) (Scotland) Act 1995.

---

1 2000 SCCR 28.

Before the jurisdiction of the High Court is excluded in relation to a category of indictable crime that exclusion must be express or necessarily implied. The best authority for this proposition seems to be *McPherson v Boyd*,[2] in which Lord Justice-General Dunedin said:

> "[T]here is an underlying universal jurisdiction in both the Sheriff Court and this Court, and it seems to me, therefore, to be quite settled by long practice that where Parliament is going to give jurisdiction to courts other than the Sheriff Court or the Court of Justiciary it must say so."

The most obvious—and perhaps the only significant current—example of the exclusion of the jurisdiction of the High Court relates to offences which can be prosecuted only under summary procedure, as a necessary consequence of the fact that the High Court sits only under solemn procedure. The exception to this occurs where a summary offence is, in terms of the 1995 Act s 292(6), prosecuted on the same indictment as an offence which can be dealt with under solemn procedure.

"Scotland"

"Scotland" for the purposes of criminal jurisdiction includes the territorial sea, the breadth of which is now 12 nautical miles.[3]

It is, however, not always obvious when a crime has been committed in Scotland. It may be, for example, that a false representation is made by post or telephone from another jurisdiction and takes effect in Scotland in that a person in Scotland is induced to act on that representation. For example, a payment may be sent from Scotland to the other jurisdiction. Alternatively, it may be that the pretence is made from Scotland to another jurisdiction. There are many possible permutations.

The leading case on this sort of situation is *Laird and Goddard v HM Advocate*.[4] That case involved a fraudulent scheme, hatched in Scotland, under which the accused pretended, by telex and telephone from Scotland to a company in England, that they could supply steel of a particular quality. They delivered steel of a different quality and covered up the difference by uttering (that is, passing) forged documents. The delivery and uttering took place in England. Refusing their appeal against conviction, during which it had been argued that the Scottish court had no jurisdiction, Lord Justice-Clerk Wheatley said:

> "[I]t seems to me that where a crime is of such a nature that it has to originate with the forming of a fraudulent plan, and that thereafter various steps have to be taken to bring that fraudulent plan to fruition, if some of these subsequent steps take place in one jurisdiction and some in another, then if the totality of the events in one country plays a material part in the operation and fulfillment of the fraudulent scheme as a whole there should be jurisdiction in that country."

This is, of course, expressed with particular reference to a fraudulent scheme but there seems to be no reason why it should not apply to any criminal scheme. The test would seem to be whether the totality of the events in Scotland plays a material part in the scheme as a whole.

---

2 (1907) 5 Adam 247.
3 Territorial Sea Act 1987 s 1(1)(a).
4 1984 SCCR 469.

Laird and Goddard proceeded under reference to three much older cases. These were *HM Advocate v Bradbury*,[5] *HM Advocate v Allan*[6] and *HM Advocate v Witherington*.[7]

In *Bradbury* the accused wrote letters from England to persons in Scotland. In them he made fraudulent representations and induced the recipients to send goods to him in England. The court took the view that there was jurisdiction because the loss occurred in Scotland. *Allan* concerned an accused who had, from London, placed fraudulent advertisements in Scottish newspapers. Persons in Scotland were induced to send money to London. It was objected that there was no jurisdiction in the Scottish court because the accused's actings were all in London but *Bradbury* was followed and the objection was repelled. Lord Ardmillan said:

> "[i]f a man, for instance, standing in one country shoots a man across the border, thus committing a crime which takes effect in another country, or if he commences a theft or fraud in one country and continues its perpetration into another, *he is amenable in either case to the jurisdiction of the courts of both countries*" (emphasis added).

Witherington was a full bench decision (that is, a decision by a number of judges greater than the quorum for an appeal and therefore particularly authoritative) on similar facts to *Bradbury* in which the Appeal Court confirmed the approach taken in *Bradbury*.

Although *Bradbury*, *Allan* and *Witherington* were not cited in *Clements and Gouner v HM Advocate*,[8] it is possible to discern in that case a similar understanding of the concept of territoriality. The facts were that the two appellants had been charged with, and convicted of, being concerned in the supplying of controlled drugs, which were delivered (by others) from the London area to Edinburgh. The two appellants represented the London end of the operation; neither of them had been in Scotland (at least in connection with the offence) and Gouner did not even know that the drugs were destined for Scotland. It was argued on their behalf that the Scottish courts had no jurisdiction. However, the Appeal Court upheld their convictions. Explaining that decision, Lord Justice-General Hope pointed out that where a criminal enterprise of this sort exists there is an obvious connection between the activities of all of the participants and the point of supply, where the harmful act is to occur. Lord Hope could see no reason why the courts of one part of the United Kingdom should be precluded from exercising jurisdiction in relation to all participants (though he left open the possibility of a different result if international borders were involved). In this he was to some extent influenced by what Lord Griffiths had to say in *Somchai Liangisiriprasert v Government of the United States of America*[9] (a Privy Council case relating to extradition from Hong Kong):

> "Unfortunately in this century crime has ceased to be largely local in origin and effect. Crime is now established on an international scale and the common law must face this new reality. Their Lordships can find nothing in precedent, comity or good sense that should inhibit the common law from regarding as justiciable in England inchoate crimes

5 (1872) 2 Couper 311.
6 (1873) 2 Couper 402.
7 (1881) 8 R(J) 4.
8 1991 SCCR 266.
9 [1991] 1 AC 225.

committed abroad which are intended to result in the commission of criminal offences in England."

Limited exceptions exist to the principle that jurisdiction is territorially based. The main exceptions are set out in the 1995 Act s 11 and the Criminal Law (Consolidation) (Scotland) Act 1995 s 16B. Section 16B of the Criminal Law (Consolidation) (Scotland) Act 1995 gives jurisdiction over certain sexual offences against children, committed outside the United Kingdom by a British citizen or resident, provided that the conduct is also recognised as an offence in the place where it took place. So far as the 1995 Act s 11 is concerned, by subsection (1), any British citizen or British subject who, in a foreign country, commits what would have been murder or culpable homicide had it been committed in Scotland is guilty of that crime in Scotland. Subsection (2) applies only to those British citizens and subjects employed in the service of the Crown. If such a person, in a foreign country, when acting or purporting to act in the course of his employment, does anything which would constitute an offence punishable on indictment had it been done in Scotland, that person is guilty of that crime in Scotland. By subsection (3), persons affected by subsections (1) and (2) can be prosecuted in Scotland. In addition, by subsection (4), a person who has in his possession in Scotland property which he has stolen in another part of the UK or who in Scotland receives property stolen in another part of the UK may be dealt with, indicted, tried and punished as if he had stolen the property in Scotland.

It should be understood that this list of exceptions is not exhaustive and also that there seems to be an increasing readiness on the part of the legislature to take extraterritorial jurisdiction over serious offences.

SHERIFF COURT JURISDICTION

The jurisdiction of the sheriff court is more restricted than that of the High Court.

Offences

The 1995 Act s 3(6) sets out the offences with which the sheriff may deal under solemn procedure:

> "Subject to any express exclusion contained in any enactment, it shall be lawful to indict in the sheriff court all crimes except murder, treason, rape and breach of duty by magistrates."

The effect of this is to restrict to the High Court prosecution of the particular crimes mentioned; but all other indictable offences committed within Scotland may be indicted in the sheriff court. The sheriff court also has the extraterritorial jurisdiction established by the 1995 Act s 11 to the extent that it applies to offences other than those mentioned in s 3(6). However, the sheriff court does not have any other extraterritorial jurisdiction unless it is expressly granted by statute. In *McCarron v HM Advocate*[10] it was held that the Criminal Law (Consolidation)

---

10 2001 SCCR 419.

(Scotland) Act 1995 s 16B only sufficed to give the High Court jurisdiction and did not create a sheriff court jurisdiction.

In relation to summary prosecutions, the 1995 Act s 4(4) gives the sheriff concurrent jurisdiction with all other courts of summary jurisdiction (that is, the JP court) and accordingly any matter which can competently be prosecuted on summary complaint can be so prosecuted in the sheriff court.

Territorial jurisdiction

There are six sheriffdoms in Scotland (Grampian, Highland and Islands; Tayside, Central and Fife; North Strathclyde; Lothian and Borders; Glasgow and Strathkelvin; South Strathclyde, Dumfries and Galloway) and each of these is divided into sheriff court districts. So, for example, in the Sheriffdom of Lothian and Borders there are district sheriff courts at Edinburgh, Livingston, Haddington, Jedburgh, Duns, Peebles and Selkirk.

It is the practice to prosecute crimes within the sheriff court district in which they are committed. The only requirement in law, however, is to try an offence within the sheriffdom in which it is committed. By the 1995 Act s 4(2), where an offence is alleged to have been committed in one district in a sheriffdom it is competent to try that offence in any other district in that sheriffdom. It is suggested that *Laird and Goddard* and the earlier cases which that case followed are good law in relation to the jurisdiction of the sheriff court in cases of crime which involve two (or more) national jurisdictions.

Multiple sheriffdoms

It is suggested that *Laird and Goddard* is also authoritative as between sheriffdoms and this proposition derives support from *Lipsey v Mackintosh*[11] where a letter was sent from one sheriff court district to another and it was held that both sheriff courts had jurisdiction.

Where an offence is committed in a harbour, river, arm of the sea or other water, tidal or otherwise, which runs between or forms the boundary of two or more courts, the 1995 Act s 9(1) permits the offence to be tried by any one of those courts. An offence committed within 500 metres of the boundary of the jurisdiction of two or more courts may be tried by any of those courts in terms of the 1995 Act s 9(2). By the 1995 Act s 9(3), which is expressed in somewhat antiquated language, an offence committed against any person or in respect of any property in or on a carriage, cart, or vehicle employed in a journey by road or railway, or on board any vessel employed in a river, loch, canal or inland navigation, may be tried by any court through whose jurisdiction the journey passes. On the wording of the subsection this will be so even though it may be possible to show that the conveyance concerned was, at the time of the offence, in some district other than that in which the case is prosecuted.

In terms of the 1995 Act s 10, where a person is alleged to have committed crimes within the application of the section in more than one sheriff court district, he may be indicted in respect of all of them in whichever sheriff court district the Lord Advocate selects. The section applies (a) to a crime committed partly in

11 1913 SC(J) 104.

one sheriff court district and partly in another (the most obvious examples of which would be a continuing offence such as reset or the *Lipsey v Mackintosh* type of case); (b) to crimes "connected with each other" (an expression which is undefined) "but committed in different sheriff court districts"; and (c) to crimes committed in different sheriff court districts in succession which, if they had all been committed in a single district could have been tried under one indictment. The precondition that they should all be capable of being tried under a single indictment excludes the operation of the section where one of the offences has already been prosecuted and the accused has been convicted, even if sentence has been deferred and the offence has therefore not been finally disposed of.

An example of the kind of situation contemplated in (c) is to be found in *Mackie v HM Advocate*.[12] The appellant was indicted in Glasgow Sheriff Court in respect not only of offences in Glasgow but also in respect of a charge of theft committed in Edinburgh. No attempt was made to argue that this was incompetent and, standing the terms of the statutory predecessor of s 10, any such argument would have received short shrift. What was argued, however, was that the fact that the prosecutor had deserted (that is, dropped) the "Glasgow" charges against the accused before the jury was empanelled, leaving only the "Edinburgh" charge meant that Glasgow Sheriff Court no longer had jurisdiction. The High Court held on appeal, however, that jurisdiction does not depend on what charges are remitted to the knowledge of the assize (that is, what charges are on the indictment when the jury takes its oath at the start of the trial) but on whether the accused is lawfully indicted to the court. What happens thereafter is irrelevant.

JP COURT JURISDICTION

By the Criminal Proceedings etc Reform (Scotland) Act 2007 s 62, a JP court has territorial jurisdiction in respect of offences committed within the sheriff court district in which it is located, and any other district in the same sheriffdom. It is competent for proceedings for an offence committed in one district in a sheriffdom to be taken in a JP court in any other district in the sheriffdom.

The JP court may, in terms of the 1995 Act s 6(2) be constituted by a stipendiary magistrate (who is legally qualified) or by one or more justices (who need not be so qualified but occasionally are). By the 1995 Act s 7(5) a JP court which is constituted by a stipendiary magistrate has not only the jurisdiction of a JP court but also the full summary criminal jurisdiction and powers of a sheriff. Accordingly, the remainder of what is said here about the jurisdiction of the JP court relates to such courts when constituted by justices.

The 1995 Act s 7(3) provides that the JP court has jurisdiction to try any offence which is triable summarily except in so far as any enactment provides otherwise. Section 7(8) precludes it from dealing with murder, culpable homicide, robbery, rape, wilful fire-raising (or an attempt thereat), theft by housebreaking or housebreaking with intent to steal, offences of dishonesty where the value exceeds level 4 on the standard scale provided for by the 1995 Act s 225 (£2,500 at the time of writing), assault causing the fracture of a limb, assault with intent to ravish,

---

12 1969 JC 20.

assault to the danger of life, assault by stabbing, uttering forgeries or offences under the Acts relating to coinage. The JP court is, however, specifically empowered (by the 1995 Act s 7(4)) to deal with theft, reset, fraud and embezzlement, provided the amount concerned does not exceed level 4.

3 The Prosecution of Crime

The Scottish criminal justice system is an adversarial one, with the initiative being taken by the prosecution. Very considerable reliance is placed on the integrity and judgment of the public prosecutor, especially in the early stages of a prosecution. We must, therefore, understand the prosecution system if we are to understand the criminal justice system as a whole.

The overwhelming majority of prosecutions in Scotland are public prosecutions at the instance of either the Lord Advocate or the procurator fiscal. Cases under solemn procedure are prosecuted in the name of the Lord Advocate and those under summary procedure in the name of the procurator fiscal. By the 1995 Act s 133(5), all summary prosecutions are to be brought at the instance of the procurator fiscal unless statute expressly provides to the contrary.

Although it is possible for an individual who has suffered a personal wrong to apply to the court for authority to institute a prosecution, this procedure (known as a bill for criminal letters) is invoked rarely and hardly ever succeeds. Accordingly, the proportion of Scottish criminal cases which do not involve either the procurator fiscal or the Lord Advocate as prosecutor is so small that, in an introductory text such as this, they can safely be ignored.

THE LORD ADVOCATE

The principal prosecutor in Scotland is the Lord Advocate. He (or she) and the Solicitor General for Scotland are members of the Scottish Government[1] and the Scottish Parliament does not have the legislative competence to remove the Lord Advocate from his or her position as head of the system of criminal prosecution.[2] The Lord Advocate is required to take any decision in that capacity independently of any other person[3] but is disabled from doing any act which is incompatible with the Convention rights or with Community Law.[4]

All indictments run in the name of the Lord Advocate whether they are tried in the High Court of Justiciary or the sheriff court. The only exception to this arises, in terms of the 1995 Act s 287(2), when the Lord Advocate's office is vacant. During such a vacancy, indictments are in the name of the Solicitor General.

The Lord Advocate's office is an ancient one and in 1587 he was empowered by an Act of Parliament to instigate criminal proceedings notwithstanding the wishes of the parties.

---

1 Scotland Act 1998 s 4(1)(c).
2 Scotland Act 1998 s 9(2)(e).
3 Scotland Act 1998 s 8(5).
4 Scotland Act 1998 s 7(2).

ADVOCATE DEPUTES

The Lord Advocate and Solicitor General are assisted in prosecution matters by the advocate deputes, who prosecute cases in the High Court and give instructions on behalf of the Lord Advocate to procurators fiscal in connection with criminal cases. Advocate deputes are either members of the Faculty of Advocates or solicitor advocates with a High Court right of audience and they are drawn from both private practice and the Crown Office and Procurator Fiscal Service. Typically, they serve for a term of three years. The Lord Advocate, Solicitor General and advocate deputes are known collectively as "Crown Counsel".

PROCURATORS FISCAL

Brief history and functions

The procurator fiscal is a civil servant qualified as a solicitor, solicitor advocate or advocate and employed within the Scottish Administration. He or she is:

> "an independent public prosecutor, who receives and considers reports of crimes and offences from the police and over 40 other agencies and decides whether or not to take criminal proceedings in the public interest. He or she investigates the more serious cases and prosecutes all cases in court except the High Court".[5]

The existence of the office of procurator fiscal is recorded from 1584 but it certainly existed even before that.

Originally, the sheriff combined both investigative and judicial functions, much like a continental examining magistrate. The procurator fiscal was originally an agent (procurator) employed by the sheriff to collect fines and pay them into the sheriff's treasury (the "fisc"). However, the sheriff's investigative functions were gradually delegated to the procurator fiscal and his status as public prosecutor in the sheriff court was recognised by the Criminal Procedure Act 1701. His appointment was vested in the Lord Advocate by the Sheriff Courts and Legal Officers (Scotland) Act 1927.

Relationship with police and other investigators

Chief constables, and hence the police as a whole, must, by statute, obey the instructions they receive from the prosecutor in relation to the investigation of crime and cannot at their own hand commence a prosecution. Section 17(3) of the Police (Scotland) Act 1967 provides:

> "in relation to the investigation of offences the chief constable shall comply with such lawful instructions as he may receive from the appropriate prosecutor".

In similar vein, the 1995 Act s 12 provides:

> "The Lord Advocate may, from time to time, issue instructions to a chief constable with regard to the reporting, for consideration of prosecution, of offences alleged to have been committed within the area of such chief constable, and it shall be the duty of a chief constable to whom any such instruction is issued to secure compliance therewith."

5 *Crown Office and Procurator Fiscal Service Annual Report* 1991–92 p 1.

It is rare for these statutory provisions to be invoked explicitly but their existence underlies the whole relationship between Scottish prosecutors and the police.

The responsibility of the police as to reporting to the fiscal was considered in *Smith v HM Advocate*,[6] a murder by stabbing in which the police omitted to tell the fiscal that they had found at the locus not only the murder weapon but also a second knife. They reasoned that the second knife was irrelevant, as indeed it probably was. On appeal Lord Justice-Clerk Thomson had this to say about the duties of the police:

> "[I]t is their duty to put before the Procurator Fiscal everything which may be relevant and material to the issue of whether the suspected party is innocent or guilty ... a cautious officer will remember that he is not the judge of what is relevant and material and will tend to err on the safe side."

There are no equivalent provisions with regard to non-police reporting agencies such as environmental health departments or the Health and Safety Executive. To such agencies, the procurator fiscal can only offer advice. However, bearing in mind that such agencies have no right to initiate criminal proceedings themselves but must depend upon the procurator fiscal to do so, one can usually expect that compliance with such advice will be prudent.

When anyone aged 16 or over is charged by the police, whenever the police have evidence which they think justifies charging a person they cannot find and whenever another investigating agency considers it appropriate to commence a prosecution, a report is submitted to the procurator fiscal. So far as the police are concerned, this follows from the Police (Scotland) Act 1967 s 17(1)(b), which provides:

> "[I]t shall be the duty of the constables of a police force ... (b) where an offence has been committed ... , to take all such lawful measures, and make such reports to the appropriate prosecutor, as may be necessary for the purpose of bringing the offender with all due speed to justice."

So far as other investigating agencies are concerned, the need to report to the procurator fiscal arises from the fact that there is no other way to commence criminal proceedings.

THE DECISION TO PROSECUTE

When the procurator fiscal receives a report of a crime it is his or her duty to consider it and decide whether or not to prosecute. This decision is taken under reference to such guidance and instructions as the Lord Advocate may have given either in general or, through Crown Counsel, in relation to the particular case. The Lord Advocate's general guidance to procurators fiscal is not published and, whilst the effect of particular instructions will become apparent to the accused and his representatives from the course which the prosecution takes, those instructions themselves will be treated as confidential.

The general approach which the procurator fiscal will apply is set out in the *Prosecution Code* which at the time of writing is available at the Crown Office and

6 1952 JC 66.

Procurator Fiscal Service website.[7] The most fundamental assessment which the procurator fiscal will make as part of the decision-making process is whether or not there is sufficient evidence to prove a crime. This need not be the same crime with which the accused has been charged by the police. The procurator fiscal is in no sense bound by the assessment made of the case by the reporting agency. If the procurator fiscal is not satisfied, even after calling for such further information as may be helpful, that there is sufficient evidence to prove a crime, it is improper for him to commence proceedings or take any other steps. His only option is to mark the report "no proceedings".

Once satisfied that there is sufficient evidence to proceed, the procurator fiscal's discretion comes into play. That discretion is considerable. By contrast with certain continental European jurisdictions, he is under no obligation to prosecute in every case in which a crime can be proved. There are alternatives to prosecution. However, his exercise of that discretion is something for which he is answerable only to the Lord Advocate and procurators fiscal generally decline to explain their decisions to anyone else.

Notwithstanding that, procurators fiscal have a discretion to disclose reasons in exceptional cases—for example, the fiscal might consider it appropriate to explain to the complainer in a sexual assault case why a prosecution cannot proceed where there is insufficient evidence.

ALTERNATIVES TO PROSECUTION

No proceedings, warning letters and diversion

In some cases, the fiscal will decide that although there is sufficient evidence to proceed, the case is so trivial that further action is not needed. Such cases are simply marked "no proceedings". In other cases, a warning letter may be sent. Such a letter does not say that the fiscal has decided that the accused is guilty. What it does say is that the person has been reported to the fiscal and that there is enough evidence to proceed, but that the fiscal has decided that court action is not necessary, though if the person is reported again for a similar offence there might well be a prosecution. In other cases, diversion to the social work department or another similar agency might be a constructive way forward. The details of such schemes vary from place to place and from time to time. These are all informal options.

Fixed penalties, compensation offers and work orders

Sections 302 to 303ZB of the 1995 Act make provision for three formal options short of prosecution.

Fixed penalties (or "conditional offers") are dealt with by s 302, which empowers a procurator fiscal, who receives a report that a "relevant offence" (essentially, one which can be tried in the JP court) has been committed, to send the alleged offender a notice giving particulars of the alleged offence and stating the amount of the appropriate fixed penalty for that offence and the arrangements for payment by instalments. The appropriate fixed penalty is selected by the procurator fiscal

---

7 http://www.crownoffice.gov.uk.

from a sliding scale laid down in the Criminal Procedure (Scotland) Act 1995 Fixed Penalty Order 2008,[8] and ranging from £25 to £300. It is up to the alleged offender whether to elect to pay the penalty or not. If he accepts the conditional offer, either by paying the first instalment of the fixed penalty or simply by failing to refuse the offer, he cannot then be prosecuted for the offence but will be liable to pay the full penalty. If the conditional offer is not accepted, the fiscal can (and probably will) commence a prosecution. Acceptance of the offer of a fixed penalty does not constitute a conviction but can be disclosed to the court in any proceedings for an offence committed within the next two years.

Section 302A provides for "compensation offers". The arrangements parallel the fixed penalty arrangements rather closely except that the payments made are transmitted to the complainer. The maximum amount for a compensation offer is £5,000.[9]

By s 302B the procurator fiscal may send to an alleged offender a combined offer of an opportunity to pay a fixed penalty and compensation.

Section 303ZA provides for the procurator fiscal to send the alleged offender the offer of an opportunity to perform between 10 and 50 hours' unpaid work under the supervision of the local authority. The arrangements are, again, modelled on those for fixed penalties.

CHOICE OF PROCEDURE

Once the decision is made that the case should be prosecuted, the procurator fiscal must decide whether the case requires solemn procedure or summary and, if summary, whether the sheriff court or the district court. That decision taken, he will commence proceedings.

THE PROSECUTOR AS "MASTER OF THE INSTANCE"

Throughout the proceedings, until the accused is convicted (or acquitted) the prosecutor is in charge of his own case and not subject to the directions of the court in its handling. So, in *Howdle v Beattie*[10] where a sheriff refused to allow a case to be called in Dumfries Sheriff Court because he thought that it would have been administratively preferable for it to be prosecuted in Kirkcudbright Sheriff Court, it was held that a prosecutor has the right to decide whether a case will call in court on a given day and the sheriff cannot stop him from calling the case. Moreover it was decided in *Strathearn v Sloan*[11] that the prosecutor is not bound to accept a plea of guilty even to the whole indictment or complaint but may insist on proceeding to trial (as might happen if a fundamental disagreement on the circumstances of the offence was anticipated). In *Kirkwood v Coalburn District Co-operative Society*[12] it was held that a prosecutor is not bound to accept a plea to the minor of two alternative charges but is entitled to insist on leading evidence

---

8 SSI 2008/108.
9 Criminal Procedure (Scotland) Act 1995 Compensation Offer (Maximum Amount) Order 2008 (SSI 2008/7).
10 1995 SCCR 349.
11 1937 JC 76.
12 1930 JC 38.

with a view to obtaining a conviction on the major alternative. And, according to *Clark v Donald*,[13] the prosecutor is even entitled to substitute a new complaint for one which was still current.

The limits on the prosecutor's rights as master of the instance were set out in *HM Advocate v O'Neill*[14] in which it was alleged to be oppressive for the Crown to proceed to trial against two accused and then indict the third separately. Lord Justice-General Hope said, in deciding the case:

> "[T]here is no doubt that in the ordinary case the Court will only with the greatest reluctance interfere with the discretion of the Crown. But its power to do so is beyond question, and in all these cases where oppression is alleged, or where it is suggested that there is a material risk of grave prejudice to the accused, the ultimate decision must rest with the Court."

In the *O'Neill* case the court decided that there was no oppression, by contrast with *Normand v McQuillan*[15] in which a sheriff held that where the accused pled not guilty to a summary complaint and was remanded in custody it was oppressive to substitute a petition two weeks later containing no new charges. The petition is the document which commences a prosecution under solemn procedure under which, as we shall see, the period during which the accused can be kept in custody before trial is longer than that under summary procedure. On the other hand, in *HM Advocate v Griffiths*,[16] Temporary Judge C J Macaulay QC held that there was no bar to the Crown substituting an indictment for causing death by dangerous driving for a summary complaint charging careless driving where the initial decision had been reconsidered in the light of CCTV footage of the accident which became available. By contrast with *Normand v McQuillan* (which was not cited or discussed in *Griffiths*), the summary complaint was withdrawn before it called in court and the accused had not spent time remanded in custody.

---

13 1962 JC 1.
14 1992 SCCR 130.
15 1987 SCCR 440 (Sh Ct).
16 [2009] HCJ 1.

4 Investigation of Crime

INTRODUCTION

The first contact which a complainer or alleged offender will have with the criminal justice system will almost certainly be with the police or another investigating agency. In the course of their investigations, such agencies frequently require to use powers granted to them by the law which are not available to private citizens. These include powers of entry to premises, of search and seizure and of detention and arrest. Plainly, such powers require to be regulated, because they affect the liberty of the individual and his or her right to the enjoyment of his property and liberty without undue interference by the state. That regulation is provided in an over-arching way by aspects of the Convention rights (that is, those articles of ECHR which are given effect directly in national law) and otherwise takes the form in part of detailed provision as to the extent of such investigative powers (especially in Part II of the 1995 Act) and in part of a tendency to refuse to admit in evidence material which has been obtained by means which violate those provisions or which are regarded as unfair in the circumstances of the case. Our consideration of investigative functions therefore incorporates elements of both procedure and evidence.

The police have the right to use their powers to investigate any crime. The powers granted to other investigating agencies are so granted only in relation to a limited range of crimes and can only properly be exercised in relation to those crimes. Whatever the basis and extent of the powers which are exercised by particular investigators, the principles which the law will apply to the exercise of those powers are common. Perhaps the most fundamental of these is the principle that, since powers of this sort do tend to infringe the liberty of the subject, they will be construed strictly and powers which Parliament has not given expressly are unlikely to be implied by the courts.

EFFECT OF IRREGULARITY IN INVESTIGATION

It would be a mistake to assume that the fact that an investigator has exceeded his or her powers will automatically mean that the evidence which he or she has obtained thereby will be inadmissible. As we shall see, the courts are prepared, in deciding questions relating to admissibility of evidence, to excuse some excesses of zeal, especially where the investigator has acted in good faith but made an honest mistake. This can be illustrated by contrasting two cases. The first is *Lawrie v Muir*[1] in which a Milk Marketing Board inspector obtained entry to

1 1950 JC 19.

premises by a misrepresentation and the subsequent conviction was quashed. The court pointed out that an irregularity in the method by which evidence has been obtained does not necessarily make that evidence inadmissible and that whether a given irregularity should be excused depends on its nature and the circumstances, an important consideration being fairness to the accused. They declined to make any distinction in this between statute and common law offences. On the facts of *Lawrie v Muir*, the Appeal Court took the view that the use of a positive misrepresentation did not justify excusing the irregularity.

The other case is *Fairley v Fishmongers of London*[2] in which the appellant had been charged with possession of salmon contrary to a particular regulation. Essential evidence was the result of a search by an inspector charged with the enforcement of that regulation, accompanied by an officer charged with the enforcement of other regulations. The inspector had not obtained a warrant (though he could have done). The officer had obtained a warrant, but not under the regulations relating to salmon. It was held, applying *Lawrie v Muir*, that the evidence, although obtained irregularly was admissible. Lord Justice-General Cooper said, in the course of his judgment:

> "I can find nothing to suggest that any departure from the strict procedure was deliberately adopted with a view to securing the admission of evidence obtained by an unfair trick, and in the circumstances of this case the appellant's assumption of the guise of a champion of the liberties of the subject failed to elicit my sympathies."

The correct approach, therefore, is to examine the exercise of a power to see, first, whether it has been exercised in accordance with the law or irregularly and, second, if there has been irregularity, whether that irregularity is one which may be excused or whether it is fatal to the admissibility of the evidence. It is important in this regard to note that, while Convention rights law provides much material which is relevant to the question whether evidence has been obtained regularly or not, it has no automatic consequences for the admissibility of evidence as the European Court of Human Rights made clear in *Khan v United Kingdom*.[3]

In terms of practice, it is worth knowing about *McAnea v HM Advocate*.[4] The appellants had been convicted at the High Court at Edinburgh of various charges of forging and counterfeiting bank notes and other documents. At the trial, the advocate depute had called a scenes-of-crime officer, who gave evidence of having gone to an address in Beith Street in Glasgow for the purpose of taking photographs. At that point there was an objection to the line of evidence on the basis that "the taking of photographs in Beith Street followed an illegal warrant and that all action in respect of Beith Street [was] in fact invalid, including the taking of any photographs there". Counsel went on to explain that the objection did not simply apply to the search warrant for the Beith Street premises but to 14 other warrants. All of the warrants were on a pre-printed form correctly headed "Search Warrant under the Forgery and Counterfeiting Act 1981" but the crave was for a warrant "in terms of the Forgery and Counterfeiting Act 1989, Section 24(1)". The justice of the peace "granted warrant as craved". There is in fact no Forgery and Counterfeiting Act 1989 and so the warrant was granted in terms of a non-existent section of a non-existent Act.

2 1951 JC 14.
3 (2001) 31 EHRR 45.
4 2000 SCCR 779.

The trial judge sustained the objection and the advocate depute asked for an adjournment overnight to consider the position. The following day, he argued that the trial judge had ruled that the search warrants were invalid and that the effect of that was that the productions seized and photographs taken as a result of execution of the search warrants had been irregularly obtained. He then asked the trial judge to exercise his discretion to excuse the irregularities and admit the evidence. After argument and taking time to consider, the trial judge did just that. The issue for the Appeal Court was whether, having sustained the defence objection to the line of evidence, the trial judge could, in the face of defence opposition, subsequently hear further Crown submissions on the admissibility of the evidence and, in the light of those additional submissions, in effect repel the objection and admit the evidence.

The court took the view that it was plain that the trial judge had, in the first debate, not simply decided that the warrants were invalid but also that the line of evidence relating to the searches and related matters was, accordingly, inadmissible. His decision the following day to admit that evidence was therefore a decision to reverse his earlier decision. Neither the Crown nor counsel for the appellants was able to refer to any authority dealing with the competency of a trial judge reversing a ruling on a defence objection to a line of evidence in such circumstances. The court concluded that a decision on a defence objection once formulated and stated in open court is final and cannot be reconsidered. Whilst the court did not hold that the rule thus established by practice may not admit of rare exceptions, it considered that it should not sanction a departure from the rule simply to repair an omission by the prosecutor and on the prosecutor's plea that it is necessary to serve the ends of justice.

REGULATION OF INVESTIGATORY POWERS

Article 8 ECHR insists that there must be no interference with the right to respect for the private and family life, the home and correspondence, except such as is in accordance with the law. In a series of cases[5] the European Court of Human Rights has made it clear that this means that the investigative measures used by the police must, if they interfere with the right protected by Article 8, have a clear basis in domestic law—that is, that there must be law which says that they *can* use the technique. It is not enough that they are not prohibited from using it.

The qualification that this applies only to activities which interfere with the rights protected by Article 8 is important. There is no reasonable expectation of privacy and hence no Article 8 issue in relation to things done in a public place. In *Connor v HM Advocate*[6] objection was taken to the leading of evidence of observations made on the street entrance of the common close in which the appellant lived. That objection failed precisely because those observations could not be described as a breach of the appellant's right to respect for his private and family life and home in terms of Article 8.

In cases in which the Article 8 rights are engaged, the European Court has reasoned that, since the implementation in practice of surveillance measures is not

5 *Malone v United Kingdom* (1984) 7 EHRR 14; *Kruslin v France* (1990) 12 EHRR 528; *Khan v United Kingdom* (2001) 31 EHRR 45.
6 2002 SCCR 423.

open to scrutiny by the individuals concerned or the public at large, it would be contrary to the rule of law for the legal discretion granted to the executive to be expressed in terms of an unfettered power. Consequently, the law must indicate the scope of any such discretion conferred on the competent authorities and the manner of its exercise with sufficient clarity, having regard to the legitimate aim of the measure in question, to give the individual adequate protection against arbitrary interference. So, in *Khan v United Kingdom*, the court found against the UK on the basis that the existence of Home Office Guidelines to govern surveillance did not constitute the necessary "law" for the purposes of Article 8. The court noted that, since such guidelines were neither legally binding nor directly publicly accessible, there was no domestic law regulating the use of covert listening devices at the relevant time and held that the interference could not, therefore, be considered to be "in accordance with law".

This is the issue which the Regulation of Investigatory Powers (Scotland) Act 2000 and the corresponding Regulation of Investigatory Powers Act 2000, passed by the UK Parliament, set out to address.

The heart of the Scottish Act is s 2, which provides that conduct to which the Act applies shall be lawful for all purposes if an authorisation under the Act confers an entitlement to engage in the conduct in question and the conduct is in accordance with the authorisation. This is critical. If what is done is not within the ambit of the authorisation, it will not be rendered lawful by the Act. If it is not rendered lawful by the Act and if there is no other positive rule of law authorising what is done, the evidence obtained will, in terms of *Khan*, be obtained in breach of Article 8 and hence irregularly. The usual rule will then apply—before irregularly obtained evidence can be admitted, the irregularity will have to be excused

The Acts are concerned with covert investigation techniques and seek to ensure that the law clearly covers the purposes for which such techniques may be used, which authorities can use the powers and who should authorise each use of the powers. The Scottish Act applies primarily to the police, though there is an order-making power to extend it to other agencies. It also provides for independent judicial oversight and a means of dealing with complaints and redress for the individual. Covert surveillance is that which is undertaken in a manner calculated to ensure that the person subjected to it is not aware that it is taking place. The Act does not seek to regulate less intrusive forms of surveillance of which the public is in any event generally aware. CCTV in town centres is the most obvious example.

The Acts are concerned with three sorts of surveillance. In practice, they will often overlap. The approach which is taken is to provide for the development of statutory codes of practice (which will be capable of being updated quickly to take account of technological developments) and to put in place a framework of authorisations. This approach reflects the pattern of English legislation such as the Police and Criminal Evidence Act 1984.

The first of the Acts' concerns is "directed surveillance", which is surveillance undertaken in relation to a specific investigation in order to obtain information about a particular person. The second is the use of "covert human intelligence sources". In essence, this unattractive mouthful denotes undercover officers and participating informants. The use of either of these techniques will require authorisation from a police superintendent and will only be available for the purpose of preventing or detecting crime or preventing disorder; in the interests of public safety; or for the purpose of protecting public health. This language clearly reflects aspects of Article 8.2 ECHR. Another possibility under the UK Act, however, is that authorisation may be granted "for any purpose ... which is specified ... by an order made by the Secretary of State".[7] This startlingly wide provision is not, of course, the blank cheque which it at first appears because the legislation will have to be construed so as to be compatible with the Convention rights[8] and Ministers act unlawfully if they do anything which is incompatible with those rights.[9] That means that any Order made would itself have to specify a purpose consistent with Article 8.2. The obvious additional purpose would be the protection of the rights and freedoms of others.

The third sort of surveillance is "intrusive surveillance" which is surveillance carried out into things which are happening on residential premises or in any private vehicle. Authorisation for such surveillance will have to be given by a chief constable and only where necessary for the prevention or detection of serious crime. That authorisation will be subject to review by a surveillance commissioner. Serious crime is defined as that which might reasonably be expected to result in imprisonment of three years or more for a first offence, or which involves the use of violence, or which results in substantial financial gain, or which involves a large number of persons in pursuit of a common purpose. These are, of course, intrinsically subjective judgments but it should not be thought that they are incapable of being reviewed. Article 8.2 ECHR goes on to require that any interference with the rights which Article 8 protects should be "necessary" and that includes the concept of proportionality. Chief constables are public authorities for the purposes of the Human Rights Act 1998, s 6 and, even in a case of serious crime, a chief constable who authorises disproportionate surveillance will act unlawfully.

It is clear from *Klass v Germany*[10] that the rule of law implies, *inter alia*, that an interference by the executive authorities with an individual's rights should be subject to an effective control which should normally be assured by the judiciary, at least in the last resort, judicial control offering the best guarantees of independence, impartiality and a proper procedure. The Act therefore builds on the office of surveillance commissioner established by the Police Act 1997. Except in case of urgency, no intrusive surveillance will become effective until approved by a commissioner. Moreover, the Chief Surveillance Commissioner will review the use of directed surveillance and of human resources. For the individual, redress will be available before the tribunal established by the UK Act.

DETENTION AND ARREST

We begin consideration of the remainder of the law on investigation with detention and arrest, because changes in the other types of powers exercised by the police and customs officers tend to flow from changes in the status of the suspect. It is worth remembering, however, that considerable investigative work may have been done before detention or arrest takes place. In particular, there may already have been searches carried out.

---

7 Regulation of Investigatory Powers Act 2000 s 28(3)(g).
8 Human Rights Act 1998 s 3.
9 Human Rights Act 1998 s 6.
10 (1980) 2 EHRR 214.

Detention

The 1995 Act s 14(1) provides as follows:

> "Where a constable has reasonable grounds for suspecting that a person has committed or is committing an offence punishable by imprisonment, the constable may, for the purpose of facilitating the carrying out of investigations—
>
> (a) into the offence; and
> (b) as to whether criminal proceedings should be instigated against the person,
>
> detain that person and take him as quickly as is reasonably practicable to a police station or other premises and may thereafter for that purpose take him to any other place and, subject to the following provisions of this section, the detention may continue at the police station, or as the case may be the other premises or place."

Officers of Customs and Revenue have an identical power in terms of the Criminal Law (Consolidation) (Scotland) Act 1995 s 24 and the cases on detention by police officers apply equally to that power. No other investigators have such a power to detain. It should be noted, however, that "constable" is not confined to officers of ordinary police forces. *Smith v Dudgeon*[11] decided that officers of the British Transport Police were also constables for the purposes of the section and officers of other special police forces, such as the Ministry of Defence Police, would also be included on the same reasoning.

Reasonable grounds for suspicion

The constable must have "reasonable grounds for suspecting" that the person to be detained has committed or is committing an offence. It is clear from *Houston v Carnegie*[12] that the constable must have those grounds *himself*. In that case, a constable was held to have acted unlawfully when he detained the suspect simply because a senior officer told him to do so. But the same case also establishes that what matters is whether the officer had *grounds for* suspicion. He does not require to actually *be* suspicious. The enquiry is into the constable's state of knowledge, not his state of mind.

What will amount to such reasonable grounds will vary infinitely with the circumstances of the case but the phrase is one which appears commonly in legislation which grants the police particular powers and is quite well understood in practice. It requires to be interpreted in light of Article 5.1(c) ECHR, the leading case on which (for these purposes) is *Fox, Campbell and Hartley v United Kingdom*.[13] In that case it was said that reasonable suspicion in that Article refers to the existence of facts or information that would satisfy an independent observer that the person concerned might have committed the offence.

The phrase was earlier considered by the Appeal Court in *Wilson v Robertson*[14] in which it was argued that in the particular circumstances the constables concerned could not have had such grounds. The facts were that police officers saw that the fire door of a club had been interfered with by someone from the inside at some time before a theft in the club. The accused had been the only strangers in the club at the relevant time and had been the last to leave. Moreover, they were in the

---

11 1983 SLT 324.
12 1999 SCCR 605.
13 (1990) 13 EHRR 157.
14 1986 SCCR 700.

vicinity of the club car park when the club was locked for the night. The sheriff considered that these facts provided reasonable grounds for the relevant suspicion and the Appeal Court agreed. Lord Justice-General Emslie said:

> "We are concerned here not with evidence as to guilt. We are concerned here simply to know whether there were reasonable grounds on which a police officer might entertain a suspicion that the appellants had committed the offence".

In *X v Austria*,[15] the European Court of Human Rights too rejected the proposition that full proof is necessary before a suspicion can be regarded as a reasonable one.

The standard required seems, therefore, to be quite low and that receives some confirmation from cases like *Dryburgh v Galt*[16] in which an anonymous telephone call was held to be a sufficiently reasonable ground for police officers to suspect that a man had been drinking and driving and to operating the power under the Road Traffic Acts to require the provision of a specimen of breath for a breath test. In that case, the court followed *McNicol v Peters*,[17] *Copeland v McPherson*[18] and *Allan v Douglas*[19] and Lord Justice-Clerk Wheatley summarised the effect of these cases thus:

> "[T]he fact that the information on which the police officer formed his suspicion turns out to be ill founded does not in itself necessarily establish that the police officer's suspicion was unfounded. The circumstances known to the police officer at the time he formed his suspicion constitute the criterion, not the facts as subsequently ascertained. The circumstances may be either what the police officer has himself observed or the information which he has received."

It seems clear, then, that it is incorrect to judge the adequacy of the grounds according to the ordinary rules of evidence and equally incorrect to judge with hindsight.

The suspicion must relate to the commission of an offence which is punishable by imprisonment. This includes all common law offences. Where the offence suspected is a statutory offence, the potential penalty will be set out or referred to in the statute.

Entering property

Where the criteria are satisfied, a constable may "detain" the person. *Gillies v Ralph*[20] establishes that there is no right implicit in s 14 to enter property without a warrant. Accordingly, if the police wish to detain a person who is in his home and who refuses to come out, they will need to seek a search warrant.

Information to be given to suspect

At the time when a constable detains someone he is required, by s 14(6), to inform that person of his suspicion, of the general nature of the offence suspected and of the reason for the detention. The person detained is not obliged to answer any question other than to give his name and address and must be told so.

---

15 (1989) 11 EHRR 112.
16 1981 SCCR 26.
17 1969 SLT 261.
18 1970 SLT 87.
19 1978 JC 7.
20 2008 SCCR 887.

Taking of suspect to police station

A person who has been detained must be taken as quickly as is reasonably practicable to the police station or other premises.

The meaning of the phrase "as quickly as is reasonably practicable" was considered in *Menzies v HM Advocate*.[21] In that case the appellant had been detained outside Airdrie Police Station by police officers from Dunfermline. They did not take him into Airdrie Police Station but took him instead to Dunfermline Police Station, where he made an incriminating statement. It was objected that the statement should not have been admitted and argued that the requirement to take the suspect to a police station as quickly as is reasonably practicable meant that the police had to take him to the nearest police station.

On appeal, the court did not agree. It considered that the phrase "as quickly as is reasonably practicable" is conditioned by what is reasonably practicable, according to the circumstances as they present themselves at the time to the constable by whom the person is detained". In *Menzies* there was evidence that there was substantial documentation relevant to the case at Dunfermline and also that the interviewing facilities in Airdrie Police Station were under considerable pressure at the relevant time. The Appeal Court characterised these as "understandable operational reasons" and held that there was no breach of the requirements of the section.

"Other premises" is not defined and has not been judicially considered.

After the detainee has been taken to the police station or other premises he may then be taken "to another place" where the detention may continue. The purpose of this is to allow for him to be taken to hospital, for example, if he requires treatment or to a place where he has offered to point out evidence to the police.

Questioning

On arrival at the police station he is entitled in terms of the 1995 Act s 15 to be told that he has a right to have a third party and solicitor informed of the detention and where he is being held. Whilst he is there, certain matters, such as his time of arrival and the nature of the offence, must, by virtue of the 1995 Act s 14(6), be recorded. There are forms available to the police for making that record but it was held in *Cummings v HM Advocate*[22] that it is enough if the record is made in the officer's notebook. In that case the Appeal Court was disparaging about the proposition that failure to make the record renders inadmissible any evidence obtained during the detention but did not require to decide the point.

The purpose of detention is to allow the constable to put questions to the detainee and to exercise the same powers of search which could be exercised following arrest. The 1995 Act s 14(7) empowers the police to do both of these things. In terms of s 15A, he is entitled to a private interview with a solicitor at any time during questioning.

The right to question is expressed to be without prejudice to existing rules of law as regards the admissibility in evidence of any answer given. Lord Cameron gave effect to this in *HM Advocate v Bell*,[23] holding that the legislation did not rule out the admissibility of a comment made by a suspect or an accused person when that comment related to something said by a police officer in answer to a question asked by the suspect himself.

21 1995 SCCR 550.
22 1982 SCCR 108.
23 10 September 1981, High Ct Glasgow; unreported.

Section 14(9) of the 1995 Act requires that the suspect is told upon being detained that he is not obliged to answer any question other than to give his name and address and the relationship between that and subsection (7) has required comment by the courts.

The most important case is *Tonge v HM Advocate*.[24] The facts of that case were somewhat complex but for present purposes it is enough to note that the police relied on the forerunner of subsection (9) rather than giving a full caution. This was a significant factor in the Appeal Court's decision that the answers obtained were inadmissible and Lord Justice-General Emslie finished his judgment with the words:

"I would strongly urge police officers throughout Scotland who proceed to accuse a detainee or to question him or to take from him a voluntary statement to rely not at all on the efficacy of the warning described in [the legislation]."

At an earlier stage of his judgment he had referred to the provision that the right to question is without prejudice to any relevant rule of law regarding the admissibility in evidence of any answer given and said:

"[t]he position is, accordingly, that the admissibility in evidence of anything said by a detainee falls to be determined by the common law and where the common law and proper practice would require, in the interests of fairness and fair dealing, that a full common law caution be given, the omission to give it before questioning a suspect who has received no more than the limited warning prescribed by [the Act] will, at the very least, on that account alone, place the admissibility of any evidence elicited from the suspect in peril".

The converse situation, in which the statutory warning was not given but a common law caution was, arose in *Scott v Howie*.[25] Lord Justice-General Hope treated the omission of the statutory warning as being of no significance and, on the basis that the common law caution had been given, held that the evidence of the statement made was not open to objection. Commenting on this decision, Sir Gerald Gordon has said "[t]he court do not specifically indicate whether a failure to give a ... warning renders the detention unlawful and/or deprives the police of their right to hold the detainee for questioning, but their decision suggests that it does not".[26]

Termination of detention

By the 1995 Act s 14(2) detention cannot be continued beyond 12 hours and must in any event cease if the grounds for it cease. At the end of that time the accused must be arrested or released unless some other statutory power to detain (as for terrorism) supervenes or a "custody review officer" authorises a further 12-hour period. It does not follow, however, that failure to follow this procedure precisely will inevitably render evidence obtained inadmissible. *Grant v HM Advocate*[27] was a case in which an appeal was taken against the admissibility of evidence of a reply made by the appellant while he was detained under the section during the statutory six-hour period. It was said that he had not been arrested on the charge until some 20 minutes after the expiry of the statutory period and that this rendered his reply inadmissible in evidence. The High Court held that there

24 1982 SCCR 313.
25 1993 SCCR 81.
26 1993 SCCR 86, commentary.
27 1989 SCCR 618.

was no express provision in the section which retrospectively invalidated processes carried out within the statutory period if that period was by chance exceeded and that no such consequence could be implied.

Arrest

Arrest goes beyond detention. It is much less temporary and has more far-reaching consequences. In 1973, Lord Cameron considered the concept in *Swankie v Milne*[28] and, although the words he used have been rendered more liable to confusion by the introduction of a specific statutory power of detention, read with care they are still of considerable value. The "detention" to which Lord Cameron referred was a thoroughly informal affair. He said:

"An arrest is something which in law differs from a detention by the police at their invitation or suggestion. In the latter case a person detained or invited to accompany police officers is, at that stage, under no legal compulsion to accept the detention or invitation. ... I think it is important always to keep clear the distinction between arrest, which is a legal act taken by officers of law duly authorised to do so and while acting in the course of their duty, carrying with it certain important legal consequences, and the mere detention of a person by a police officer. ... Once arrested not only is the freedom of action of the person arrested circumscribed but he is also placed in the protection of the law in respect eg of questioning by a police officer."

The arrest of a person is a serious step, and one which, if challenged, requires to be justified; though this is by no means the same as saying that an invalid arrest will operate as a bar to prosecution.

Where a warrant has been granted by a court for the arrest of a person a police officer is unlikely to have much difficulty in justifying that course, especially if Stoddart is right to define a warrant as "an *order* by a judge ... that an individual ... authorised by law to execute a deliverance of the court shall put it into effect".[29]

Arrest without warrant

In terms of the 1995 Act s 21 any constable may take into custody without warrant any person whom he sees committing or has reason to believe has committed any of the offences mentioned in Schedule 1 to the Act, if the constable does not know and cannot ascertain his name and address or if there is reasonable ground to believe he will abscond. The offences mentioned in Schedule 1 are various sexual offences and offences involving bodily injury to a child under 17.

There are wide powers of arrest at common law but their limits have never been defined clearly. The case law tends to be concerned with civil actions for damages in respect of wrongful arrest and contains no fully satisfactory statement of the law for criminal law purposes. This is partly because a wrongful arrest does not render subsequent proceedings void (since the procurator fiscal is not bound by the actions of the police) and does not inevitably render evidence obtained as a result of the arrest inadmissible. Any understanding of this area of law must be informed by Article 5 ECHR because the police are clearly a public authority for the purposes of the Human Rights Act 1998 s 6 That means that a constable who acts in breach of a Convention right acts unlawfully. Article 5.1(c) ECHR

28 1973 JC 1.
29 Charles N Stoddart, *Criminal Warrants* (2nd edn, 1999) p 1 (emphasis added).

and its application to detention was discussed above and that discussion applies equally to arrest.

Telling the suspect he has been arrested

It has always been understood that an arrested person is entitled to know that he has been arrested and to be told the nature of the charge, at least in general terms. Article 5.2 ECHR makes this explicit. In *Forbes v HM Advocate*[30] the accused had been taken into custody under the Prevention of Terrorism (Temporary Provisions) Act 1984 but since that legislation referred to the "detention" of a person the word "arrest" was not used. Nor was he told in words what the nature of the charge was but he was allowed to read a search warrant which contained that information.

Lord Justice-General Hope gave the judgment of the court and dealt first with the issue of telling the accused that he had been arrested. He said that the word "arrest" need not itself be used though it is desirable that it should be because "it is necessary that it should be made clear to the person concerned that he is under legal compulsion and that his freedom of action is being curtailed". He desiderated the use of clear and simple language for this purpose but, citing *Alderson v Booth*,[31] said that any form of words will do if they bring to the notice of the person concerned that he is under compulsion and he submits to that compulsion. The actions of the police officer, he said, may themselves be enough to convey the nature of what he is doing.

So far as information about the nature of the charge was concerned, Lord Hope said that a mere statement that the appellant had been detained under the 1984 Act s 12 would not have been enough but that allowing him to read the search warrant was "sufficient, when taken together with the words used by the police officers, to provide the appellant with the information which he was entitled to have as to the general nature and true ground of his arrest".

Article 5.2 ECHR requires that a person who has been deprived of his or her liberty should be informed "promptly" (which means as soon as possible unless the person is in such a condition that he cannot understand what he is being told[32]) in a language which he understands (fluency is not necessary) of the reasons for his arrest and of any charge against him. In *Fox, Campbell and Hartley v United Kingdom*[33] it was held that the Article 5.2 guarantee means that the person must be told in simple, non-technical language that he can understand the essential legal and factual grounds for his arrest so as to be able, if he sees fit, to challenge its lawfulness under Article 5.4. This formula suggests that a high degree of legal precision is not required; and, indeed, it has been held in that case and others[34] that if the process of questioning itself makes the charge clear, Article 5.2 will be satisfied.

Interview with solicitor

In terms of the 1995 Act s 17, an arrested person is entitled to have a third party and a solicitor told of the arrest; but there is no entitlement to an interview

30 1990 SCCR 69.
31 [1969] 2QB 216.
32 *Clinton v United Kingdom*, Committee of Ministers Resolution DH(95)4, 11 January 1995.
33 (1990) 13 EHRR 157.
34 Eg *Delcourt v Belgium* 10 YB 238 (1967).

whilst in police hands. Such an entitlement only arises, as a result of subsection (2), before the accused appears in court. However, in *Cadder v HM Advocate*,[35] the Supreme Court held that Article 6 ECHR requires that a person who has been detained by the police has the right to have access to a lawyer prior to being interviewed, unless in the particular circumstances of the case there are compelling reasons to restrict that right. As a general rule, evidence of such interviews is inadmissible.

Action following arrest

Following arrest, in terms of the 1995 Act s 21(2) one of three things may be done with the person who has been arrested. He may be liberated on a signed, written undertaking to present himself at a specified court at a specified time. Failure to answer such an undertaking is an offence. Or he may simply be liberated. Or, finally, he may be kept in custody in which event he must be placed before the court on the first lawful day after he has been taken into custody (except in terrorist cases where the period allowed is 48 hours or five days with the authority of the Secretary of State). The next lawful day is simply the next day on which the court sits and the practice is to convene a court in the middle of any extended public holiday (such as at Christmas) in order to deal with persons arrested and kept in custody. It seems probable that compliance with Article 5.4 ECHR requires a hearing within four days.[36] There is, of course, nothing to prevent the fiscal simply ordering the release of an accused person—it is consistent with the general rule that the police cannot bind the fiscal and they cannot oblige him to proceed in court against anyone.

QUESTIONING OF SUSPECTS AND OTHERS

Initial investigation

When investigators begin their enquiries into a crime it may well be that all they know is that a crime has been committed. Their information may be sparse and, in particular, they might have no idea who committed the crime. Accordingly, Lord Justice-General Cooper said in *Chalmers v HM Advocate*,[37] "at the stage of initial investigation the police may question anyone with a view to acquiring information which may lead to the detection of the criminal".

Inevitably, those whom the police question will sometimes include the person whom they come to suspect of being the perpetrator of the crime. Sometimes, indeed, it will be that person's replies to their questions during initial investigation which focus their attention upon him. Thus in *Miln v Cullen*[38] the accused had been pointed out to police officers as the person who had been driving a car which had been involved in an accident. They asked him, without cautioning him, whether that was so and his reply, that it was, was held admissible. And in

---

35 [2010] UKSC 43.
36 *Brogan v United Kingdom* (1989) 11 EHRR 117.
37 1954 SLT 177.
38 1967 JC 31.

Wingate v McGlennon[39] police officers saw the accused carrying a pick-axe handle. They asked him why, without cautioning him first, and he told them he had been assaulted and was looking for those responsible. He was arrested, charged, prosecuted and convicted of possession of an offensive weapon. It was held that the reply was admissible.

Particular suspicion

There comes a point, however, at which the investigators begin to have suspicions about a particular person. This progression was recognised in *Chalmers* and, immediately after the passage quoted above the Lord Justice-General went on to say:

> "When the stage has been reached at which suspicion, or more than suspicion, has in their view centred upon some person as the likely perpetrator of the crime, further interrogation of that person becomes very dangerous and if carried too far, eg to the point of extracting a confession by what amounts to cross-examination, the evidence of that confession will almost certainly be excluded."

Chalmers has been the subject of considerable critical comment over the years but Lord Cooper's remarks nevertheless provide a convenient basis for consideration of the essentials of the law. As he made clear, once suspicion has centred upon a person investigators are more constrained but neither Lord Cooper nor any succeeding judge has said that the answers to questions at that stage will certainly be excluded. Such exclusion depends upon questioning being taken too far, such as into cross-examination. It was on this that Lord Avonside was commenting in *Hartley v HM Advocate*[40] when he said:

> "Firstly, police officers may question a suspect so long as they do not stray into the field of interrogation. Secondly, and most importantly, cross-examination is just what it means. It consists in questioning an adverse witness in an effort to break down his evidence, to weaken or prejudice his evidence, or to elicit statements damaging to him and aiding the case of the cross-examiner."

In similar vein, in *Jones v Milne*[41] Lord Justice-General Emslie said:

> "The mere fact that a suspected person is asked a question or questions by a police officer before or after being cautioned is not in itself unfairness and if answers are to be excluded they must be seen to have been extracted by unfair means which place cross-examination, pressure and deceit in close company."

The fairness test

What the courts do consistently is emphasise that the test is one of fairness. One of the clearest expressions of this came in *Brown v HM Advocate*[42] in which Lord Justice-General Clyde said:

> "It is not possible to lay down *ab ante* the precise circumstances in which answers given to the police prior to a charge being made are admissible in evidence at the ultimate trial or

---

39 1991 SCCR 133.
40 1979 SLT 26.
41 1975 SLT 2.
42 1966 SLT 105.

where they are inadmissible. This is so much a question of the particular circumstances of each case and those circumstances vary infinitely from one another. But *the test in all of them is the simple and intelligible test which has worked well in practice—has what has taken place been fair or not?* Just for this reason, because the circumstances in each case vary so much from one another, I do not consider that it is helpful to examine in detail the circumstances leading up to the confession in this case. A meticulous examination of these circumstances only leads in future cases to the creation of subtle distinctions between one decision and another on a matter where the true criterion is neither subtle nor complicated, but is the broad principle of fair play to the accused" (emphasis added).

The courts also stress the issue of fairness to the public interest and we may remind ourselves of Lord Wheatley's remarks in *Milne v Cullen*:[43]

"[I]t is the function of the court to seek to provide a proper balance to secure that the rights of individuals are properly preserved, while not hamstringing the police in their investigation of crime with a series of academic vetoes which ignore the realities and practicalities of the situation and discount completely the public interest."

It is important, however, to note that Lord Wheatley was rejecting an approach which concentrated on detailed criteria rather than common sense. In *B v HM Advocate*[44] the Appeal Court made it clear that if an interview is unfair that is an end of the matter. The public interest does not justify admitting its fruits. In *Thompson v Crowe*,[45] it was conceded that, where the fairness of an interview is challenged, it is for the Crown to satisfy the judge, on the balance of probabilities, that the interview was fair.

Cautioning and compulsory powers

Many considerations will be relevant to what is fair but in *Tonge v HM Advocate*[46] the Appeal Court laid particular stress on the giving of a caution. Lord Justice-General Emslie said:

"[W]here the common law and proper practice would require, in the interests of fairness and fair dealing, that a full common law caution be given, the omission to give it before questioning a suspect ... will, at the very least, on that account alone, place the admissibility of any evidence elicited from the suspect in peril."

Tonge came a few years after *HM Advocate v Von*,[47] a case in which Lord Ross had to deal in the course of a trial with an objection to the admissibility of a confession. The objection was based on the fact that no caution had been given and, in sustaining that objection, Lord Ross said: "I do not consider that a statement can be regarded as being fairly obtained if the accused was never advised of the fact that under our law no person is required to incriminate himself."

This is subject to modification where statute empowers an investigator to ask questions which must be answered. The most common example of this is probably the Road Traffic Act 1988 s 172, which empowers police officers to require

43 1967 JC 21.
44 1995 SLT 961.
45 1999 SCCR 1003.
46 1982 SCCR 313.
47 1979 SLT (Notes) 62.

certain persons to tell them who was driving a motor car at the time of an alleged offence and which makes it an offence to fail to do so. In considering the statutory predecessors of s 172 the High Court held in both *Foster v Farrell*[48] and *Tudhope v Dalgliesh*[49] that in such cases a caution is not only inappropriate, but positively wrong. It would, of course, be a nonsense to tell someone that he is not obliged to answer a question when the law prescribes a criminal penalty for declining to do so. *Brown v Stott*,[50] a Privy Council decision, established that a s 172 requirement and the use of the answer in evidence does not breach the right to silence derived from Article 6.2 ECHR.

The point arose in another context in *Styr v HM Advocate*.[51] That was an insider dealing case in which inspectors were appointed under the Financial Services Act 1986 s 177, which provides that such inspectors may require "all assistance" and examine persons on oath. Subsection (6) provides explicitly that a statement made by a person in compliance with the section may be used in evidence against him. It was argued by the defence that a caution should have been administered. In giving the judgment, Lord Justice-Clerk Ross said:

> "When an inspector appointed under s 177 is carrying out an investigation … [into insider dealing] … he is fully entitled to put any questions which he thinks are appropriate to the person whom he is examining on oath … there was no need to administer a caution in the present case. We would stress that the investigation which the inspectors were carrying out was quite different from police enquiries. In police enquiries the person being questioned is not placed on oath, he cannot be compelled to answer, and he commits no offence if he refuses to answer."

It is clear from *HM Advocate v Friel*[52] that a caution will not be a universal panacea for otherwise unfair practice. In that case, customs officers subjected the accused to a 16-hour interview and, during the latter part of that interview, conducted what amounted to a cross-examination of him. That, it will be recalled, was one of the practices which was to be deprecated in *Hartley*. The evidence was held to be inadmissible. Nevertheless, a caution having been given, it may be difficult for the defence to argue successfully that the evidence should not be allowed. In *Heywood v Smith*[53] a person was detained because she smelt of cannabis. One officer searched her and found a suspicious substance, which the suspect promptly swallowed. In the presence of another officer the first officer cautioned and charged the suspect with attempt to pervert the course of justice to which she made an incriminating reply which was held admissible. The fact that, without the reply there would have been insufficient evidence against her availed her nothing.

Not only that, but a reply to a charge of committing one crime will be admissible at trial in relation to a different crime of the same category (violence, dishonesty etc) arising out of the same *species facti*, at least if the crime actually prosecuted is less serious than that originally charged (and perhaps even if it is more serious).[54] Thus in *Willis v HM Advocate*[55] a reply made to a charge of murder was allowed in

48 1963 SLT 182.
49 1986 SCCR 559.
50 2001 SCCR 62.
51 1993 SCCR 278.
52 1978 SLT (Notes) 21.
53 1989 SCCR 391.
54 *McTavish v HM Advocate* 1975 SLT (Notes) 27.
55 1941 JC 1.

a trial for culpable homicide; and in *McAdam v HM Advocate*[56] a reply to a charge of assault to severe injury was allowed at a trial for attempted murder.

Questioning after charge

Once the police have charged the accused person, replies to further questions which they ask about that charge will be inadmissible. In *Stark and Smith v HM Advocate*[57] two men who had been charged with theft were questioned about that charge whilst in the police cells and the evidence of the reply one of them made was held to be inadmissible. This was followed in *Wade v Robertson*[58] in which a man was in custody charged with the theft of whisky. Whilst he was incarcerated his lodgings were searched and a stolen bottle was found. He was confronted with this and cautioned whereupon he made an incriminating statement. This too was held inadmissible. *Jack v HM Advocate*[59] is, perhaps, the most extreme case imaginable. The Appeal Court had no difficulty in rejecting as inadmissible a remark made to a police officer acting as dock escort during the trial itself.

It should be noted, however, that *Johnston v HM Advocate*[60] is authority for a (short) delay in charging after arrest during which there may be questioning. The accused in a murder case was at first interviewed, without caution, as a prospective witness. What he said was suspicious and he was at that point cautioned. He made a highly incriminating statement and was arrested. After arrest but before charge he was interviewed, having been reminded of the caution. He was asked specific questions about the weapon and damage to his own clothing and made certain admissions.

The court found it hard to understand why the police had arrested the accused rather than detaining him but was not persuaded by a defence argument that a person who has been arrested cannot then be questioned. The heart of the decision seems to be a passage in Lord Justice-Clerk Ross's judgment:

> "[A]rrest may be justified on less material than is required for charge and ... there is no justification for a general rule of law that arresting a person would debar the police from ordinary questioning provided that the questioning was not unfair. In the present case the appellant was arrested and told the general nature of the charge on which the arrest was made. Thereafter in my opinion the police were entitled to question the appellant provided that the ordinary rules of fairness were observed ... the trial judge left the issue of fairness to the jury and in my judgment he was entirely correct to do so."

None of this prevents the police from asking questions about other matters. In *MacDonald v HM Advocate*[61] the accused had been charged with conspiracy to commit robberies and with committing a particular robbery. His answers to questions about other robberies were allowed in evidence.

Tape-recorded interviews

The practice of tape-recording interviews with accused persons was first noted in a reported case in *Lord Advocate's Reference (No 1 of 1983)*[62] and that case proceeded

56 1960 JC 1.
57 1938 JC 170.
58 1948 JC 117.
59 1999 SCCR 296.
60 1993 SCCR 693.
61 1987 SCCR 581.
62 1984 SCCR 62.

upon the basis that admissibility was to be determined according to the ordinary test of fairness, described above. Frequently, nowadays, the interview is also video recorded.

Once proceedings have been commenced, the tapes are transcribed by the procurator fiscal's office and, if the transcript is served on the accused at least 14 days before the trial, a certified transcript is to be received in evidence and is sufficient evidence of the making of the transcript and of its accuracy, all in terms of the 1995 Act s 277, unless the accused serves notice under s 277(2) that he challenges the making of the transcript or its accuracy. In a trial on indictment the tape will usually be played as part of the Crown case (though in *Hudson v Hamilton*[63] the proposition that it should be played during the evidence of the second interviewing officer also was described by the Appeal Court as a pure formality and a waste of the court's time).

It often happens that a recording includes inadmissible material, such as the disclosure of previous convictions. In such a case, the transcript is edited and the inadmissible material is not played at the trial. *Tunnicliffe v HM Advocate*[64] is authority for the proposition that the playing of the whole, unedited tape cannot be cured by directions.

SEARCH

The other investigative tool enjoyed by the police and other agencies is search of persons and of premises.

Is it a search?

Before any attempt is made to apply the law of search to the recovery of material it is as well to be sure that what has been done actually has amounted to a search. In *Devlin v Normand*[65] a prison officer formed the suspicion that a visitor had something in her mouth. He asked her to open her mouth and to give him the package which he saw there. She did so and it turned out to be cannabis resin. The defence argued that this was an unlawful search and that the evidence was therefore inadmissible; but the Appeal Court held that no search took place at all within the proper meaning of that expression. Rather, the court characterised what happened as a request complied with voluntarily, basing the distinction on the absence of any element of force in what was done. Accordingly, the evidence was admissible.

The decision in *Devlin* was in line with *Davidson v Brown*,[66] in which police officers, for another purpose, stopped a car in which the appellant was a passenger. They saw a closed plastic bin in her possession and asked to see inside it. She handed it to them and they found it to contain stolen property. Objection was taken and repelled. The Appeal Court held, as it was to do in *Devlin*, that there was no search but merely a voluntary act on the part of the accused. In this, it founded on an opinion delivered by Lord Justice-General Emslie in *Lucas v Lockhart*[67] in which he said:

63 1992 SCCR 541.
64 1991 SCCR 623.
65 1992 SCCR 875.
66 1990 SCCR 304.
67 1980 SCCR Supp 256.

"[i]f the sheriff had thought that ... the appellant was a volunteer in the matter of search he would not have had to waste his time or ours upon a consideration of the statutory warrant under which the search purported to be carried out".

Baxter v Scott[68] is an example of another situation which was held not to be a search. Police officers arrested the accused on a drink/driving charge. They took possession of his car pending him becoming fit to drive and, since they were responsible for its safekeeping, checked its contents. They found stolen property. The Appeal Court held that the police were entitled to check the car routinely, that there had been no search as such and that the evidence that particular property had been found in the course of the checking of the vehicle was admissible. The court did not adopt the approach urged by the Crown, which was to treat what happened as a search which was lawful because the accused had been arrested under the Road Traffic Act 1988. By contrast, in *Forrester v HM Advocate*[69] where police officers saw the appellant acting suspiciously as he put a package into the boot of a car, the Appeal Court doubted whether the lifting of the boot lid by the police constituted a search but said that in any event "the circumstances were plainly such that ... immediate, on the spot, and thus lawful investigation was reasonably required".

These cases concerned action by officers of law (broadly defined). *Urquhart v Higson*[70] and *Wilson v Brown*[71] are contrasting cases involving staff at licensed premises. In *Urquhart* the appellant had (reluctantly) complied with the demand of the licensee of a bar that he should hand over the substance he was offering for sale in the toilets. It turned out to be temazepam, which is a controlled drug. The Appeal Court said:

"[H]owever reluctant the appellant may have been, the appellant actually handed over the container. ... In those circumstances we cannot say that the appellant was searched. For that reason, no question as to the lawfulness of the search arises."

In *Wilson*, on the other hand, stewards at a dance ejected the appellant and subsequently searched him outside without his consent. They discovered temazepam. It was held that what they had done was to carry out a search and was unlawful.

In *Lucas* and *Wilson* there was no hint of voluntariness on the part of the person searched. In the other cases, it was possible for the trial court to take the view that there had been voluntary compliance with a request. The Appeal Court has been reluctant to go behind the trial court's assessment even where what has been done plainly involved a significant amount of pressure. (In *Urquhart*, for example, the licensee made it clear to the appellant that he was not going to be allowed just to walk away.)

Was the search lawful?

It being established that what has happened in a given case is in fact a search properly so called, the question will be whether that search was lawful. In the

68 1992 SCCR 342.
69 Appeal No 808/01, 15 February 2002.
70 1998 GWD 18-889.
71 1996 SCCR 470.

absence of a warrant, search of premises is likely to be irregular and evidence obtained at risk of being held to be inadmissible.

Many statutes make specific provision for search warrants. The most commonly encountered statutory search warrant is probably that provided for by the Misuse of Drugs Act 1971 s 23(3). We examine it briefly here both for its own importance and as an example of a type.

Section 23(3) permits the granting of a warrant by a justice of the peace, a magistrate or a sheriff, who is satisfied by information on oath that there is reasonable ground for suspecting either (a) that there are controlled drugs in the possession of a person on premises in contravention of the Act or regulations made under it, or (b) that a document relating to a drugs offence is in the possession of a person on premises. The warrant may be executed within one month of the date of its grant and allow a constable to enter the premises, if need be by force, to search the premises and anyone found thereon and to seize and detain drugs or any document fitting the description in the application.

Like all Scottish search warrants, the s 23(3) warrant takes the form of an application which narrates the essential facts and is followed by a docquet signed by the grantor to the effect that he or she "grants warrant as craved". The s 23(3) warrant can only be granted if the grantor is satisfied by evidence on oath that the criteria are fulfilled and that oath and satisfaction are narrated on the face of the application and warrant.

Even if there is no statutory provision for a warrant, the procurator fiscal is always entitled, even in relation to a statutory offence, to seek a warrant at common law from the sheriff unless statute specifically excludes that right in the particular circumstances. In *McNeill, Complainer*[72] a procurator fiscal sought such a warrant but the sheriff refused on the ground that the particular statute said to have been contravened did not provide for a search warrant. The Appeal Court held that this was an incorrect approach.

The sheriff is, of course, perfectly entitled to refuse to grant a warrant if, after considering in light of Article 8.2 ECHR the balance to be struck between the public interest in the detection of crime on the one hand and the interest of the citizen whose property it is intended to search on the other, he or she is not satisfied that it would be proportionate or otherwise necessary or appropriate to grant the warrant. Such a refusal has been reported[73] where it was apparent that the true purpose of the search was not directly proof of the offence which had been reported to the police (indecent assault during a consultation with an aromatherapist) but an attempt to recover a list of other customers in the hope that interviewing them would discover other offences so as to enable the *Moorov* doctrine to be invoked (a matter dealt with below).

Common law search warrants can be obtained by the procurator fiscal by *ex parte* application to the sheriff. This means that the application is made in private and without application being intimated either to the holder of the material or to the suspect, neither of whom has any opportunity to make representations about whether or not it should be granted. The procedure is available both before and after the institution of proceedings, in relation to any offence whatever and in relation to any type of material.

---

72 1984 SCCR 450.
73 *Green's Criminal Law Bulletin*, June 1993.

Defective warrants

The obvious question which arises in relation to a warrant is what happens when it is defective. The first point to be made about this is that the Appeal Court has discouraged efforts to invoke latent defects. In *Aziz v HM Advocate*,[74] the court noted that the warrant which was attacked was *ex facie* valid. The court thought it appropriate to apply "the normal presumption as to the regularity of the proceedings" and could find nothing to suggest any impropriety. This built on the decision in *Allan v Tant*,[75] in the context of a warrant under the Misuse of Drugs Act 1971 s 23(3), that where a warrant is *ex facie* valid it is not permissible for the trial court to hear evidence designed to show that the procedure for obtaining the warrant was not followed properly. It appears that the only remedy available to the accused in such a case will be to take a bill of suspension before the trial in an attempt to reduce the warrant, as was done in *Stuart v Crowe*.[76] *HM Advocate v Rae*[77] suggests that a bill of suspension may be pursued even during the trial.

So far as patent defects are concerned, the absence of the signature of the grantor of the warrant was held to be fatal in *HM Advocate v Bell*.[78] However, *Dickson v Crowe*[79] establishes that, where a warrant requires information on oath, leaving the space for the name of the deponent blank is not fatal because that is part of the minute of proceedings and not of the warrant. The same result was reached in *Whyte v Vannet*[80] where the wrong name was inserted.

Failure to state the address of the premises to be searched led to the refusal of the court to hold evidence admissible in *HM Advocate v Cumming*.[81]

It is not clear whether it is absolutely necessary for the date of granting the warrant to appear except where there is a statutory time limit on the execution of the warrant when it certainly is essential. Warrants under the Misuse of Drugs Act 1971 s 23(3) are an example of this.

Other defects may be excusable and the test, as so often in relation to the admissibility of evidence, will be that of fairness. If there is no material prejudice to the accused, the defect is likely to be excused. So, for example, failure to give the name and designation of the sheriff who granted the warrant was not fatal in *HM Advocate v Strachan*.[82]

Was the search within the scope of the warrant?

Whatever kind of search is in contemplation and whatever the kind of warrant obtained, the question which will arise is whether the search which was carried out was within the scope of the warrant. A relatively relaxed view of this is taken by the courts and the cases of *Lawrie v Muir* and *Fairley v Fishmongers of London* will be recalled. There are, however, limits. In *Singh v HM Advocate*[83] a search warrant authorised entry by four persons. Eight entered. The search was held to

74 1998 SCCR 736.
75 1986 SCCR 175.
76 1992 SCCR 181.
77 1992 SCCR 1.
78 1984 SCCR 430.
79 1998 SCCR 406.
80 1997 SCCR 461.
81 1983 SCCR 15.
82 1990 SCCR 341.
83 2001 SLT 812.

have been unlawful. The argument that only four had actually searched while the other four had interviewed the occupants of the premises was not well received by the court.

The general principle is that once the police are lawfully on premises with a search warrant or the permission of the occupier they may take any suspicious articles they happen to see, even if these are outwith the strict terms of the warrant (or permission) but they may not search actively for articles outwith the warrant or take away articles which might on further examination disclose other offences. Thus in *HM Advocate v Hepper*[84] police searched the house of a suspect without warrant but with the permission of his wife in pursuance of an investigation not connected with the subsequent charge; they saw a briefcase with someone else's name and address on it and that was plainly suspicious. It was held at the trial for theft that the removal of the briefcase had been proper and the evidence allowed.

With *Hepper*, we must contrast *HM Advocate v Turnbull*[85] in which a warrant was obtained for search of an accountant's office in relation to the affairs of a particular client but police removed a large quantity of material relating to other clients which they subsequently trawled through and found other offences. It was held that the removal of the documents which were not in themselves plainly suspicious was illegal and that evidence was not allowed.

Much depends on the particular circumstances of the case. We may contrast *Tierney v Allan*[86] and *Innes v Jessop*.[87] In *Tierney* evidence that police officers searching a house under a warrant in relation to stolen gas cylinders had found a stolen typewriter under a cot was held to be admissible. It was clear that the search had not been random. However, in *Innes* the search was under a warrant granted under the Firearms Act 1968 and the police removed a driving licence, a subcontractor's tax certificate and a number of other items which had nothing to do with anything and less to do with firearms. This was held to be a random search and the results were inadmissible. The significance of the individual circumstances of a case is carried perhaps as far as it can get by *Drummond v HM Advocate*.[88] Two police officers searched a house and the evidence of the first was that he had been looking deliberately for items not covered by the warrant. His evidence was held to be inadmissible. The evidence of the second officer, however, was that he had been looking for items which *were* covered by the warrant and he had happened upon other articles. His evidence of finding such other articles was held to be admissible.

Cases of urgency

In some cases, as the 1995 Act s 18(8) recognises, there can be a substantial risk of evidence being lost during the time it takes to get a warrant. As the law has developed, urgency has become the most common ground upon which irregular searches are excused. So, for example, it was held in *Bell v Hogg*[89] that a police

---

84 1958 JC 39.
85 1951 JC 96.
86 1989 SCCR 344.
87 1989 SCCR 441.
88 1992 SCCR 290.
89 1967 JC 49.

officer was entitled to take palm rubbings from men suspected of the theft of copper but who had not been cautioned or charged in view of the risk of the evidence being lost. A similar result was reached in *Edgley v Barbour*.[90] In that case, police officers saw the accused driving at speed. When they directed a radar gun at his car, he braked at once. They suspected that he was using a radar detection device contrary to the Wireless Telegraphy Act 1949 s 5(b)(i) and saw what appeared to be such a device on his dashboard as they stopped him. When they approached him, it had gone and he declined to open the door or step out of the vehicle. One officer opened the passenger door and opened the glove compartment where he found such a device. It was found as a fact that in view of the lateness of the hour and the remoteness of the locus it would have been impracticable for the officers to get a search warrant. The appellant could not have been detained and the time lapse would have allowed him to dispose of the device. The Appeal Court held that the officers were entitled to act as they had and that the interest of the public outweighed the relatively minor interruption of the appellant's privacy.

It is worth noting that, on the question of urgency, Lord Justice-Clerk Aitchison in *HM Advocate v McGuigan*[91] placed some emphasis on the subjective view of the officers concerned as to the need to search at once. This, of course, is consistent with what we noted in the context of detention about the test of what constitutes reasonable grounds to suspect something.

Search of the person

The reference to *Bell v Hogg* leads us to consider search of the person and we start with the 1995 Act s 18 which makes provision for the taking by the police of prints and other impressions, hair and nail clippings and swabs etc of body fluids on external parts of the body.

By s 18, where a person has been arrested and is in custody, or has been detained under s 14, a constable is allowed to take fingerprints, palm prints and such other prints and impressions of an external part of the body as the constable reasonably considers it appropriate to take in the circumstances of the suspected offence; but the samples thus taken must, by s 18(3), be destroyed if the person is not subsequently convicted of that offence.

By the 1995 Act s 18(6), with the authority of an officer of rank no lower than inspector, a constable is allowed to take from the person from the hair of an external part of the body (other than pubic hair) a sample of hair or other material by cutting, combing or plucking; from or from under a fingernail or toenail a sample of nail or other material; from an external part of the body by swabbing or rubbing, from an external part of the body a sample of blood, other body fluid, body tissue or other material. The meaning of the phrase "external part of the body" was much discussed in Parliament during the passage of the Prisoners and Criminal Proceedings (Scotland) Act 1993 (in which the provision first appeared) but never satisfactorily defined. It is thought that it means precisely what it says and that the section will permit samples from intimate parts of the body provided no degree of penetration is involved. It is to be noted that, although there is a prohibition on the taking of samples from pubic hair, the taking of a swab from the external genitalia is not excluded.

---

90 1994 SCCR 789.
91 1936 JC 16.

By s 18(6A) a constable may take, from inside the mouth, by means of swabbing, a sample of saliva or other material.

Section 18(8) of the 1995 Act provides that the provisions of that section are without prejudice to other powers of search, powers to take possession of evidence where there is imminent danger of its being lost or destroyed, or power to take prints, impressions or samples under the authority of a warrant.

Invasive search

In many cases, what the Crown will require for its investigation is a sample of the suspect's DNA and that can be obtained from a mouth swab taken under the 1995 Act s 18(6A). When forensic science was less developed, there was a need to obtain blood samples for comparison. In other cases, what was wanted was an impression of part of the body (often, the teeth, to compare with a bite mark). Sometimes, that need still arises. Such sampling requires either the consent of the person from whom the samples are taken or a warrant. This resulted in a considerable body of case law.

The starting-point is *Hay v HM Advocate*.[92] The appellant had been convicted of murder. Part of the evidence had been that there was found on the body of the victim a bite mark. The inmates of a nearby approved school were under suspicion and, after impressions of the teeth of all of the inmates, obtained with their consent, had been examined, all were eliminated except the appellant. In order to permit the carrying out of a more detailed comparison, the procurator fiscal presented to the sheriff court an application for a warrant to take dental impressions, photographs and measurements of the appellant's mouth. That warrant was granted and the samples obtained. The subsequent examination demonstrated that the appellant's dental configuration matched the mark precisely and that evidence was led at his trial.

It was argued on appeal that the granting of the warrant had been incompetent and that, even if the warrant had been competent, the evidence should not have been admitted.

The court, in dealing with the competence of the warrant, noted that the need in the public interest for "promptitude and facility in the identification of accused persons and the discovery on their persons or on their premises of indicia either of guilt or innocence" was to be held in balance with the need to protect the liberty of the subject from any undue or unnecessary invasion. This is, of course, the balance which we have noticed on several occasions and which, as we shall see, is the whole theme of the area of law now under consideration.

The court went on to say that warrants of this sort, sought before the accused has been arrested, will be granted only in special circumstances and that the hearings on such applications are by no means formalities. However, after reviewing a number of early authorities, the court expressed the unequivocal view that such warrants are competent.

This decision is of high authority. It was a full bench decision by five judges and, indeed, the trial judge had heard argument on the point with two other judges to assist him before repelling the defence objection. In all, therefore, eight judges, including the Lord Justice-General and Lord Justice-Clerk were unanimous that such warrants are competent. It is not seriously possible to argue that they are not.

92 1968 SLT 334.

The issue next appears in the reports as *HM Advocate v Milford*,[93] a sheriff court decision. The allegation was rape and the procurator fiscal sought a warrant to take a sample of blood from the accused for comparison with blood on the inside of the fly of his trousers. By contrast with *Hay*, the accused had been arrested and appears to have been committed for further examination at least. It was argued in opposition to the application that the medical process involved went beyond the mere taking of impressions and was truly invasive. This, it was said, was an unprecedented invasion of personal liberty.

The sheriff noted that the offence alleged was a very grave one and that the taking of a blood sample is comparatively innocuous. He decided that balance was in favour of him granting the warrant, which was neither too wide nor too oppressive.

There was no appeal in *Milford* but that case was reviewed by the Appeal Court in *Wilson v Milne*,[94] an assault case in which a warrant to take a sample of blood from the accused had been granted. It was argued that *Milford* had been wrongly decided but the court, far from disapproving *Milford*, treated it as authoritative when read along with *Hay*. The need for a balance was again stressed and the court pointed out that it was in fact in the interests of the accused, as well as of justice, that the blood found on his boots and the victim's clothing should either be reconciled or distinguished.

An attempt was made by the defence in *Morris v McNeill*[95] to argue that the above line of authority is confined to cases where the crime is particularly serious, a proposition which was rejected by the sheriff and not insisted on before the High Court on appeal. That case was one of theft by housebreaking where blood had been found at the point of entry. It was, however, argued on appeal that the sheriff had erred in granting the warrant where the circumstances were not "special". The Appeal Court, however, indicated that the high value of the property taken and the fact that the procedure would help to clear up the housebreaking and either eliminate or implicate the appellant were sufficient to make the case special. We may note, on this, Sir Gerald Gordon's observations that:

"[t]he offence in the instant case was certainly serious, if hardly comparable to murder. It remains to be seen how far down the calendar of crimes the courts will be prepared to go in cases of this kind",

and, on the matter of the possibility of analysis exculpating the accused:

"with the emphasis on the result of the comparison as the focus of interest, the conclusion sounds a little disingenuous. ... It has to be said, however, that there are not likely to be many cases in which an innocent suspect will be so attached to his constitutional rights as to object to giving blood or hair, or whatever, in order to establish his innocence".[96]

In deciding *Morris*, the court reiterated the test in words which have come to be quoted regularly in the context of applications for warrants such as this. It said:

"Although it is competent to grant a warrant such as was sought in the present case to take a blood sample from an accused or a suspect, such a warrant will not be

93 1973 SLT 12.
94 1975 SLT 26.
95 1991 SCCR 722.
96 1991 SCCR 726 and 727, commentary.

lightly granted and will only be granted where the circumstances are special and where the granting of the warrant will not disturb the delicate balance that must be maintained between the public interest on one hand and the interest of the accused on the other."

In other words, the Crown cannot expect the court to "rubber stamp" such applications and this was made even clearer by *Hughes v Normand*[97] in which the Appeal Court suspended such a warrant where it was not known whether the stain found on the suspect's shirt was blood at all and, if it was, whether it was that of the victim. The application was regarded as premature. However, a further application was made by the procurator fiscal for such a warrant against Hughes and one of his co-accused. The application for that warrant narrated that the staining had been identified as blood and that there had been certain comparisons made, the results of which were given. It was further stated that it was necessary in the interests of justice to ascertain whether the blood could have come from the accused. The warrants were granted and appealed.

On this occasion (also reported as *Hughes v Normand*),[98] it was not argued that the application was premature—patently it was not—but it was contended that it was not justified since at best the results would, in the particular circumstances, be in favour of the accused or neutral. The court took the view, however, that it was desirable that the comparison process should be completed and refused to suspend the warrants.

Gordon has observed on this that:

> "[T]he High Court said nothing about the circumstances being exceptional or about balancing the rights of the accused and that public interest. We have probably now reached the stage at which the Crown will be entitled to obtain warrants of this kind in any case in which they can show that they have information which indicates that the samples sought will be useful evidence."[99]

It is not only blood samples for which the Crown has sought warrants of this type. In *Lees v Weston*[100] a warrant was sought to fingerprint the accused where the police had omitted to do that when he was arrested in connection with drugs offences. The sheriff refused the warrant, on the basis that the police had had their chance and that it was not appropriate to grant a warrant such as this to allow the Crown to improve their case by trying to get round a "police blunder". The Appeal Court took a different view on appeal, pointing out that the taking of finger impressions involved a relatively minor invasion of bodily integrity, which was outweighed by the public interest. Again, in *Smith v Cardle*[101] the procurator fiscal recovered a video recording of a fatal assault; it was known that the perpetrator must be either the complainer (in this bill of suspension) or his identical twin brother. A warrant was sought to obtain precise physical measurements for comparison with the video, although by definition the complainer was not yet the suspect. The Appeal Court held that the balance was in favour of the public interest and that there would be no bodily invasive procedures or any great inconvenience. Accordingly the sheriff was entitled to grant the warrant.

---

97 1992 SCCR 908.
98 1993 SCCR 69.
99 1993 SCCR 74, commentary.
100 1989 SCCR 177.
101 1993 SCCR 609.

With these cases must be contrasted *McGlennan v Kelly*.[102] That case concerned an allegation of rape. A pubic hair, which could not have come from the victim, was found at the locus but at the time of the offence the particular comparison of such hairs which was necessary was not known to be scientifically practicable. It became so before the accused was brought to trial and an application for a warrant to take such a sample was presented almost two years after the offence.

The sheriff refused the application and it was of some importance to the decision that the accused had provided such samples at the time of the initial investigation of the offence and they had been examined within the limits of the technology then available. The sheriff took the view that the balance in these circumstances was against granting the warrant, a decision which the Appeal Court declined to disturb. Lord Dunpark said:

> "[t]he grant or refusal of a warrant of this nature is ultimately a matter for the discretion of the sheriff and, unless it can be shown that he failed to exercise a proper balancing exercise in the public interest and in the interest of the respondent, there was no wrong exercise of the discretion".

That balancing exercise will, of course, require to take account of the fact that invasive techniques are a clear interference with rights under Article 8 ECHR and, accordingly, only justifiable where they are shown to be necessary (including, in particular, proportionate).

102 1989 SCCR 352.

5 Petition Procedure

Solemn procedure usually starts with a document called the "petition", though it is competent to raise an indictment without any prior petition. An attempt was made to argue the contrary in *O'Reilly v HM Advocate*[1] but the Appeal Court gave this short shrift. They did, however, point out the effect of a petition, saying:

> "[A] petition is required in order to obtain from the court a variety of orders, such as an order for the accused to be committed or for warrants of one kind or another to be granted. Normally the prosecutor will wish to obtain such things from the court and so it is in his interests to have a petition in the appropriate form served on the accused. This is the normal procedure but if it is not followed and no petition is served it does not mean that the Lord Advocate cannot indict. What it does mean is that the accused cannot be committed or arrested on warrant or have his property searched, because court orders authorising such things cannot be obtained in the absence of a petition which brings the accused before the court."

The court might have qualified this last sentence because, as we have seen, search warrants can be obtained other than as an ancillary to petition. Its point, however, was that a petition is a package. Petition procedure is dealt with in the 1995 Act Part IV. To deal with it here means departing from the order of the 1995 Act, because Part III of the Act deals with bail. However, that subject makes much better sense once petition procedure is understood.

In the petition the procurator fiscal informs the court that "from information received" by him "it appears, and he accordingly charges" that the accused person named committed a particular offence or offences. The petition goes on to ask the court, amongst other things:

(a) to grant warrant to search for and apprehend the accused—in short, to arrest him;
(b) to imprison the accused either for further examination or until liberated in due course of law;
(c) to search the person and property of the accused; and
(d) to grant warrant to cite witnesses for precognition.

Most of these will only be of significance if the accused is not yet in custody for the offence but the warrant to imprison the accused will be significant in all cases.

Where the accused is not in custody, the procurator fiscal will present the petition to the sheriff, obtain a signature to the warrant, and issue it to the police for execution by arresting the accused.

---

1 1984 SCCR 352.

Where the accused has been arrested on a petition warrant, or where the procurator fiscal has decided to proceed on petition against an accused who has been arrested without warrant, the accused will appear in court on the next day on which it sits. This follows from the Police (Scotland) Act 1967 s 17(1) which obliges the police to bring offenders before the court without detaining them unreasonably or unnecessarily and from the 1995 Act s 135(3), which provides that a person apprehended shall wherever practicable be brought before a court competent to deal with the case not later than in the course of the first day after he has been taken into custody, where that is not a Saturday, Sunday or court holiday.

The appearance will be in private, in the sheriff's chambers, or (more usually) in a closed courtroom which will be regarded as chambers. A copy of the petition will have been handed to the accused in the cells. The accused and his solicitor are entitled to an interview in private before he appears before the sheriff, in terms of the 1995 Act s 17(2).

Procedure in relation to appearance on petition bears the marks of its history. At a time when the investigation was in the hands of the sheriff, the appearance on petition was the occasion on which the accused was examined as to his account of the events relevant to the offence and he was entitled to make a declaration. That declaration would in due course be part of the evidence at trial and, since the accused was at one time not allowed to give evidence at the trial, the declaration was his only chance to give his side of the story. Now that the accused is (and for many years has been) a competent witness at his own trial and the Crown case will have only an embryonic form when most accused persons appear on petition, it is rare, though not entirely unknown, for the accused to make a declaration.

If the accused is going to make a declaration, he must do so himself, in his own words. In *Carmichael v Armitage*[2] the accused's solicitor had noted his client's account of relevant events and then edited it—the word used was "structured"— to make it "reasonable". The Appeal Court held that the basic rules of evidence applied to such a declaration and that something edited by the solicitor had become a precognition (that is, a statement prepared by one engaged on behalf of one of the parties in preparing the case for trial) and so not admissible.

After the sheriff clerk has asked the accused to confirm his identity it is usual for the accused's solicitor to say that his client makes "no plea or declaration" and the sheriff then looks to the procurator fiscal to hear what the Crown wishes to do. The first question is whether the fiscal wishes to conduct a judicial examination. Once that has been dealt with, the fiscal may either seek the committal of the accused for further examination (in custody or on bail) or seek his full committal (in custody or on bail).

JUDICIAL EXAMINATION

The judicial examination procedure was originally introduced by the Criminal Justice (Scotland) Act 1980 and is now set out in the 1995 Act ss 35 to 39.

2 1982 SCCR 475.

Scope of questioning

In terms of the 1995 Act s 36 the accused may be questioned by the prosecutor in so far as such questioning is directed towards eliciting any admission, denial, explanation, justification or comment which the accused may have as regards three things. The first of these (subsection (2)) is whether any account which the accused can give ostensibly discloses a defence and, if so, the nature and particulars of that defence. The second (subsection (3)) is the alleged making by the accused, to or in the hearing of an officer of police, of an extrajudicial confession (whether or not a full admission) relevant to the charge and a copy of which has been served on the accused. The third (subsection (4)) is any declaration made by the accused.

Where the accused discloses an ostensible defence, the 1995 Act s 36(10) obliges the prosecutor to secure the investigation of that defence, though it may be thought that any competent prosecutor would do so anyway. It was argued for the appellant in *McDermott v HM Advocate*[3] that the apparent failure of the procurator fiscal to make full investigation of the alibi which he stated should have precluded the advocate depute from cross-examining the appellant on that alibi and that the failure to investigate was prejudicial so that the trial judge should have directed the jury to acquit. That argument was rejected and the Appeal Court said that the provision is administrative in character and belongs to the stage of proceedings before the case goes to trial. The court also rejected the suggestion that the Crown should have led evidence about the extent of the investigation made.

Confessions

In the early years after the judicial examination procedure was introduced, questioning about statements to the police generated some appeal business, essentially about what amounts to a confession. In *McKenzie v HM Advocate*,[4] following an identification parade the accused had said "just my luck, I knew I'd be picked out". The accused said that he saw his remark as an expression, not a confession. He sought to have those words omitted from the transcript to be read to the jury and on appeal Lord Robertson said:

> "The wording of this particular section does not appear to be as clear as it might have been. There is no definition of 'confession' in the statute and it is accordingly doubtful as to exactly what is intended. The wording 'extrajudicial confession' (whether or not a full admission) relevant to the charge suggests that the confession referred to is something less than a full admission and must be susceptible of interpretation provided the statement is relevant to the charge. In the context it seems to me that the definition of 'confession' must be that the statement is clearly susceptible of being regarded as an incriminating statement. ... In the present case the statement allegedly made is perhaps not a full admission but in my view it cannot be said that the statement was not or cannot be susceptible of being regarded as an incriminating statement."

Lord Robertson went on to say that the accused always has the opportunity at trial to challenge the admissibility of such a statement.

In some cases, of course, such as *Moran v HM Advocate*[5] it will only be possible to determine whether something is a confession in light of other evidence and

---

3 2000 JC 291.
4 1982 SCCR 545.
5 1990 SCCR 40.

in such cases the court will be inclined to let the matter go to the jury with an appropriate direction.

Moran concerned a statement said to contain "special knowledge", a concept to be considered below. For now, it may be noted that there will be sufficient evidence for a conviction if an admission contains information which the accused could only have known if he was a party to the crime, and which is proved to be true by evidence from another source. Objection was taken, and repelled, to the reading to the jury of that part of the transcript which contained this material. On appeal, Lord Brand pointed out that whether or not the passage could be said to be an extrajudicial confession could only be decided in the light of other evidence and that it had been proper to allow it to be read to the jury. It is thought that what he meant was that whether or not the knowledge was "special" could only be decided by the jury and that only once they had heard other evidence to demonstrate both that the information given was accurate and that it was in restricted currency.

HM Advocate v Cafferty[6] is sheriff court authority that the Crown can choose which statements to put to the accused and need not put them all.

Alleged confessions made in the hearing of others, such as customs officers, are not provided for and accordingly, it is suggested, cannot form the basis of questions.

In framing his questions, the procurator fiscal is required by the 1995 Act s 35(5) to have regard to certain principles. These are that questions should not be designed to challenge the truth of anything said by the accused, that questions which the accused has refused to answer should not be reiterated and that there should be no leading questions.

Refusal to answer

By the 1995 Act s 36(8) the accused is always entitled to decline to answer questions at judicial examination, and many do so refuse. However, where at trial the accused (or any witness called on his behalf) says something, or calls a witness who says something, in evidence which could have been stated appropriately in answer to a question which he refused to answer at judicial examination his refusal to answer at judicial examination may be commented on by the prosecutor, the judge presiding at the trial, or any co-accused. The intention of the Thomson Committee, which recommended the introduction of the judicial examination procedure, was that this provision would make it difficult for the accused to decline to answer[7] but the view which Lord Dunpark took in *Gilmour v HM Advocate*[8] was rather different. In that case, he pointed out to the jury that the accused had refused to answer questions on the advice of his solicitor and that he had the right to remain silent. He therefore advised the jury to ignore the judicial examination altogether. However, the Appeal Court seems to have taken a different approach in the appeal in *Alexander v HM Advocate*[9] (though the absence of a recorded judgment is unhelpful). There, the three accused had made no reply at judicial examination beyond what has become something of a standard formula: "On the instructions of my lawyer I don't wish to say anything." At trial, they put forward

6 1984 SCCR 444.
7 Criminal Procedure in Scotland (Second Report) 1975, Cmnd 6218, para 8.19.
8 1982 SCCR 590.
9 1988 SCCR 542.

alibis. The trial judge (Lord Brand) told the jury that the failure to disclose the alleged alibis at judicial examination was a matter for it to assess in weighing the evidence. There was an appeal on the basis that this was a misdirection but the appeal was refused. Sir Gerald Gordon comments[10] that this indicates that Lord Dunpark's approach in *Gilmour* was incorrect. However, in *McEwan v HM Advocate*[11] the Appeal Court counselled restraint in the way in which trial judges should comment to juries on this sort of point.

Role of defence solicitor

The role of the defence solicitor at a judicial examination is rather limited. The 1995 Act s 36(5) lays upon the sheriff the responsibility of ensuring that all questions are fairly put to, and understood by, the accused and, whilst the accused must be told by the sheriff that he may consult his solicitor before answering any question,[12] the solicitor is not entitled to intervene by way of objection to questions. What he can do, by the 1995 Act s 36(7), after the completion of the procurator fiscal's questions, is ask the accused questions designed to clarify any ambiguity in an answer given by the accused to the prosecutor at the examination or to give the accused an opportunity to answer any question which he has previously refused to answer.

Transcript

Judicial examination is recorded and, by the 1995 Act s 37(6), a copy of the transcript must be served on the accused and his solicitor within 14 days. There is provision in the 1995 Act s 38 for application to the court for rectification of any perceived errors in the transcript.

COMMITTAL

Once the judicial examination is completed the procurator fiscal will move the court either to commit the accused for further examination or to commit him until liberated in due course of law. Committal until liberated in due course of law is usually referred to as "full committal".

Full committal

Full committal is committal for trial. In times past the sheriff would at this stage be shown the "precognition", which is the volume of statements taken by the Crown. That practice fell out of use a long time ago and modern practice is that the procurator fiscal, by moving for full committal, is in effect saying to the sheriff that he is satisfied that there is a *prima facie* case, at least on paper. The procurator fiscal provides a "custody statement" which is an informal document which was originally intended to summarise the evidential basis of the case so that the defence

---

10 1988 SCCR 545 commentary.
11 1990 SCCR 401.
12 1995 Act s 36(6)(a).

can, if desired, dispute the assessment of the sufficiency of the case on paper. In practice, custody statements are extremely brief and uninformative. In *Brown v Selfridge*[13] an argument that the production of such a statement is prejudicial and renders the petition incompetent was rejected in short order.

Provided that the petition contains a relevant charge the sheriff will almost always order full committal without further enquiry, though the sheriff does retain the jurisdiction to refuse to do so. The few occasions where this happens are cases where the sheriff considers that in the particular circumstances the motion is oppressive or frankly incompetent. So, for example, in *Normand v McQuillan*[14] a sheriff refused full committal in a case in which the Crown substituted a petition for a summary complaint a fortnight after the accused had been remanded in custody to await trial on that complaint. This the sheriff regarded as oppressive in the circumstances. In refusing the motion for full committal the sheriff rejected an argument by the procurator fiscal that it is incompetent for the defence to challenge the competency of a petition, observing:

"For present purposes I am satisfied that complaints of unfairness and oppression can be entertained by the court at any stage of the prosecution procedure. The prevention of such ills must surely be a primary justification for the presence of a judge."

An example—perhaps the only example—of refusal of a motion to commit as frankly incompetent is to be found in *Herron v A, B, C and D*[15] in which the sheriff noticed that the time limit between committal for further examination and full committal had been exceeded. The judgment is worth reading for its description of just how far things can go wrong when all parties assume that the fact that sheriffs scarcely ever refuse full committal means that it is no more than an administrative rubber stamp.

It should be understood that refusal of a motion to commit does not prevent the Crown from subsequently serving an indictment and proceeding to trial.

Committal for further examination

Committal for further examination is used where the fiscal does not consider that he is yet in a position to take the responsibility for full committal. It may be that he is working from a summary of the evidence and wants to see the full statements which the police have taken; or he may expect that there are further charges to come; or he may consider that further enquiries are necessary to provide a sufficiency of evidence.

Committal for further examination happens only once. If the accused is granted bail at committal for further examination, it operates for practical purposes as full committal as a result of the 1995 Act s 23(3). Where the accused is kept in custody he must be brought back to court for full committal. The period within which that must be done depends on an understanding of the Criminal Procedure Act 1701 which provides, *inter alia*:

"And farder Discharges all closs imprisonments beyond the space of Eight dayes from the commitment."

13 1999 SCCR 809.
14 1987 SCCR 440.
15 1977 SLT (Sh Ct) 24.

Sheriff Macphail (as he then was)[16] analysed the effect of this in *Herron v A, B, C and D* and the Appeal Court approved his reasoning in *Dunbar, Petitioner*.[17] The effect is that no longer than eight days may elapse between committal for further examination and full committal but neither of the days on which one of these committals takes place counts towards that total. Accordingly, an accused who is committed for further examination on a Monday, if he is to be fully committed must be so committed on the Wednesday of the following week at the very latest. If the Monday is the first of the month, the Wednesday on which full committal takes place will be the tenth.

16 Later Lord Macphail.
17 1986 SCCR 602.

6 Bail

BAIL APPLICATIONS

When the accused first appears in court, one question which will be prominent in his mind is whether he is going to get bail—that is, to be liberated pending his trial. Part III of the 1995 Act deals with bail. By contrast with former procedure, all crimes and offences are now bailable.[1]

The procedural starting-point is s 22A which imposes a duty on the court before which an accused is first brought to give the accused and the prosecutor an opportunity to be heard and then either admit or refuse to admit the person to bail. The court is required to take the initiative in this and not to wait for the accused to apply for bail. If that is not done within 24 hours of first appearance, the accused is entitled to be liberated.

On subsequent appearances in court, by s 23(1), any person accused on petition of a crime is entitled to apply to the sheriff for bail. The prosecutor is entitled to be heard against that application. By subsection (2), the sheriff is entitled in his or her discretion to refuse the application. By s 23(4) and (5) of the 1995 Act bail may be sought after full committal even if it has been refused at committal for further examination.

Under summary procedure, by subsection (6), any judge having jurisdiction to try the offence (in other words, sheriffs and JPs) may, at his discretion, on the application of the accused and after giving the prosecutor an opportunity to be heard, admit or refuse to admit the accused to bail. Subsection (7) requires bail applications under subsection (5) or (6) be dealt with within 24 hours after presentation to the judge, failing which the accused must be liberated forthwith. In *Gibbons, Petitioner*[2] an application lodged at 11.30 am one day was, for administrative reasons, not dealt with until 11.50 am the following day, when it was refused. It was held that the time limit is mandatory and the release of the accused was ordered.

RELEVANT CONSIDERATIONS

The framework for the court's consideration of bail applications is set out in ss 23B to 23D of the 1995 Act. It used to be that, where the Crown consented to bail, the bail application would always be granted. Now, it is provided explicitly by

---

1 Criminal Procedure (Scotland) Act 1995 s 4(1).
2 1988 SCCR 270.

s 23B(5) that the attitude of the prosecutor does not restrict the court's exercise of its discretion and s 23B(6) gives the court power to request the prosecutor, or the defence solicitor (or counsel) to provide information relevant to the question (which usually means a copy of any schedule of previous convictions). The starting-point for consideration, by s 23B(1), is that bail is to be granted except where, by reference to s 23C and having regard to the public interest, there is a good reason for refusing bail. Section 23D makes special provision where the applicant for bail is charged under solemn procedure with a violent or sexual offence or drug trafficking or has previous convictions on indictment for violent or sexual offences or drug trafficking.

The Act gives little guidance about the public interest aspect of these criteria. Section 23B(3) states that it includes reference to the interests of public safety, though that might have been regarded as self-evident. Section 23C, however, sets out a list of grounds which constitute "good reason for refusing bail". What they do is to put into statutory form considerations which were expressed (rather more succinctly) by Lord Justice-Clerk Wheatley in *Smith v McCallum*[3] and by the European Court of Human Rights in *Letellier v France*,[4] *Toth v Austria*[5] and *Tomasi v France*.[6]

The considerations which constitute good reason for refusing bail, in terms of s 23C(1), are as follows. The risk in each case must be "substantial":

(a) the person might abscond or fail to appear at court;
(b) a risk that the person will commit further offences whilst on bail; or
(c) a risk that the person will interfere with witnesses or otherwise obstruct the course of justice.

To these, the Act adds:

(d) "any other substantial factor which appears to the court to justify keeping the person in custody".

This last consideration is, as expressed, singularly unilluminating but there are two sources of help. The first is that, in *Burn, Petitioner*,[7] the Lord Justice-General (Rodger) pointed out that:

"[T]he Crown must provide sufficient general information relating to the particular case to allow the sheriff to consider the merits of their motion that the accused should be committed to prison and detained there ... where, for example, the Crown oppose bail on the ground of the risk that the accused would interfere with witnesses, the procurator fiscal depute should be in a position to explain the basis for that fear."

The context for that was consideration of what will be required to justify refusal of bail at committal for further examination but the requirement for the Crown to provide information does not depend on that context. It is suggested, too, that the proposition that the procurator fiscal should be in a position to explain the basis for

3 1982 SLT 421.
4 (1992) 14 EHRR 83.
5 (1992) 14 EHRR 551.
6 (1993) 15 EHRR 1.
7 2000 SCCR 384.

the fear expressed goes wider than the situation in which it is said that the accused will interfere with witnesses. *Burn* was decided several years before ss 23B to 23D were enacted but it is suggested that the principle holds good. The mere *ipse dixit* of the Crown is not enough to establish any of the s 23C(1) factors, including the enigmatic "any other substantial factor".

The second source of help comes in s 23C(2), which provides that the court must have regard to all material considerations "including … the following examples", which at least gives some sort of framework for understanding what is meant by "any other substantial factor":

(a) the nature of the offences before the court and the probable disposal of the case (ie sentence) if the person was convicted of the offences;

(b) whether the person was subject to a bail order when the offences are alleged to have been committed;

(c) whether the offences are alleged to have been committed while the person was subject to another court order, on licence or parole or subject to a deferred sentence;

(d) the character and antecedents of the person including the nature of any previous convictions, whether he has previously contravened a bail order or other court order, whether he has previously breached the terms of a release on licence or parole and whether he has recently served a sentence of imprisonment in connection with any of these things; or

(e) the "associations and community ties" of the person.

The reference to associations and community ties is not a legislative expression of the proverb that those who "flee wi' the craws will be shot wi' the craws". Rather, it is a reference to *Letellier v France* and to *Maznetter v Austria*[8] in which the European Court of Human Rights pointed out that the danger of a person absconding will vary with the strength of his ties with the jurisdiction and that the court should consider financial guarantees (such as money bail, which will be discussed shortly) as a means of offsetting the risk.

Section 23D(1) expresses what appears to be a restriction on the granting of bail where the applicant for bail is charged under solemn procedure with a violent or sexual offence or drug trafficking or has previous convictions on indictment for violent or sexual offences or drug trafficking. In those cases, the section provides that the person "is to be granted bail … only if there are exceptional circumstances justifying bail". That reads very much as an automatic restriction on bail, transferring the burden to the applicant to demonstrate that there are exceptional circumstances. The difficulty which that reading creates is that the provision has to be read compatibly with Article 5.3 ECHR, in terms of which there is an entitlement to release on bail which the prosecution has to overcome before bail can be refused. *Caballero v United Kingdom*[9] makes it absolutely clear that an automatic refusal of bail will breach Article 5.3.

It appears from the Explanatory Notes to the Criminal Proceedings etc (Reform) (Scotland) Act 2007, which introduced s 23D, that it was enacted in the belief that:

8 (1979–80) 1 EHRR 198.
9 (2000) 30 EHRR 643.

"under article 5(3) of the ECHR, detention would usually be justified when someone with a previous conviction for a grave offence is charged with a second such crime on the basis that this demonstrates a need to prevent further offences whilst on bail".[10]

That, however, represents an inadequate understanding of the Convention law. Certainly, the European Court of Human Rights held in *Toth v Austria* that previous convictions *could* be relied on as giving reasonable grounds to fear that further offences would be committed but the court certainly did not say that the existence of a previous conviction for a grave offence *would usually* justify refusal of bail. The furthest the European Court went was to say that, on the basis of Mr Toth's previous convictions, the national courts "could reasonably fear" that he would commit new offences (para 70). In *Letellier v France*, the European Court said that the court before which the accused is brought must consider "all the facts arguing for and against the existence of a genuine requirement of public interest" for the remanding of the accused in custody. In an English case in the House of Lords, *R (O) v Crown Court at Harrow*[11] Lord Brown of Eaton-under-Heywood explained that:

> "The two key requirements imposed by article 5(3) are, first, that the prosecution must bear the overall burden of justifying a remand in custody—it must advance good and sufficient public interest reasons outweighing the presumption of innocence and the general presumption in favour of liberty; and, secondly, that the judge must be entitled to take account of all relevant considerations pointing for and against the grant of bail so as to exercise effective and meaningful judicial control over pre-trial detention."

In *M v Watson*,[12] Lord Brodie had to consider the meaning of s 23D(1). He reasoned that the norm will be that persons having previous convictions on indictment for the same sort of offence with which they are charged will not be granted bail. Accordingly, if, having regard to all the relevant facts, they are admitted to bail the circumstances will indeed be "exceptional" in the sense that the norm has been departed from. The court must assess all the information before it with a view to determining whether there is good reason for refusing bail having regard to the relevant risks and the relevant level of these risks as identified in s 23C. In every case, if bail is to be refused, good reason must be shown for the refusal. In enacting s 23D Parliament has reminded the court of the risks normally attendant upon the grant of bail to a person to whom the section applies. In terms of this, what s 23D does is to impose an evidential burden on the accused: there are factors applying to him which would lead the court to refuse bail. He needs to point to some circumstances which should lead the court to grant bail notwithstanding those factors.

CONDITIONS

By the 1995 Act s 24(4) and (5) the court in granting bail must impose the "standard conditions" of bail. These are:

- that the accused appears at the appointed time at every diet in the case of which he is given due notice;

10 Paragraph 18.
11 [2007] 1 AC 249.
12 2009 SCCR 847.

- that he does not commit an offence whilst on bail;
- that he does not interfere with witnesses or otherwise obstruct the course of justice;
- that he does not behave in a manner which causes, or is likely to cause, alarm or distress to witnesses;
- that he makes himself available for interview for reports to assist the court in dealing with him for the offence; and
- that where the offence is a sexual offence listed in s 288C (effectively, all sexual offences) he does not try to obtain a precognition or statement from the complainer except through his solicitor.

The court must also impose such conditions as it considers necessary to ensure that the standard conditions are observed and that the accused makes himself available for an identification parade or for prints, impressions or samples to be taken from him. By s 24(6), except where bail is being granted because the prosecutor has missed one of the custody time limits discussed in the next chapter, a requirement for money bail to be lodged may be made where that is appropriate to the "special circumstances" of the case. That might arise where the court is concerned about a lack of associations and community ties but considers that the lack may be offset by money bail. There is an example in *Urquhart, Petitioner*[13] in which the accused person was a French citizen and he was required to lodge money in euros. Section 29 provides for forfeiture of the money where there is a breach of bail conditions.

Section 27 of the 1995 Act creates offences in relation to breach of bail conditions. These are substantive offences rather than matters of evidence or procedure and are therefore not dealt with in this book.

A bail order will continue in force until the disposal of the case in relation to which it was made unless it is actually recalled. In particular, if the trial is adjourned in the absence of the accused that does not cause the bail order to fall (the situation and result in *Walker v Lockhart*[14]).

BAIL APPEALS

Section 32 of the 1995 Act grants rights of appeal to both the accused and the prosecutor, both as to the decision allowing or refusing bail and as to the amount of bail fixed (if any). However, s 24(7)(b) provides that any reference to the amount of bail fixed is to be construed as a reference to conditions. So s 32 does not actually mean what it says. It means that an appeal can be taken both as to the decision allowing or refusing bail and also as to conditions.

Marking and intimation

The marking of a bail appeal is not subject to any time limit, though for obvious reasons it is usually (and, in the case of a prosecution appeal, always) done at once upon the court of first instance making the order which it is desired to review. In

13 2003 GWD 26-735.
14 1993 SCCR 148.

the case of the prosecutor, there will be a desire on the part of the authorities to get the benefit of that part of the 1995 Act s 32(2) which provides that the accused "shall not be liberated ... until the appeal by the prosecutor is disposed of". In the case of the accused there will be a compelling desire to secure his liberty as soon as that can be accomplished.

In either event, the 1995 Act s 32(3) requires that written notice of appeal is to be immediately given to the opposite party by the party appealing. This is probably of more practical importance in the case of a defence appeal, which might not be marked immediately, than in the case of a prosecution appeal, where the reason for the continued incarceration of the accused will quickly become apparent to his advisers even if they do not see the procurator fiscal physically marking the appeal. Nevertheless, the provision is mandatory and ensures that the opponent has the chance to prepare for the appeal, which, by the 1995 Act s 32(7) must be heard within 72 hours (Sundays and public holidays do not count) in terms of subsection (8). If this time limit is not met, the accused is to be liberated.

By the 1995 Act s 32(4) a bail appeal is to be disposed of by the High Court or "any Lord Commissioner of Justiciary in court or in chambers after such inquiry and hearing of parties as shall seem just". The practice is that such appeals are dealt with in the High Court building in Edinburgh, by a single judge in chambers, before the start of the other business of the court. (The 2009 Gill Report on civil justice recommended that there should be a new Sheriff Appeal Court with a jurisdiction which would include bail appeals, so things might change.) The Crown is represented by an advocate depute, instructed by a member of the Procurator Fiscal Service from Crown Office. The accused, unless he represents himself, is not entitled to be present[15] but is represented by an advocate or a solicitor advocate.

The appeal is usually a brief affair, decided on *ex parte* statements. If a defence bail appeal is successful, the High Court interlocutor is sent (by fax) to the clerk of court of first instance, who (again by fax) sends it to the prison in which the accused is held. The accused signs a form of acceptance of the conditions and is then released.

BAIL REVIEWS

At the instance of the accused, any court can review its own decision on bail or on bail conditions in terms of the 1995 Act s 30. A material change in circumstances, or material information which was not available when the decision was made, is required. What is clear is that, where there has been a bail appeal, the court of first instance cannot review the decision taken by the High Court. In *HM Advocate v Jones*[16] a sheriff refused to entertain a motion to review bail where the case had been the subject of a bail appeal, holding that any review would have to proceed in the High Court. This decision was approved by Lord Cameron in *Ward v HM Advocate*,[17] with the proviso that the court of first instance can review other elements of the bail order, such as conditions, which were not at issue in the High Court.

15 *DL v HM Advocate* 2007 SCCR 472.
16 1964 SLT (Sh Ct) 50.
17 1972 SLT (Notes) 22.

By the 1995 Act s 31 the prosecutor has an equivalent right to seek review of a court's decision to grant bail but this is limited explicitly to those cases where the prosecutor puts before the court "material information" which was not available to it when it granted bail. The procedure is by application to the court and, by subsection (2), on receipt of such an application, the court must do three things. First, it must intimate the application to the person granted bail; second, it must fix a diet for hearing the application and cite the person on bail to attend that diet; and, third, "where it considers that the interests of justice so require" it must grant warrant to arrest that person. On hearing an application the court may, by subsection (3), either withdraw the grant of bail and remand the person in custody or may grant bail, or continue the grant of bail, varying the conditions if it sees fit.

BAIL APPEAL AFTER CONVICTION

The accused who has been convicted, made the subject of a deferred sentence and remanded in custody, or on bail with conditions which he finds unacceptable, has a right of appeal in terms of the 1995 Act s 201(4). The prosecutor has no equivalent right to appeal against the liberation of a person on deferred sentence.

An appeal by an accused person under this provision can only be marked within 24 hours of the remand and is by note of appeal presented to the High Court. In *Long v HM Advocate*[18] the accused, upon whom sentence had been deferred in custody for reports had, for reasons which are not disclosed, not marked a bail appeal within the 24 hours allowed. An attempt was made to operate the bail review provisions instead but Lord Justice-Clerk Wheatley held that they apply only to pre-trial procedure and have no application to the accused after conviction.

18 1984 SCCR 161.

7 Solemn Proceedings

OUTLINE

After the appearance of the accused on petition the procurator fiscal prepares the case for the Crown and an indictment is served. That indictment contains the charge and lists of productions and witnesses. There are rules about each of these aspects. The indictment also calls the accused to a first diet, followed by a trial (in the sheriff court) or to a preliminary hearing at which the trial date will be fixed (in the High Court). Some aspects of the case have to be resolved at the first diet or preliminary hearing.

CROWN PRECOGNITION

Precognition on authority of petition warrant

After full committal, the procurator fiscal will conduct such precognition as he or she thinks necessary. The witnesses will, upon the authority of the warrant to cite for precognition which is contained in the petition warrant, be cited to attend the procurator fiscal's office and will there be interviewed in private by the procurator fiscal himself, a procurator fiscal depute or a precognition officer (who is a paralegal). The result of that interview is a document known as a "precognition". It is not signed by the witness and indeed is not usually shown to him. It is highly confidential to the Crown and (except in the case of applications at the instance of the Scottish Criminal Case Review Commission) that confidentiality can only be lifted by the court in cases of overwhelming necessity.[1] It was made clear in *Carmichael v B*[2] that a witness is not entitled to be accompanied by a solicitor when being precognosced and it has long been recognised that witnesses should not be precognosced in one another's company.[3] Certainly the representatives of the accused have no right to be present.[4]

Following completion of the Crown precognitions, the whole case is reported to Crown counsel, in the form of a volume or volumes known as "the Precognition". Crown counsel, with the assistance of an analysis and recommendation by the

---

1 *Donald v Hart* (1844) 6 D 1255; *Scottish Criminal Cases Review Commission v HM Advocate* 2000 SCCR 842.
2 1991 SCCR 715.
3 Hume ii 82; *Reid v Duff* (1843) 5 D 656.
4 Hume ii 82.

procurator fiscal and with assistance also from members of the Procurator Fiscal Service in the Crown Office High Court Unit, decide the future course of the proceedings. Most fundamentally, they consider whether the state of the evidence is such that the case can and should proceed further. They determine whether the case is to remain under solemn procedure or be reduced to summary procedure by the procurator fiscal serving a summary complaint on the accused. In a case which remains under solemn procedure, they decide the charges which will appear on the indictment and they decide whether the case will be indicted in the High Court or in the sheriff court.

As *Kelly v Vannet*[5] made clear, precognition can continue even after service of the indictment and may extend even to the solicitor who has acted for the accused if the circumstances are such that confidentiality no longer applies.

Precognition on oath

The High Court said in *HM Advocate v Monson*[6] that it is every citizen's duty to co-operate with the Crown in this process. That, however, is a duty which is not attended by a sanction and it quite often happens that a witness will fail to attend for precognition. In that event the procurator fiscal may petition the court for warrant to cite the witness to attend for precognition on oath. Where such a warrant is granted, the witness will be interrogated in the presence of a sheriff and what he or she says will be transcribed and subsequently signed by the witness and the sheriff.

A person who is precognosced on oath cannot thereafter be prosecuted for the offence.[7] Indeed *Mowbray v Crowe*[8] seems to establish that it will be oppressive for the Crown to commence proceedings against a person who has been interviewed by the procurator fiscal at all in connection with a case. In that case the fiscal was considering a report against the appellant and wrote inviting her to attend for a discussion about the case. During the discussion which took place the appellant disclosed her version of events. The fiscal decided to prosecute.

It seems that what the fiscal had in mind was to give a warning if the appellant had admitted the offence. However, as the court pointed out, discussions with the accused are not normally undertaken when a warning is contemplated and, in a criminal justice system which is adversarial, the prosecutor and the accused are to be at arm's length. The appellant had not been told that she could bring a solicitor to the interview. As one who had been cautioned and charged she could not have been interviewed by the police and it was equally wrong that she should have been interviewed by the procurator fiscal. The court took the view that there had been oppression and directed the district court to sustain a plea in bar of trial.

DISCLOSURE

Since the passing of the Human Rights Act 1998 and the Convention rights provisions of the Scotland Act 1998, there has been a steady move towards disclosure

---

5 2000 SLT 75.
6 (1893) 1 Adam 114 at 135.
7 Alison ii 138.
8 1993 SCCR 730.

of much more material by the Crown than occurred previously. Part 6 of the Criminal Justice and Licensing (Scotland) Act 2010 makes detailed provision for a scheme of disclosure, based on the recommendations made by Lord Coulsfield in the *Review of the Law and Practice of Disclosure in Criminal Proceedings in Scotland*, published in 2007, but departing from them in some respects. The essence of the arrangements is that, in terms of the 2010 Act s 121, where the accused appears for the first time on petition or on indictment or where a plea of not guilty is recorded on a summary complaint, the prosecutor must review all of the information that may be relevant to the case of which the prosecutor is aware and determine whether any of it would:

(a) materially weaken or undermine the prosecution case,
(b) materially strengthen the accused's case, or
(c) be likely to form part of the prosecution case.

If the information falls into any of these categories, the prosecutor must disclose the information to the defence, except that the prosecutor may apply to the court in terms of the 2010 Act s 145 for an order preventing disclosure where there is a real risk of substantial harm or damage to the public interest and the fairness of the trial would not be compromised by non-disclosure.

DEFENCE PRECOGNITION AND IDENTIFICATION PARADE

It has been usual for the Crown to give the defence a provisional list of witnesses at an early stage so that they too can proceed to precognosce. Defence precognition has become less frequent and less comprehensive as a result of the Crown's more recent practice of providing copy statements. Nevertheless, the right to precognosce remains. It should be noted that the defence cannot insist on tape recording the Crown witnesses and, in the case of police officers at least, cannot insist on seeing the witnesses outwith the presence of more senior officers.[9]

Occasionally, the defence will wish to operate the 1995 Act s 291, which empowers a sheriff, on the application of the accused, to grant warrant to cite for precognition on oath any person who is alleged to be a witness in relation to any offence of which the accused has been charged. The test which the sheriff must apply is whether it is "reasonable" to require such precognition on oath in the circumstances and it was held by sheriffs in *Low v MacNeill*[10] and *Cirignaco v Lockhart*[11] that the reasonableness test applies not merely to the requirement for a precognition—which could be satisfied in almost every case—but also to the requirement that it be given on oath. The reasoning was that the defence need to find out that what Crown witnesses are going to say in evidence is catered for adequately by other existing law and practice, leaving the possibility of defence precognition on oath for "unusual and exceptional circumstances". In *HM Advocate v Campbell*[12] the Appeal Court doubted the appropriateness of an application to precognosce a police officer witness on oath where the purpose was to obtain information to allow the defence to cross-examine another witness about

9 *Drummond, Petitioner* 1998 SCCR 42.
10 1981 SCCR 243.
11 1995 SCCR 157.
12 1996 SCCR 419.

transactions between the two witnesses with a view to attacking the credibility of that other witness. The question was not, however, resolved.

The defence might also wish to invoke the 1995 Act s 290 which provides that, on the application of the accused, the sheriff may order that the prosecutor shall hold an identification parade. Three criteria must be satisfied, these being that the prosecutor has not already held such a parade, that the accused has requested him to do so but that the prosecutor has refused or unreasonably delayed and that the sheriff considers the application to be reasonable. *Beattie v Hingston*[13] seems to have proceeded on the basis that the defence require to offer reasons why an identification parade is needed, though the correctness of that approach was not reasoned out in the case.

PLEA OF GUILTY BEFORE SERVICE OF INDICTMENT

At any time after he has appeared on petition, the accused can intimate in terms of the 1995 Act s 76 that he intends to plead guilty, in which case he will be served with an abbreviated form of indictment (unless an indictment has already been served) and a notice to appear at a diet of the appropriate court not less than four clear days after the date of the notice. A s 76 indictment does not contain any list of witnesses or productions. The "appropriate court" means either the High Court or the sheriff court where no indictment has been served or the court in which the case has been indicted if an indictment has already been served.

At the s 76 diet if the accused does in fact plead guilty, he will be sentenced on that basis. Submission of such a s 76 letter does not, however, bind him and if he does not plead guilty, or pleads guilty only to a part of the indictment and the prosecutor is not prepared to accept a restricted plea, the s 76 indictment must be deserted *pro loco et tempore*—that is to say, the court, on the motion of the prosecutor, dismisses the case but with the possibility of re-indicting.

TIME LIMITS

It has for centuries been a feature of solemn procedure in Scots law that the prosecutor does not have unlimited time to serve the indictment and bring the case to trial. There is a general entitlement, in terms of Article 6.1 ECHR, to a trial within a reasonable time and that is discussed below. However, the 1995 Act ss 65 and 66 set out particular time limits, the purpose of which is, according to Lord McCluskey (speaking in *Gardner v Lees*[14]):

"to require the Crown to proceed with deliberate expedition in cases where the circumstances are serious enough to warrant procedure on indictment and/or the detention of the accused in custody awaiting trial".

These time limits provide a framework within which the Crown must work.

In reading the case law about the time limits, it should be kept in mind that they were changed when the Criminal Procedure (Amendment) (Scotland) Act 2004

13 1999 SLT 362.
14 1996 SCCR 168.

overhauled the procedure in the High Court, introducing preliminary hearings. The principles underlying the rules remain essentially the same, so some of the earlier cases are still relevant, but the time limits themselves have been varied.

The broad outline is as follows.

In the sheriff court, if the accused is in custody, the indictment must be served within 80 days of full committal; the first diet must take place between 10 and 15 days before the trial; the trial must start not less than 29 days after service of the indictment; and the trial must start within 110 days of full committal.

In the High Court, if the accused is in custody, the indictment must be served within 80 days of full committal; the preliminary hearing must take place within 110 days of full committal; and the trial must start within 140 days of full committal.

In both courts, whether the accused is in custody or on bail, the trial must start within 12 months of the first appearance of the accused on petition. In the High Court, whether the accused is in custody or on bail, the preliminary hearing must take place within 11 months of first appearance on petition.

All of these periods can be extended by the court, which explains why the 11- and 12-month periods may in theory (and very occasionally in practice) apply in custody cases as well as those on bail. It is, for example, possible for High Court preliminary hearings to be continued repeatedly, even with the accused in custody, so that the 140-day period for starting the trial keeps being extended until the 12-month time limit also becomes an issue. Such cases are highly exceptional and cause the court grave concern.

In more detail, the time limits are now as follows.

Service of indictment

Accused in custody: time allowed after full committal

By the 1995 Act s 65(4) an accused who is in custody must be served with the indictment within 80 days of full committal, which failing he is entitled to be admitted to bail. This provision does not, however, affect the validity of the indictment. In *McCluskey v HM Advocate*[15] an attempt was made to argue the contrary but the Appeal Court rejected that argument, observing that if the appellant had been unlawfully detained he might have a civil remedy, but that nothing in the legislation provided him with protection from prosecution.

As well as being significant for the situation with which it dealt, *McCluskey* also highlights the fact that acquittal on the substantive charge is not the inevitable remedy for any procedural defect.

A single judge of the High Court (but not a sheriff) may, for what the 1995 Act s 65(5) calls "any sufficient cause", extend the 80-day period. In *Farrell v HM Advocate*[16] it was held that it is competent to grant such an extension retrospectively.

All cases: induciae

By the 1995 Act s 66(6), the indictment must in all cases be served on the accused not less than 29 clear days before the trial diet. This is to allow the accused time to prepare his defence. The reference to "clear days" means that neither the day the

---

15 1992 SCCR 920.
16 1984 SCCR 301.

trial starts nor the day the indictment is served counts towards the computation of the 29 days. Moreover, in a case to be tried in the sheriff court, there must be at least 15 clear days between service of the indictment and the first diet. The Appeal Court held in *HM Advocate v McDonald and Others*[17] that failure to meet the 29-day time limit does not render the indictment fundamentally null and also that it is open to the defence to waive the 29-day *induciae*. The court also held that the failure of the defence to object to the failure to meet the time limit in that case by the procedure provided by the predecessor of the 1995 Act s 72 (which is considered below) meant that it was incompetent for them to take objection at the trial diet. This was on the ground that it was (and, by the 1995 Act ss 72 and 79, still is) provided that matters which can be dealt with by preliminary plea under s 72 cannot thereafter be raised except by leave of the court on cause shown.

Preliminary hearing

By the 1995 Act s 65(4)(aa)(i), where the accused is in custody the preliminary hearing must commence within 110 days of full committal, which failing he is entitled to be admitted to bail. By the 1995 Act s 65(1) in the High Court an accused cannot be tried on indictment at all unless the preliminary hearing is commenced within 11 months of the first appearance of that accused on petition in respect of that offence.

It is important to note that the 110-day period runs from full committal and the 11-month period runs from first appearance on petition at which, of course, the accused might have been committed for further examination, with full committal happening only (about) eight days later.

Both periods may be extended in terms of s 65(5). The law on extensions is discussed below.

Commencement of trial

By the 1995 Act s 65(4), in the High Court the trial of the accused who is in custody must be commenced within 140 days of full committal. In the sheriff court, the period is 110 days. Failure to meet these time limits entitles the accused to bail. The periods may, however, be extended (in terms of s 65(5)), in which case the accused is not entitled to bail until the extension runs out. Extensions can and do happen more than once.

In reading the cases on these time limits, it helps to remember that until 2004 the 110-day period applied in both the High Court and the sheriff court and the result of a failure to meet the time limit (as extended, if that happened) was that the accused was entitled to be liberated forthwith and thereafter he was to be "forever free from all question or process for that offence". In other words, missing the time limit operated as an absolute bar on further prosecution of the particular accused for the crime in question.

In *JTAK and Anr v HM Advocate*[18] the 110-day rule was held to apply to two children who were committed for trial and sent initially to prison on unruly certificates but afterwards were granted bail on condition that they resided in a

---

17 1984 SCCR 229.
18 1991 SCCR 343.

List D school, it being held that the bail order was in that case merely a procedural device for locking them up in the List D school.

HM Advocate v Meechan[19] decides that any period during which the accused is serving a substantive sentence for another offence does not count towards these time limits. Nor, in terms of *Bickerstaff v HM Advocate*,[20] does any period during which the accused is confined in a mental hospital as being insane in bar of trial. So, in *Wallace v HM Advocate*[21] where an accused was, after full committal, sentenced to two years' imprisonment on another charge it was held that the running of the custody time limit was interrupted when the accused began his sentence of two years' imprisonment, as his detention after that date was not referable to the committal order.

HM Advocate v McCann[22] establishes that the release of an accused from custody, on the authority of the prosecutor, at any point during his incarceration interrupts the running of the time limit.

Also by s 65(1) an accused cannot be tried on indictment for any offence unless the trial is commenced within a period of 12 months. This, of course, applies almost exclusively where the accused is on bail, though it is theoretically possible that the 110- or 140-day custody time limits might be extended to a full year.

There is an exception to the 12-month time limit (in terms of s 65(2)) in the case of an accused for whose arrest a warrant has been granted for failure to appear at a diet in the case. Parliament did not intend to provide an encouragement for accused persons to abscond in the hope that, if they could stay at large for over a year, they could thus obtain immunity from prosecution.

The Appeal Court made it clear in *McCulloch v HM Advocate*[23] that the date on which the accused appeared on petition is to be discounted in calculation of the 12-month period. In that case, the first appearance was on 6 October 1993 and the 12 months was, accordingly, due to expire on 6 October 1994 (and not on 5 October). This follows the decision in *Keenan v Carmichael*[24] which established that this is the correct approach to take to the computation of any period of time in a Scottish criminal context.

Extensions

As we have noted, the time limits can be extended. The majority of the case law relates to extension of the 11- and 12-month periods under s 65(3).

Such extensions are essentially a matter for the discretion of the court, no definitive test being laid down in the Act. However, some assistance may be gained from the cases. The most important of these is *HM Advocate v Swift*.[25] In that case, the Lord Justice-General (Emslie) explained that a judge faced with an application for an extension of the time limit should ask him or herself two questions:

"[T]he first question for the judge concerned is ... 'Has a sufficient reason been shown which might justify the grant of an extension?' The second question is: 'Ought I, in

19 1967 SLT (Notes) 75.
20 1926 JC 65.
21 1959 JC 71.
22 1977 SLT (Notes) 19.
23 1995 SLT 918.
24 1991 JC 169.
25 1984 SCCR 216.

the exercise of my discretion in all the relevant circumstances of the case, to grant the extension for that reason?'"

Although the precise terms of the statute have changed since Lord Emslie made these remarks, the courts still treat what he said as defining the issues and these are, accordingly, the matters which both Crown and defence need to have in mind when debating an application for an extension.

The cases give examples of the things that the court will regard as significant, and those which it will not. In *Hogg v HM Advocate*,[26] it was held that, where there were three accused placed on petition and it turned out after precognition that the case against one of them depended on evidence which the other two might give, it was a proper exercise of the Crown's discretion to proceed against those other two and then precognosce them and reassess the case against the third. It was also held that an extension of the 12-month period to permit that was proper.

In *Warnes v HM Advocate*[27] it was held that pressure of business on the court is not a good reason to grant an extension. The court noted, under reference to ECHR case law, that there is an obligation on the Scottish Executive "to organise our legal system so as to allow the courts and all other components in the system to bring cases to trial within the time limit set down by Parliament".

In *Watson v HM Advocate*[28] it was learned that the accused had decamped from his domicile of citation, possibly to the Republic of Ireland. A further petition warrant was granted and issued to the police for enforcement in relation to other charges. Efforts to trace him were unsuccessful and it was learned that he had failed to comply with bail conditions in England. The Crown, instead of serving an indictment at the domicile of citation which they knew to have been abandoned, sought and obtained an extension of the 12-month period. The accused appealed against the grant of that extension (though since it appears from the report that at the time of the appeal hearing he was still untraced it is not clear how he managed to do so).

The ground of appeal was that the extension was unreasonable since the indictment could have been served timeously at the domicile of citation. In support of this it was argued that, if the accused had failed to appear for trial having been so cited a warrant could have been obtained for his arrest and the extension was therefore not necessary. The Appeal Court, however, was persuaded by the Crown's argument that it is not in the public interest to require jurors and witnesses to come to court for a trial diet which is almost certain not to proceed because of the absence of the accused. The appeal was refused.

With some hesitation, the court supported the Crown's position in *McGinty v HM Advocate*[29] where the indictment was not served timeously because of the unforeseen illness of the police officer tasked with effecting service and an extension had to be sought. The court did point out in that case that mere pressure of business will not justify an extension. However, whilst it is one thing for the Crown to take a considered decision not to serve the indictment at the domicile of citation (as in *Watson*) or to be caught out by something unforeseen (as in *McGinty*), it is quite another for the Crown to seek an extension where it has itself made what Lord

26 2002 SCCR 18.
27 2000 SCCR 1127.
28 1983 SCCR 115.
29 1984 SCCR 176.

Justice-General Emslie was to call "repeated inexcusable and major errors"—the situation in *HM Advocate v Swift*.

In that case, the Crown twice made a mistake as to the accused's domicile of citation and left service copy indictments at an address which the accused had long since left and which had never been his domicile of citation. These indictments were, accordingly, never served and the Crown, when it discovered its error, had to attempt to serve a new indictment for yet another trial diet. However, there were less than 29 clear days available before the expiry of the 12-month period and so they could not comply with the requirement to give a 29-clear-day *induciae*. An application was made for an extension but the sheriff refused it and the Crown appealed.

The appeal was refused. The Appeal Court did not exclude the possibility of an extension even though the Crown may have been at fault but Lord Justice-General Emslie did say that "any particular fault on the part of the prosecutor and its nature and degree will be relevant considerations". In this case there was considerable and inexcusable fault and the court did not consider that the seriousness of the charges was enough to override that.

A similar conclusion was reached in *Lyle v HM Advocate*[30] in which the Crown made an error in the calculation of the expiry of the 12-month period and applied for an extension which was granted. On appeal the court held that in the circumstances of the case the error was inexcusable and, in respect that the charges were not of an unusual or exceptional gravity, that the wider public interest lay in favouring the observance of the statutory time limit. The appeal was allowed.

With *Swift* and *Lyle* must be contrasted *Black v HM Advocate*[31] in which the failure of the Crown to serve at the correct domicile of citation was attributable not to the fault of the Crown but to the fact that the change in domicile had not been intimated to the Crown. In that case the extension was granted.

The Crown is, of course, quite likely to get an extension if the delay in bringing the case to trial is attributable to the defence. In *HM Advocate v Brown*[32] the sheriff granted a defence motion for an adjournment of the trial but refused to grant an unopposed application by the Crown to extend the 12-month period. Her reasoning was that the Crown still had time to proceed within the 12-month period and that pressure of court business occasioning difficulty in finding court time to do so was not a sufficient reason for an extension. Lord Justice-General Emslie characterised this as "wholly unreasonable" and the Crown appeal was granted. Similarly, in *Duffy v HM Advocate*[33] the Appeal Court upheld a decision by the trial judge to extend the 12-month period in the absence of the appellant at the diet. The appellant was legally detained in England and the Appeal Court held that the delay in trying the case in Scotland was attributable to the appellant, not to the Crown.

In *HM Advocate v M*[34] the High Court held that it is competent to extend the 12-month period retrospectively.

These cases are all concerned with the 11- and 12-month periods; but s 65(7) permits the extension of the custody time limits on cause shown. Such extensions are commonly sought and granted where parties—especially the defence—still

---

30 1991 SCCR 599.
31 1990 SCCR 609.
32 1984 SCCR 347.
33 1991 SCCR 685.
34 1986 SCCR 624.

have preparation to do which cannot be completed within the time limit. An obvious example is the obtaining of an expert's report. *Young v HM Advocate*[35] provides an example of the extension because of the illness of the judge and the illness of two co-accused.

THE INDICTMENT

The indictment which is served on the accused sets out the charge and must be accompanied by a list of the names and addresses of the prosecution witnesses and a list of the productions, all as provided for by the 1995 Act s 66(4).

Certain things are implied in charges, even where not explicitly stated. One of the more important of these things is the allegation that the accused acted either as principal or art and part—so the fact that a charge does not specify that he was "acting along with others" does not prevent the Crown from presenting its case on the basis that he was involved with others in the commission of the crime.[36] We shall look at the law about the way in which charges are framed later in this chapter, under the heading of "preliminary pleas".

The list of witnesses is governed by the 1995 Act s 67. By that section the list must provide the names of the witnesses together with an address at which they can be contacted for precognition. It is in general not open to the Crown to call any witness whose name does not appear on the list or refer to any production not included in the list of productions. However, by the 1995 Act s 67(5), it is competent, with leave of the court, for the prosecutor to examine such witnesses or refer to such productions, provided that written notice has been given to the accused. In the High Court that notice must be given not less than seven clear days before the preliminary hearing. If that deadline is missed, the notice can be given at any time before the jury is sworn to try the case but only on cause shown. In the sheriff court, the notice must be given not less than two clear days before the jury is sworn to try the case. Notices of this sort are very common.

PRODUCTIONS

It is sometimes argued that the law requires that absolutely any object mentioned in the course of evidence should be produced in court. There are many cases about this question and they demonstrate that the law makes no such requirement. Rather, it discriminates between those things which truly add to the reliability of the evidence and those which do not.

The best starting-point is *Maciver v Mackenzie*,[37] in which a man was charged with taking wreck (pit props, battens and logs) without delivering it to the Receiver of Wreck. The wreck was not produced at trial. Lord Justice-General Normand said in the course of the judgment:

"The learned counsel for the appellant asserted that there was an obligation on the prosecutor to produce any article which was referred to in an indictment or complaint

---

35 1990 SCCR 315.
36 *HM Advocate v Meikleham and Parker* 1998 SCCR 621.
37 1942 JC 51.

unless it was beyond his power to do so. There is certainly no such rule. It is no doubt the proper practice to produce any article referred to in the indictment or complaint where there is no practical difficulty in doing so. There are, however, many cases where it is inconvenient, though not wholly impossible, to make articles productions in the case because of the size of the articles. Livestock cannot conveniently be made productions in all cases. Perishable goods cannot be made productions and there are other examples. *The question in each case is whether the real evidence is essential for proving the case against the accused*" (emphasis added).

The final sentence is the key to this whole area of law. If the article—what Lord Normand referred to as "the real evidence"—is essential to proof of the case, it should be produced unless that is impracticable. In *Tudhope v Stewart*[38] the Appeal Court distinguished the proof of the case from making it possible for the defence to test credibility by reference to the articles. In that case there was evidence that the accused had been seen running from a shop carrying clothing. The defence wished to demonstrate the improbability of that by reference to the bulkiness of the clothing. It was held that it did not have to be produced. The Appeal Court said that the test is "whether the real evidence was essential for proving the case against the accused, not for the purpose of testing credibility".

This must be seen in the light of the 1995 Act s 276. Although in general it could be argued that the production in court of biological material, such as blood, is undesirable on health grounds and not necessary to proof (since no-one ever analyses a blood sample in the courtroom), s 276(1) puts the matter beyond doubt by providing that evidence as to the characteristics and composition of such a sample is admissible notwithstanding the fact that neither the material nor a sample of it is lodged as a production.

The position reached in *Maciver v Mackenzie* was reaffirmed in *McKellar v Normand*[39] in which the appellant had been charged with reset of a bed and blanket which were not produced and it was held that, whilst it is good practice for items which are the subject of this sort of charge to be produced if it is convenient to do so or, failing production, for labels relating to them to be produced in their place, the question is always whether injustice is likely to result from failure to produce them. In *McKellar* the court took the view that it was not and upheld the conviction.

In *Hughes v Skeen*[40] a man was convicted of theft of 78 newspapers which were not produced at the trial. In upholding the conviction the Appeal Court observed that it was not explained what purpose in the interests of justice would have been served by the production of the newspapers and that such production was neither necessary, convenient nor practicable.

We may contrast *Anderson v Laverock*,[41] a poaching case in which the manner in which fish had been taken was essential to the charge and was proved by distinctive marks on the fish. Fish being perishable, the prosecution did not produce them at trial and for that the court did not make any criticism. However, the prosecution went further and destroyed the fish without giving the defence any opportunity to have them examined. This, it was held, was prejudicial and the conviction was quashed.

---

38 1986 SCCR 384.
39 1992 SCCR 393.
40 1980 SLT (Notes) 13.
41 1976 SLT (Notes) 14.

Where, however, the original material is made available, it is open to the Crown to use derivatives of that material to produce the evidence. In *Hamilton v Grant*,[42] for example, fingerprint lifts were made on vinyl sheets at the locus but photographs of those lifts were used by forensic scientists for comparison with the fingerprints of the accused. The vinyl sheets were lodged as productions at the trial but the sheriff upheld a no case to answer submission on the basis that the best evidence rule required that vinyl lifts should have been used for comparison. The Crown appeal against the sheriff's decision was allowed, though the court did not issue an opinion and we cannot therefore know the reasoning. We do know that in *HM Advocate v Dennison*[43] a trial judge allowed evidence to be led of sellotape lifts from prints on a cigarette packet, on the ground that there was nothing distinctive about the packet itself, though he regretted the absence of the packet.

It may be said, then, that the other party is entitled to an opportunity to test the accuracy of any assertion made about an article. Usually that opportunity will be given by producing the article at court; but if that is impracticable the party making the assertion imperils his case if he voluntarily does or acquiesces in anything which deprives his opponent of that chance. It does not, however, appear to be necessary to allow an opponent to test the proposition that an article exists (eg the newspapers in *Hughes v Skeen*). This principle is preserved for biological material by the 1995 Act s 276(2), which requires that a party wishing to lead evidence of the characteristics or composition of such material but not lodging it as a production, must make it available for inspection by the other party unless the material constitutes a hazard to health or has been destroyed in the process of analysis.

The point has sometimes been taken that the party wishing to lead evidence about the results of examination of an article needs to have that article in court to have it identified by both the person who speaks to the circumstances in which it was found and the person who made the examination. The argument goes that it is only in this way that it can be proved that the article examined is that which was found in circumstances of significance to the case.

Such was the argument made in *Williamson v Aitchison*,[44] a drink driving case in which the evidence related to a blood sample which was not produced at court. The appellant argued that this made it impossible for a constable to give evidence that the blood referred to in the analyst's certificate was that taken by the doctor from the accused, thereby breaking the link between the blood taken and that analysed. The court observed that whilst it would be usual to produce the sample it was not the only way to make the link and held that the analyst's and doctor's certificates taken with the evidence of the police that one part of the sample taken by the doctor had been sent to the analyst were enough to make the link. The conviction was upheld.

Documentary productions

Particular rules apply to documents which are to be productions with a view to proof of their contents. Issues arise in relation to copy documents and to business records.

---

42 1984 SCCR 263.
43 1978 SLT (Notes) 79.
44 1982 SLT 399.

Copy documents

The general rule, and the starting-point for our consideration, is that a copy is secondary evidence. The best evidence is the original. Therefore in a criminal case, unless the absence of the original can be explained satisfactorily as by its loss or destruction, the copy is inadmissible. This rule, for which there was more justification when copies were handwritten copies than nowadays when they are produced photographically, has been heavily modified by statute. Nevertheless, it must be borne in mind because if the statutory requirements are not met it will express the law which applies.

The statutory modification is to be found in Schedule 8 to the 1995 Act, which is based on work done by the Scottish Law Commission in a report entitled *Evidence: Report on Documentary Evidence and Proof of Undisputed Facts in Criminal Proceedings.*[45]

The root of the objection to the copy document seems to be Dickson's remark[46] that:

"[C]opies are often inaccurate from inadvertence, ... admitting them would afford opportunities for misleading the jury, and ... a party is most likely to tender such secondary evidence in order to gain an improper advantage from a discrepancy between it and the original document."

The Commission pointed out the inapplicability of the risk of inadvertent error in light of the existence of the photocopier and thought that the risk of deliberate deception could be sufficiently met by a power in the court to direct production of the original where it is desirable for the court to see the original or where there is any genuine dispute as to its appearance. This was substantially the approach taken for civil evidence in the Civil Evidence (Scotland) Act 1988 s 6.

Accordingly, paragraph 1 of Schedule 8 provides:

"For the purposes of any criminal proceedings a copy of, or of a material part of, a document, purporting to be authenticated in such manner and by such person as may be prescribed, shall, unless the court otherwise directs, be—

(a) deemed a true copy; and
(b) treated for evidential purposes as if it were the document, or the material part, itself,

whether or not the document is still in existence."

By paragraph 2 it is immaterial how many removes there are between a copy and the original.

Essentially, the effect of this is that a copy, provided that it bears what purports to be a proper authentication and the court does not "otherwise direct", is not only to be deemed a true copy but is to be treated as if it were the original.

It is also worth noting that in this provision, as throughout the Schedule, "document" is not confined to written documents. It includes maps, plans, graphs, drawings, photographs, sound recordings and visual recordings (such as videotapes).

---

45 Scot Law Com No 137.
46 Paragraph 279.

Authentication, by rule 26.1, is to be carried out by

  (i) the author of the original document,
 (ii) a person who is or who has been in possession and control of the original or a copy of it, or
(iii) the authorised representative of such a person.

It is to be in the form provided as Form 26.1-A. It is also important to note that all that is necessary is that the copy *purports* to be properly authenticated. It is *not* necessary for admissibility that the person who authenticates the document actually compares it with the original, though if he gives evidence and it transpires that he has not done so the reliability of the document might become a matter of comment.

In some cases, failure to check the copy with the original might found an application to the court to direct that the document should not get the benefit of paragraph 1. It is emphasised that this will vary from document to document. A banker might well be entitled to assume the accuracy of a copy statement produced from the bank's computer without making any comparison. Indeed there might be little with which it could be compared as the "original" is electronic and there is a good case for saying that such a printout is itself an original, rather than a copy.

Other kinds of documents might be less inherently reliable. Two cases in particular require care. The first of these is the production of a monochrome copy of a coloured original, where loss of the coloured material may alter the meaning (for example, where a plan distinguishes different areas by colour). The second applies where what is produced is a copy of a material part of a document. It might well be possible to demonstrate that another part materially alters the meaning of what is produced.

This brings us to the obvious issue of the circumstances in which the court will "otherwise direct". On the basis that any other approach would defeat the purpose of the statute, it is thought that the court will only "otherwise direct" where there is some particular reason to doubt the reliability of the copy produced. Some assistance may be derived from the consideration of the Law Commission, who observed that the mere fact that it is a copy which is produced should not be enough to induce the court to make a direction. As they said,

> "[T]he mere fact that the copy, if admitted, will be adverse to the party seeking to demonstrate unfairness is irrelevant since Parliament by enacting the legislation will have impliedly decided that there is nothing intrinsically unfair about the admission of a copy. It will not normally be unfair that there is no opportunity to cross-examine the operator of the copying machine or to examine the original of a tape or other device containing computer instructions or data which would be likely to be meaningless to the court".[47]

It is thought that, since the thrust of the paragraph is to make the use of copies a normal occurrence, it will be up to the party seeking to challenge the use of a copy to persuade the court to make such a direction. This will be reasonably straightforward where there is a patent defect on the face of the document. There might, for example, be obvious and material alterations and it might be unclear

---

47 *Evidence: Report on Documentary Evidence*, p 34.

whether they exist on the original. If the authenticator is a witness, he or she might be able to resolve that matter but, otherwise, the court might require to direct that the copy is not to get the benefit of the paragraph.

A more difficult question will arise where the party against whom the copy document is sought to be led in evidence maintains that it contains a latent defect. It may be said, for example, that the authentication is not what it purports to be or it may be that serious doubts about the reliability of the copy emerge in the course of evidence, perhaps because it has not been checked with the original. Here, it is thought, the court could be persuaded to make a direction but perhaps the best time to raise the issue in a case under solemn procedure would be at a preliminary diet or first diet.

Business documents

Paragraph 1 of Schedule 8 relates to copies of all kinds of documents. Paragraph 2, by contrast, is specific to documents relating to businesses and undertakings and the holders of paid and unpaid offices—though, as we shall see, this is scarcely a major limitation. Paragraph 2(1) provides:

> "Except where it is a statement such as is mentioned in paragraph 3(b) and (c) below, a statement in a document shall be admissible in criminal proceedings as evidence of any fact or opinion of which direct oral evidence would be admissible, if the following conditions are satisfied—
>
> (a) the document was created or received in the course of, or for the purposes of, a business or undertaking or in pursuance of the functions of the holder of a paid or unpaid office;
>
> (b) the document is, or at any time was, kept by a business or undertaking or by or on behalf of the holder of such an office; and
>
> (c) the statement was made on the basis of information supplied by a person (whether or not the maker of the statement) who had, or may reasonably be supposed to have had, personal knowledge of the matters dealt with in it."

This too is derived from the Scottish Law Commission Report. The Commission treated the law as to business documents as a branch of the law relating to hearsay, essentially because they contain a record of what someone has said or done. After reviewing the existing law, the Commission came to the conclusion that it was "not well suited to the needs of a society which increasingly depends on information kept or generated by a growing variety of technical methods".[48] The Commission then looked at the English legislation on the subject and at the effect of the Criminal Evidence Act 1965 which remained in force for Scotland, though not for England and Wales. They were able to identify numerous shortcomings.

In its Discussion Paper, the Commission noted that:

> "[T]he system of recording transactions, communications and other events in business and administrative documents will usually be one on which organisations themselves will depend in everyday practice and, therefore, the evidence so generated is likely to be trustworthy. Moreover, in many instances business documents will also be the best evidence, particularly those recording very detailed or unexceptional facts or events of which witnesses are unlikely to have any recollection."[49]

---

48 *Evidence: Report on Documentary Evidence*, p 3.
49 *Criminal Evidence: Affidavit Evidence*, p 52.

What the Commission was saying, in other words, is that business records, far from being an inherently unreliable type of evidence, are in fact likely to be highly reliable. They form the basis for just those sorts of important decisions in their own affairs to which juries are invited to have regard when being charged as to the meaning of the concept of reasonable doubt. On such an analysis, reform was overdue.

This approach was carried through to the Report itself and in particular the Commission identified three tests of reliability for statements in business documents. First, the statement would have to be based on someone's personal knowledge, so that it would be derived from someone who knew what he was talking about; second, the statement should have been made for the purposes of a business; and third, the document containing the statement should have been kept by a business.[50] The point of these requirements was that if a person was making a statement for the purposes of a business and the document was important enough to be kept, there would be a strong incentive to accuracy. These three tests underlie the three conditions which must be satisfied before paragraph 2 can apply.

Where these conditions are satisfied, a statement in the document is admissible in criminal proceedings as evidence of any fact or opinion of which direct oral evidence would have been admissible. The statement in the document stands as evidence in its own right and it does not require to be "spoken to" by a witness; the sole functions of the witness are to establish that the conditions are met and (perhaps) to interpret a statement which is couched in the jargon of a particular business. In *Al Megrahi v HM Advocate*,[51] the Appeal Court said that the conventional approach to documentary evidence consisting of records regularly kept by a business is to regard them as reliable unless some specific reason exists to doubt their credibility.

This contrasts with the general rule which is that statements in documents are not evidence unless they are "spoken to" by a witness. In *Forsyth and Smith v HM Advocate*[52] it was held that a trial judge should not have allowed an advocate depute to cross-examine on the basis of a document which had been lodged as a production but not spoken to by any witness.

The first test—that the document should have been created or received in the course of, or for the purposes of, a business or undertaking or in pursuance of the functions of the holder of a paid or unpaid office—requires to be satisfied by the evidence of a witness. It defines the breadth of the provision. By paragraph 8, "business" includes trade, profession or other occupation. By the same paragraph, "undertaking" includes any public or statutory undertaking, any local authority and any government department. "Holder of a paid or unpaid office" is not defined but appears to be derived from English legislation.[53] The Scottish Law Commission intended it "to cover such persons as an office bearer in an entity which is neither a business nor an undertaking, such as a charity, kirk session or club, who may keep documents for the efficient discharge of his functions".[54] It is, in short, difficult to think of any kind of record other than purely personal or private records to which the paragraph does not apply.

---

50 *Evidence: Report on Documentary Evidence*, p 6.
51 2002 SCCR 509.
52 1991 SCCR 861.
53 See *Evidence: Report on Documentary Evidence*, p 11, footnote 9.
54 *Evidence: Report on Documentary Evidence*, p 11.

The second test is that the document was kept by the business, undertaking or office holder and in terms of paragraph 4 this test can, subject to a discretion in the court to direct otherwise, be satisfied by certification in prescribed form and purporting to be authenticated in such manner as might be prescribed either by a person authorised to do so on behalf of the relevant business or undertaking or by an office holder or a person authorised on his or her behalf, as the case may be. The certificate, by rule 26.1(2), must be in the form set out in Form 26.1-C.

The Law Commission suggested that a court would not be likely to "otherwise direct" unless the party objecting to the statutory mode of authentication put forward at least *prima facie* grounds for not accepting that the document had been kept by the business concerned.[55]

The provisions of paragraph 4 are derived from the Civil Evidence (Scotland) Act 1988 s 5. It was the Law Commission's intention to use the expression "purporting to be signed", rather than "purporting to be authenticated" and their purpose was to bring into play *Cardle v Wilkinson*[56] so that a facsimile signature would suffice.[57] It is suggested that this has been achieved, notwithstanding the draftsman's preference for "authenticated".

SERVICE OF THE INDICTMENT

In terms of the Act of Adjournal (Criminal Procedure Rules) 1996 rule 2.2 service of the indictment may be personal or by leaving it at the domicile of citation specified in the bail order (either in the hands of someone there or by fastening it to the door). It is also competent, where no proper domicile of citation has been specified, to leave the document at a place where the accused is believed, on reasonable grounds, to reside. This approach, however, is rare if not entirely unknown, since the prosecutor cannot be certain that the court will regard the grounds for the belief as reasonable and therefore cannot be certain that the indictment has been served until the accused appears for first diet or trial and does not challenge the efficacy of the citation.

In the case of an accused which is a body corporate, the indictment may be served (in terms of the 1995 Act s 70(2)) at its registered office or principal place of business in the UK. The prosecution of bodies corporate on indictment is in fact rather rare.

PRELIMINARY HEARINGS AND FIRST DIETS

After the indictment has been served and before the trial takes place there are (broadly speaking) two substantial issues which require to be resolved. One is the state of preparedness of the parties, and the other is any preliminary legal challenge. There is no point in convening a trial if (for example) there is some fundamental flaw in the indictment which should mean that the trial should not proceed at all. There is (at the time of writing) a difference between High Court

---

55 *Evidence: Report on Documentary Evidence*, p 30.
56 1982 JC 36.
57 *Evidence: Report on Documentary Evidence*, p 30.

procedure and sheriff court procedure at this point and, although the procedures have some provisions of the Act in common, it is probably easier to follow the narrative if they are described in turn. We shall do so shortly.

Defence statement

As part of the disclosure arrangements, in terms of the 1995 Act s 70A, as inserted by the Criminal Justice and Licensing (Scotland) Act 2010, the accused must lodge a defence statement 14 days before the first diet (in the sheriff court) or the preliminary hearing (in the High Court). That statement must set out:

(a) the nature of the accused's defence, including any particular defences on which the accused intends to rely,
(b) any matters of fact on which the accused takes issue with the prosecution and the reason for doing so,
(c) particulars of the matters of fact on which the accused intends to rely for the purposes of the accused's defence,
(d) any point of law which the accused wishes to take and any authority on which the accused intends to rely for that purpose,
(e) by reference to the accused's defence, the nature of any information that the accused requires the prosecutor to disclose, and
(f) the reasons why the accused considers that disclosure by the prosecutor of any such information is necessary.

In terms of the 2010 Act s 124, the prosecutor must review the disclosure position in light of the defence statement and make whatever additional disclosure is necessary. In addition, the accused may serve a further statement at any time up to the trial, to trigger further disclosure.

Seven days before the trial, the accused must lodge a statement saying that there has been no material change in the defence position or, if there has, serve a further defence statement.

Notice of special defences, defence witnesses and defence productions

The fact that the burden of proof is at all times on the Crown is reflected in the obligations placed on the Crown as to the content of the indictment, list of Crown witnesses and list of Crown productions. However, it must not be forgotten that the law aims to *balance* the interest of the accused in securing a fair trial with that of the public in securing the effective prosecution of crime, and that Scottish criminal procedure is adversarial in its nature. It is as much in the public interest that the prosecutor has fair notice of the defence case as it is that the accused has notice of the case against him; only in that way can the prosecutor in the public interest make proper investigation of any substantive case which the accused proposes to advance, to either confirm or rebut it. Accordingly, the 1995 Act s 78 provides for the giving of notice by the accused of any special defence and of any intention to defend a charge relating to specified sexual offences by reference to the complainer's consent to the act which is the subject matter of the charge or the accused's belief as to that consent. He must also give notice of any witnesses whom he proposes to call and of any productions to which he intends to refer.

Special defences

There are four classically recognised "special" defences. These are alibi, incrimination, insanity at the time and self-defence. Alibi simply means that the accused was elsewhere at the time when the alleged offence was said to be committed and so cannot have committed it. Incrimination means that the accused blames some other person for the crime. Insanity at the time negates *mens rea* and so the accused falls to be acquitted; this is properly dealt with in a text on the general principles of criminal law rather than here. It is, moreover, in the process of being replaced in terms of the Criminal Justice and Licensing (Scotland) Act 2010 by a special defence of absence of criminal responsibility on the ground of mental disorder. And self-defence means that any violence used by the accused was in legitimate defence to an attack, actual or apprehended, upon him or another. This is properly dealt with in the context of offences of violence, rather than here. *Procedurally*, however, these defences have it in common that the 1995 Act s 78 requires that in the High Court notice shall be given to the Crown and any co-accused of the plea not less than seven days before the preliminary hearing whilst in the sheriff court it must be given at the first diet. If such notice is not given, the special defence cannot be pled unless the court otherwise directs. The same is true of the leading of evidence calculated to exculpate the accused by incriminating a co-accused and, by the 1995 Act s 78(2), of the pleading of automatism (which also negates *mens rea* and is properly dealt with in a text on general principles of criminal law), coercion or (as we have seen) consent in relation to a sexual offence.

So far as evidence is concerned, the position is best summarised in the words of the High Court in *Lambie v HM Advocate*:[58]

> "The only purpose of the special defence is to give fair notice to the Crown and once such notice has been given the only issue for a jury is to decide, upon the whole evidence before them, whether the Crown has established the accused's guilt beyond reasonable doubt. When a special defence is pleaded, whether it be of alibi, self-defence or incrimination, the jury should be so charged in the appropriate language, and all that requires to be said of the special defence, where any evidence in support of it has been given, either in course of the Crown case or by the accused himself or by any witness led for the defence is that if that evidence, whether from one or more witnesses, is believed, or creates in the minds of the jury reasonable doubt as to the guilt of the accused in the matters libelled, the Crown case must fail and they must acquit."

Notice of defence witnesses and productions

The 1995 Act s 78(4) deals with defence witnesses and productions. By that section, it is not competent for the accused to examine any witnesses or to put in evidence any productions not intimated to the prosecutor at or before the first diet (in the sheriff court) or at least seven days before the preliminary hearing (in the High Court) unless the court otherwise directs.

High Court procedure

In terms of the 1995 Act s 66(6)(b), a High Court indictment is accompanied by a notice calling the accused to appear and answer to the indictment at a preliminary hearing not less than 29 clear days after service of the indictment. Although the

High Court sits as a trial court in several venues throughout Scotland, as a matter of administrative practice preliminary hearings take place only in the High Courts in Glasgow and Edinburgh. As we shall see, once the preliminary hearing business is completed, a trial will be fixed. In general, a preliminary hearing in Glasgow will tend to lead to a trial in the west of Scotland and a preliminary hearing in Edinburgh will tend to lead to a trial in the east; but there is no fixed rule and there are many exceptions. Preliminary hearing procedure is regulated primarily by the 1995 Act ss 72 to 72E. The central feature of a preliminary hearing is the written record of the state of preparation of the parties which s 72E requires them to prepare and lodge not less than two days before the preliminary hearing. The content of the written record is prescribed by Chapter 9A of the Act of Adjournal (Criminal Procedure Rules) 1996. Rule 9A.4(1) does that by prescribing a form— Form 9A-4—which requires counsel to answer a series of questions. Part 1 of the form has to be completed by the prosecutor and Part 2 by defence counsel. Some of it deals with purely practical matters such as the estimated duration of the trial. Other parts deal with legal issues and those will be explained shortly. At the preliminary hearing, the court expects counsel to deal with the questions asked on the form in order. Defence counsel is usually called upon first. Sometimes the preliminary hearing has to be continued to a later date to allow preparation to be completed or to allow the court to deal with legal argument on a preliminary plea or preliminary issue.

Once the matters which have to be dealt with at preliminary hearing are all completed, s 72A requires the court to fix a trial diet within the time limits discussed above.

Sheriff court procedure

In the sheriff court s 66(6) requires that the accused be required to attend a first diet not less than 15 clear days after service of the indictment and not less than 10 clear days before the trial diet. The matters dealt with at the first diet in the sheriff court are the same as those which are dealt with at preliminary diet in the High Court. Section 71(1) requires the court to ascertain whether the case is likely to proceed to trial on the date assigned as the trial diet and in particular the state of parties' preparation and the extent to which the duty under s 257(1) (to try to agree evidence) has been complied with. Section 71(1A) and (1B) require the court to consider whether special measures should be ordered for any vulnerable witness. Section 71(1C)(a) requires the court to ascertain which of the witnesses who are listed are required to attend the trial. In addition, s 71(1C)(b) requires the court to review the bail conditions (a matter which is not before the High Court at preliminary hearing).

Section 71(2) provides that the court shall, at the first diet, consider any preliminary plea or preliminary issue of which a party has, not less than two clear days before the first diet, given notice to the court and to the other parties.

THE MATTERS DEALT WITH AT PRELIMINARY HEARINGS AND FIRST DIETS

Most of these matters have not yet been discussed. We shall leave s 196, which relates in particular to the sentencing stage, for later consideration; but we shall address the other matters in turn here.

Preliminary issues and preliminary pleas

Section 79(2) lists preliminary pleas. They are:

(i) a matter relating to the competency or relevancy of an indictment;
(ii) an objection to the validity of the citation of a party; and
(iii) a plea in bar of trial.

Section 79(2) also lists the preliminary issues. They are:

(i) an application for separation or conjunction of trials;
(ii) preliminary objections under specified sections of the Act;
(iii) an application under the 1995 Act s 278(2) (that all or part of the record of the judicial examination should not be read to the jury);
(iv) an objection to the admissibility of any evidence;
(v) an assertion by a party that there are documents the truth of the contents of which ought to be admitted; and
(vi) any other point raised by a party which could, in his opinion, be resolved with advantage before the trial.

Challenges to competency or relevancy

Renton and Brown[59] distinguishes the concepts of competency and relevancy thus:

> "[A]n objection to competency implies that the trial of the accused person before a certain court, or at the instance of a certain prosecutor or upon a certain charge is not competent; an objection to relevancy implies that the terms of the indictment to which the accused person is asked to plead are not in accordance with the requirements of the law."

Competency

Challenges to competency are, therefore, directed essentially to the right to prosecute and the most obvious ground upon which the competency of an indictment may be challenged is lack of jurisdiction. Another ground would be that the time limits which apply once the accused has appeared on petition have expired.

Much less frequently the person in whose name the indictment runs will be found not to have a title to prosecute. The 1995 Act s 64(1) provides that all prosecutions for the public interest before the High Court or before a sheriff and jury shall proceed on indictment in name of Her Majesty's Advocate, so that anything which purports to be an indictment and which runs in another name will be incompetent except where the office of Lord Advocate is vacant when the 1995 Act s 287(2) permits indictments to run in the name of the Solicitor-General.

Relevancy

There are probably two challenges to relevancy which arise more often than any others. The first of these is that what is charged does not amount to a crime and the second is that the charge lacks specification.

---

59 Paragraph 9-02.

The purpose of a criminal trial is not to discover the truth in general but rather to discover the truth or otherwise of the proposition that the accused person committed the particular offence charged against him. It is essential, therefore, that the issue should be properly focused in the charge. The Crown must, in framing the charge, direct the attention of the accused and the court to what it offers to prove and it must do so in a way which is both relevant and, as a sub-branch of this, specific. A challenge to the relevancy of a charge alleges that even if the prosecutor proves everything contained in the charge, it does not amount to an offence. A challenge to specification alleges that the accused has not received fair notice of the allegation against him. Thus a charge will be irrelevant if an essential element of the crime is omitted or if what is charged is a statutory prohibition which does not actually create an offence. So, for example, a charge which alleged that the accused was a law student in a public place without lawful authority or reasonable excuse would not be relevant because that is not a crime.

The cases, of course, are concerned with more subtle criticisms of charges, either where there has been a mistake in the drafting and something has been left out by accident or where the Crown is pursuing a charge which has not previously been applied in quite the way it is used in the instant indictment or complaint.

Khaliq and Ahmed v HM Advocate[60] is an example of a challenge to relevancy where the Crown applied a well-recognised type of common law crime to what was then a new type of conduct. That case established that the crime of reckless conduct may be committed by the supply to children of so-called "glue sniffing kits"—solvents with containers for inhalation—in the knowledge of the intended use and that such use was injurious to health and dangerous to lives. In so deciding, the High Court took the opportunity to reiterate that it is in the nature of Scots criminal law that it does not countenance any precise and exact categorisation of the forms of conduct which amount to crime. Old crimes can be committed in new ways and the law is flexible enough to deal with them. It follows that the fact that a precise precedent for a particular charge does not exist does not necessarily mean that the charge will be irrelevant.

Article 7 ECHR should probably be seen as setting limits to this proposition. That Article prohibits conviction in respect of conduct which was not a crime at the time it was carried out. In *X Ltd and Y Ltd v United Kingdom*[61] the European Commission on Human Rights treated common law offences as unobjectionable in themselves and the development of the law by common law processes as also unobjectionable but made a distinction between that which clarifies the law and that which extends it such that it is made to "cover facts which previously clearly did not constitute a criminal offence". As regards clarification, the Commission has said in the same case that "it is not objectionable that the existing elements of the offence are clarified and adapted to new circumstances which can reasonably be brought under the original conception of the offence". This, it is suggested, is the key to understanding the relationship between Article 7 and the sort of development of the law seen in *Khaliq and Ahmed*.

As to specification, the charge must give fair notice of the allegations which the accused will have to meet and, to that end, it is required to be specific as to

---

60 1983 SCCR 483.
61 28 DR 77 (1982).

time (which means date), place and mode. The test to be applied was set out with clarity by Lord Justice-Clerk Ross in *Clydesdale Group plc v Normand*,[62] a case on specification in a charge relating to a statutory offence, when, following *Lockhart v National Coal Board*,[63] he said:

> "The appellants must be well able to anticipate what the Crown are seeking to establish, and that is the test of whether the charges are relevant and sufficiently specific."

Relevancy and specification must be considered in the light of the detailed rules contained in the 1995 Act and especially in Schedules 2 and 3, as given effect for petitions and indictments by ss 34 and 64 respectively.

Schedule 3 sets out the basic rules. We do not require to consider all of them but concentrate on the basic essentials, especially time, place and mode.

Paragraph 4 deals with specification of time, place and quantity. Quantity can be dealt with quite simply by noting that where a quantity of anything is specified in a charge the words "or thereby" are implied in terms of paragraph 4(6). Accordingly, for example, a prosecution does not fail merely because the Crown alleges the theft of £200 and proves the theft of £195. Indeed, in terms of the same provision, the words "or some other quantity to the prosecutor unknown" are implied in all statements of quantities. As a result, in the example just given the Crown can secure a conviction even if the actual amount of money stolen is left shrouded in confusion. That having been said, however, where proof of a particular quantity or the like is essential to the definition of the charge the latitude will not apply. Such will not usually be the case in theft charges and the like but an attempt to rely on the statutory predecessor of this provision in relation to the age of a victim of crime failed in *Lockwood v Walker*[64] precisely because the particular offence (lewd and libidinous practices and behaviour) was regarded as only being capable of being committed against a child under the age of puberty (a proposition upon which *Batty v HM Advocate*[65] now casts considerable doubt).

Specification of the place of the commission of the crime (often called the locus) matters not only because it is required to give the accused fair notice of the case against him but also because the jurisdiction of the court will depend upon it (as the court pointed out in *McMillan v Grant*[66]). Paragraph 4(2) implies words such as "near" in every charge so that some latitude exists as to place in every charge, again where the actual place is not of the essence of the crime. However, *Symmers v Lees*[67] makes it clear that there are distinct limits to this. In the summary complaint in that case the Crown specified three roads in South Queensferry as the loci of dangerous driving but led evidence of such driving on other roads as well. On appeal, the High Court said:

> "[I]f the Crown choose to confine themselves to three particular roads in their narrative of dangerous driving then they are confined to these particular roads unless there is some particular reason why some slight extension might be permissible."

---

62 1994 SLT 1302.
63 1981 SLT 161.
64 (1909) 6 Adam 124.
65 1995 SCCR 525.
66 1924 JC 13.
67 2000 SLT 507.

Latitude as to time is more complex. It is usually possible for the Crown to state the date of the offence with accuracy but in some cases the most that is known is that the crime occurred during a particular period. Paragraph 4(1) therefore provides that the "latitude of time … in use to be taken" is implied in all statements of time where an exact time is not of the essence of the charge.

The latitude in use to be taken was three months[68] and that is the latitude which is implied. Accordingly, a charge which alleges that an offence took place on 1 February in a given year implies the period from 1 January to 31 March, and the Crown can lead evidence of the commission of the offence at any time during that period.

This is subject to the exact time not being of the essence of the charge. There are a few offences where exact time is of the essence and the examples usually given are concerned with poaching where the taking of a creature during the closed season will be an offence but doing so during the open season will not.

It was decided in *Howman v Ross*[69] that if a defence of alibi is being pled, the prosecutor will have to be more accurate as to date; otherwise the accused is unfairly hindered in his presentation of that defence.

There are some cases in which the period of time during which the offence occurred is longer than three months and sometimes substantially so. This may be because the offence itself is covert and not discovered by the victim for some time or it may be because the victim is a child who, for whatever reason, does not disclose the offence for some time. So, for example, in *HM Advocate v Mackenzies*[70] the accused had been stealing from his employer over a period of time but had managed to conceal the fact. The latitude taken and allowed was six years. Again, where the owner of an asset does not check it for a considerable period, the Crown will libel the whole of that period. The nineteenth-century cases (*Andrew Hempseed*[71] and *Geo Douglas*)[72] on this refer to sheep on the hill. A somewhat more recent example is to be found in *Cuthill and Arbuckle v Guild*,[73] in which it was held that on a complaint libelling theft of a cheque book and uttering forged cheques, it was reasonable to fix the dates by reference to the last date when the book was seen and the date of the utterings, even though that was 17 months, because theft is in its nature a clandestine act.

An example of a victim not disclosing the offence until a late date is to be found in *HM Advocate v AE*[74] in which the Crown took latitudes of nine and a half years on one charge and five years on the other. In that case the charge was incest and the daughters of the accused had been eight and ten years old when the conduct started. The Crown was also proposing to prove a course of conduct and not just isolated acts. Nevertheless, in repelling an objection to the relevancy of the indictment Lord Justice-Clerk Aitchison said that there would be a heavy onus on the Crown to justify such a latitude.

The existence of a course of conduct was also a matter which weighed with Lord Justice-Clerk Grant in *Littlejohn v HM Advocate*[75] when he held that 22½ months

---

68 Hume ii 221, Alison ii 251.
69 (1891) 3 White 57.
70 (1913) 7 Adam 189.
71 (1832) Bell's Notes 215.
72 (1865) 5 Irv 53.
73 22 November 1989, High Ct Edinburgh; unreported.
74 1937 JC 96.
75 1970 SLT 21.

was too great a latitude in relation to each of three charges, but the brevity of the judgment makes this case less helpful than it might otherwise be.

Ultimately, it will be for the Crown to justify the taking of an exceptional latitude and inevitably that will depend on the circumstances of the particular case. The test to be met was set out succinctly by Lord Cameron in *HM Advocate v Hastings*[76] as follows:

> "The basic principle which governs decision in questions of permissible latitude of time in criminal charges is that of fairness: fairness to the legitimate interest of the person accused in being fairly tried on a relevant charge, and fairness to the interest of the public in the detection and suppression of crime."

Specification of mode is about setting out in the indictment the conduct by the accused which forms the basis of the alleged charge. By paragraph 2, it is not necessary to specify by any *nomen juris* the offence which is charged. Instead, it is sufficient that facts relevant and sufficient to constitute an offence are set forth. So, in *Dyce v Aitchison*[77] the accused's conduct in a court formed the basis of a charge of contempt of court; but contempt of court is not a crime. It is a matter *sui generis* with which the court, whether civil or criminal, has inherent power to deal. It was not, therefore, necessary for the Crown to prosecute the matter—the court could have dealt with it on its own initiative. However, the High Court considered that the facts narrated did amount to identifiable offences, even though none of them was named in the charge and the charge was therefore held to be relevant. Other examples are to be found in *Bewglass v Blair*;[78] *Strathern v Seaforth*;[79] *Coventry v Douglas*;[80] *HM Advocate v Grainger and Rae*[81] and *Cameron and Ors v HM Advocate.*[82]

Section 64(2) of the 1995 Act provides that an indictment may be in the form set out in Schedule 2 to the Act. That Schedule, which is drawn directly from nineteenth-century legislation, gives examples of charges. It is to be regretted that the examples have not been more substantially updated; they retain a quality which is now somewhat quaint and use language which does not feature in modern practice. So, for example, we still see a charge relating to the uttering of a forged certificate of character for a domestic servant, and the unfortunate Harriet Cowan, mill-worker, of 27 Tweed Row, Peebles, is still being "ravished", notwithstanding the universal use of the word "rape" in contemporary indictments for that offence. Section 138(2) gives similar effect to Schedule 5 for summary cases, which (being drawn from 1954 legislation) is less dated but still somewhat so. It is suggested that, although Schedule 5 does not in terms refer to cases on indictment, the existence of a form of charge in that Schedule will nevertheless be at least a powerful argument in favour of its relevancy where it appears on an indictment.

The essential point about these forms of charge is that if they are followed the charge will be relevant even if specification of mode is thoroughly inadequate. In Schedule 2:

76 1985 SLT 446.
77 1985 SCCR 184.
78 (1888) 1 White 574.
79 1926 JC 100.
80 1944 JC 13.
81 1932 JC 40.
82 1971 SLT 333.

"you did, while in the employment of James Pentland, accountant in Frederick Street, Edinburgh, embezzle £4,075 of money"

does not tell the reader how the embezzlement was accomplished at all, and, in Schedule 5,

"you did conduct yourself in a disorderly manner and commit a breach of the peace"

is hopelessly unspecific but is sanctioned by the Act and was given effect to by the High Court in *Anderson v Allan*.[83] Lord Justice-Clerk Ross pointed out that the appellant could find out what the case against him was about by interviewing the Crown witnesses.

Schedule 3 paragraph 11 provides:

"In an indictment or complaint charging a contravention of an enactment the description of the offence in the words of the enactment contravened, or in similar words, shall be sufficient."

This can result in greatly reduced specification, but is not a licence for the Crown to include no specification at all. We have already noted the words of Lord Ross in *Clydesdale Group plc v Normand* and can contrast two examples of the application of the principle that what matters is whether the defence can anticipate what the Crown are seeking to establish. In *Yeudall v William Baird & Company*[84] the complaint libelled a failure to produce adequate ventilation in a pit but did not specify what should have been done. It was held the complaint was relevant on the basis that it gave fair notice that the system of ventilation was said to be inadequate to perform its statutory function. In *Blair v Keane*,[85] on the other hand, the complaint libelled a contravention of the Trade Descriptions Act 1968 and specified the extravagant claims made for the vehicle in question but none of its actual defects. It was held that as the complaint did not tell the accused the defects upon which the prosecution would lead evidence it did not give fair notice and was therefore lacking in specification.

Schedule 3 paragraph 3 makes it unnecessary for the Crown to use words such as "wilfully", "maliciously" or "knowingly" in charges; such words, which apply to *mens rea*, are implied in charges. So in *Gallacher v Paton*[86] it was held that a fraud complaint was relevant without the words "falsely" or "fraudulently" and in *HM Advocate v Colquhoun*,[87] an embezzlement case, it was held to be unnecessary to narrate that the accused knew of the trust purpose for which money was received since the word "knowingly" was implied by statute.

Paragraph 3 has, however, to be read with two qualifications. The first of these is that it probably does not apply to statutory charges, where failure to libel a word contained in the offence-creating provision specifying the *mens rea* might well render the charge defective. The second is that in *HM Advocate v Flanders*[88] the trial judge (Lord Cameron) held that this provision did not relieve the Crown from the need to give notice in the indictment of its intention to lead evidence that the

83 1985 SCCR 399.
84 1925 JC 62.
85 1981 SLT (Notes) 4.
86 (1909) 6 Adam 62.
87 (1899) 3 Adam 96.
88 1962 JC 25.

accused had at some time earlier than the date of the offence evinced malice and ill will towards the victim. In so holding, he said:

> "It is no doubt true that in terms of the Act of 1887 for purposes of relevancy malice is implied in the indictment, but my experience of matters criminal is that the practice has always been that there should be an express allegation of previous malice as a matter of fair notice when it is the intention of the Crown to lead evidence of such matters. ... It seems to me that the argument against admission of this evidence without proper notice rests upon a broader and sounder foundation, namely, that the principle of fair play and of fair notice, which underlies the practice of our criminal law, forbids the introduction of evidence of this kind unless fair and proper notice is given to the accused person of the intention of the Crown to submit it to the decision of a jury."

There is, therefore, a potential distinction between the rules which apply to the indictment so far as relevancy is concerned and those which apply so far as admissibility of evidence is concerned, though in *Anderson v Allan*[89] Lord Justice-Clerk Ross was to point out that the appellant could find out what the case against him was about by interviewing the Crown witnesses and such an approach would not support the making of such a distinction except, perhaps, as to matters which would not necessarily arise in the course of such interviewing (such as malice evinced six months before the crime, as in *Flanders*).

Amendment

An issue which is related to that of the content of charges is that of amendment of charges, as provided for by the 1995 Act s 96.

Section 96(2) and (3) provides as follows:

> "(2) It shall be competent at any time prior to the determination of the case, unless the court see just cause to the contrary, to amend the indictment by deletion, alteration or addition, so as to—
>
>   (a) cure any error or defect in it;
>   (b) meet any objection to it; or
>   (c) cure any discrepancy or variance between the indictment and the evidence.
>
> (3) Nothing in this section shall authorise an amendment which changes the nature of the offence charged."

The effect of this section is that it will be open to the Crown, if they consider it necessary to do so in course of a debate about relevancy, to seek to amend the indictment so as to cure some sorts of defect.

This is a wide power but not an unlimited one. As Lord Justice-Clerk Moncrieff put it in *Stevenson v McLevy*,[90] "[h]owever wide the power of amendment ... may be, it cannot extend to the essential requisites of a criminal charge". Lord McLaren expressed a similar idea in *MacIntosh v Metcalfe*[91] when he said "[n]ow, to remedy a defect does not mean to transform into a libel what never was a libel". In *Paterson v HM Advocate*[92] the Appeal Court recognised that it is difficult to extract from the authorities what amounts to a fundamental nullity. In both *Stevenson v McLevy* and *MacIntosh v Metcalfe*, the complaints omitted to specify the locus of the alleged

89 1985 SCCR 399.
90 (1879) 4 Couper 196.
91 (1886) 1 White 218.
92 2008 SCCR 605.

offence and the sheriff had allowed them to be amended by inserting a locus; but the court held that these amendments were incompetent. This, however, must be seen in the context of *Herron v Gemmell*,[93] where the locus libelled in the complaint read "on the road on the Glasgow Inner Ring Road, at a part thereof near Charing Cross underpass" but did not say that this was in Glasgow. The procurator fiscal sought to amend by inserting the word "Glasgow" after the word "Road" and the sheriff refused to allow that amendment. The Appeal Court, however, held that the amendment should have been allowed. Lord Justice-Clerk Wheatley said that a sensible reading of the description given of the locus made it abundantly clear that it was within the jurisdiction of Glasgow Sheriff Court. He went on to distinguish the situation in which no locus is given at all from that in which (as in the instant case) the locus is very fully specified "but might be lacking in some technical point of description".

Obviously there are shades of grey between these two extremes and it will be a question for the court in each case where that particular case falls. In *Yarrow Shipbuilders Ltd v Normand*[94] it was held that "on Unit 5, Ship 1047" was inadequate to demonstrate that Glasgow Sheriff Court had jurisdiction and the procurator fiscal was not permitted to amend by adding the words "South Street, Glasgow". Lord Justice-General Hope said that "an amendment ... cannot be made if the complaint is in the first instance incompetent".

In *Paterson v HM Advocate* the indictment charged two statutory offences of lewd and libidinous conduct towards a girl aged over 12 and under 16[95] but stated the date of birth of the complainer (correctly) from which it was clear that, at the date of the offences, she had passed her sixteenth birthday. The procurator fiscal persuaded the sheriff to allow amendment of the indictment to convert these charges to breach of the peace. The Appeal Court held that the statutory charges had been irrelevant (in that the complainer's actual age took her outwith their scope) but not fundamental nullity because the facts narrated in the charge could constitute an offence at common law.

It seems, then, that if a sensible reading of what is in the charge gives the information necessary, an amendment to put the charge into a proper form will be allowed but that amendment to provide the basic information is not competent. That sort of approach was applied to the benefit of the Crown in *Duffy v Ingram*.[96] In that case the complaint had three charges. No date was given for the commission of the alleged offence in the first charge; the second charge began "date and place above libelled" and the third charge began "on said 30 November 1985". It was held that the date could be inserted in charges 1 and 2 by amendment. The High Court did not say so but, reading the charges together, it is clear that the Crown was alleging that the offences were all committed on 30 November 1985 and it is suggested that the case is to be understood on that basis.

Whether or not to allow an amendment is primarily a matter for the discretion of the court but it is clear that prejudice to the accused will be an important factor. In *Lockhart v BSM*[97] a sheriff refused to allow an amendment partly because it proposed to narrate (but not charge) a further offence by one of the accused

93 1975 SLT (Notes) 93.

94 1995 SCCR 224.

95 This offence is repealed, recast and replaced by the Sexual Offences (Scotland) Act 2009, which was about to come into force at the date this book was published.

96 1987 SCCR 286.

97 1982 SCCR 188.

(which the sheriff characterised as "a radical change to the character of the offence charged") but also because the amendment would have deprived the accused of a statutory defence which would have been available in respect of the unamended version and this he considered to be prejudicial. Again, in *Walker v HM Advocate*[98] it was held that amendment of the locus from Aberdeen Prison to Inverness Prison, whilst technically competent, should not have been allowed because in its amended form the charge would have required wider investigation by the defence than they had properly carried out based on its original form.

By contrast, in *Matheson v Ross*[99] an alteration to the date of the offence after the prosecutor's case had been closed was permitted, there being no prejudice to the accused, and he having been offered an adjournment and declined it.

Absence of prejudice to the accused also weighed heavily with the court in *Tudhope v Chung*.[100] In that case the Crown had charged the accused with having done certain things in the capacity of one who had management and control of premises; but the particular regulation contravened related to occupiers of premises. The Crown sought to amend so as to substitute the latter status for the former. The sheriff refused to allow that to be done but the Appeal Court allowed the Crown's appeal. Lord Justice-Clerk Wheatley said:

> "The character of the offence is the breach of the regulation and that has not been changed. ... This was a classical example of curing an obvious error or defect ... just the sort of things which [the section] has in contemplation. If the amendments are allowed it is the same person who is being charged with the same offence ... it was not suggested that the respondent would be prejudiced in any way in his defence on the merits if they were allowed."

Challenges to validity of citation

The whole purpose of serving the indictment on the accused is to give him notice of the charge which he is to face. Accordingly, failure to serve the indictment is fatal to the proceedings and trial on that indictment cannot go ahead. In *Hester v MacDonald and Others*[101] an accused person had been granted money bail (the usual procedure at that time), and a domicile of citation was fixed. However, he failed to lodge the money and so remained in custody. The indictment was served at the domicile of citation and the accused, who was in prison, never received it, either actually or constructively. The domicile of citation had not taken effect. The case went to trial and the accused was convicted unanimously, but when the Crown learned of the failure in service of the indictment they did not support the conviction when it was appealed. As reported, the case is concerned with the accused's (unsuccessful) attempt to get damages against the procurator fiscal and others in respect of his conviction.

Pleas in bar of trial: nonage

At common law, since it is conclusively presumed that a child aged less than eight cannot be guilty of any crime it is a valid objection to trial that the accused is below that age. The Criminal Justice and Licensing (Scotland) Act 2010 s 52(2) inserts a

---

98 1999 SCCR 986.
99 (1885) 5 Couper 582.
100 1985 SCCR 139.
101 1961 SC 370.

new s 41A in the 1995 Act to provide that a child under 12 may not be prosecuted for any offence and that a person aged 12 years or more may not be prosecuted for an offence which was committed when that person was under 12.

Pleas in bar of trial: insanity in bar of trial/unfitness for trial

The law in relation to mentally disordered persons who are accused or convicted of crime is set out in Part VI of the 1995 Act. It is notable for the complexity of its expression and Part 7 of the Criminal Justice and Licensing (Scotland) Act 2010 makes further changes and, in particular, replaces the common law rules providing for insanity in bar of trial with a new statutory plea in bar of unfitness for trial. This book does not offer a detailed commentary on the law, either here or later (in dealing with sentencing and disposal of cases). Rather, this is intended to be an outline—an introduction, as the title of the book announces its purpose to be. It is particularly important in this area that a more detailed or specialist text should be consulted if a case is encountered in practice.

At common law, the test for insanity in bar of trial remains that set out by Lord Justice-General Dunedin in *HM Advocate v Brown*.[102] It is a mental disorder which "prevents a man from doing what a truly sane man would do and is entitled to do—maintain in sober sanity his plea of innocence, and instruct those who defend him as a truly sane man would do". This is replaced with a new s 53F which provides that a person is unfit for trial if it is established on the balance of probabilities that the person is incapable, by reason of a mental or physical condition, of participating effectively in a trial. In determining that, the court will be required to have regard to the ability of the person to:

(i) understand the charge;
(ii) understand the requirement to tender a plea to the charge and the effect of such a plea;
(iii) understand the purpose of, and follow the course of, the trial;
(iv) understand the evidence that may be given against the person; and
(v) instruct and otherwise communicate with the person's legal representative.

The court will also be required to have regard to any other factor which the court considers relevant but is required not to find that a person is unfit for trial by reason only of being unable to recall whether the event occurred in the manner described in the charge.

It will often be the defence who raise the issue but, where it appears to the prosecutor that a person who is charged with an offence may be suffering from mental disorder, the prosecutor is under a duty, in terms of s 52(1), to bring before the court such evidence about the accused's mental condition as may be available. By s 52B, the prosecutor is empowered in certain circumstances to apply to the court for the making of an assessment order. An assessment order is, by s 54D, an order which authorises the detention of the accused person in hospital and which requires the responsible medical officer to submit a report on the person's mental state within 28 days.

The hearing of a plea of insanity in bar of trial or of unfitness for trial will focus on the psychiatric evidence. By the 1995 Act s 54, a court which finds an

102 (1907) 5 Adam 312 at 343.

accused to be insane in bar of trial (or, in due course, unfit for trial) must do three things. First, it must make a finding to that effect and state the reasons for that finding. Second, it must discharge the trial diet and order that an examination of facts be held. And, third, it must remand the accused in custody or on bail or, where the written or oral evidence of two medical practitioners satisfies the court that certain conditions are met about the availability of medical treatment for the person, it must remand the accused person in custody or on bail or make a "temporary compulsion order" which authorises the detention of the person in a specified hospital until after the examination of facts.

The examination of facts is regulated by s 55. Its purpose is to determine, so far as possible, whether the accused actually did the act which constitutes the offence. The point of this is that it is perceived as unsatisfactory that a person who might in fact not have done what is alleged should nevertheless be subjected to compulsory hospitalisation simply because he is not fit to stand trial. A person who is not mentally disordered and who is found not to have done the act charged would, of course, be entitled to be acquitted and Parliament's desire has been to place the mentally disordered person as nearly as possible in the same position as the sane.

So far as possible, the rules of evidence and procedure at an examination of facts are to be as nearly as possible those applicable in respect of a trial (1995 Act s 55(6)). However, those rules inevitably require some modifications, the first and most obvious of which is that, where the accused is not already legally represented the court must appoint counsel or a solicitor to represent his interests (1995 Act s 56(3)). It is axiomatic, of course, that a person who has been found to be insane in bar of trial cannot do so for himself.

The other significant alteration to the usual rules is made by the 1995 Act s 55(5) which allows the court to order that an examination of facts shall proceed in the absence of the accused if it is not "practical or appropriate" for him to attend. Ordinarily, of course, proceedings cannot competently take place in the absence of the accused (see *Walker v Emslie*)[103] unless he so misconducts himself as to prevent a proper trial from taking place, in which case the 1995 Act s 92(2) permits the court to exclude him.

At the examination of the facts the court must, on the basis of evidence, determine whether it is satisfied to the criminal standard that the accused did the act or made the omission constituting the offence. It must also determine whether it is satisfied on the balance of probabilities that there are no grounds for acquitting the accused. If it is not so satisfied—in other words, if it is not proved that the accused did the relevant act or if there is a ground for acquitting him—the court must acquit the accused of the charge. However, by s 55(4), if the court holds that the accused did the act charged but acquits him on the ground of insanity at the time (which negates *mens rea*) it must state that ground. (Insanity as a defence is abolished by the Criminal Justice and Licensing (Scotland) Act 2010 and replaced by a provision, in a new s 51A, that a person is not criminally responsible for conduct if he was, at the time, unable by reason of mental disorder to appreciate the nature or wrongfulness of the conduct.) In such cases, the court may (by the 1995 Act s 57) proceed to make a compulsion order in the same way as if the accused had been found to be insane in bar of trial (or unfit for trial).

103 (1899) 3 Adam 102.

In a case where the accused is found to be insane in bar of trial (in due course, unfit for trial) and is not acquitted at the examination of facts the court may, if it thinks fit (and provided the particular detailed conditions for the making of whatever order the court is considering are satisfied) proceed in one of the ways set out in the 1995 Act s 57(2). These are:

(1) make a compulsion order authorising the detention of the person in hospital for six months;[104] this may be combined with a restriction order in terms of s 59, which applies special restrictions in terms of Part 10 of the Mental Health (Care and Treatment) (Scotland) Act 2003, in which case the compulsion order is without limit of time;[105]

(2) make an interim compulsion order, which authorises the detention of the person in hospital for 12 weeks;[106]

(3) make a guardianship order, which places the person under the guardianship of the local authority, as if the order had been made under the Adults with Incapacity (Scotland) Act 2000;[107]

(4) make a supervision and treatment order in terms of Schedule 4 to the 1995 Act; or

(5) make no order.

There are cases in which a person who has been found to be insane in bar of trial (or unfit) subsequently recovers. In such cases, it is open to the Crown to reactivate the prosecution, upon the basis that it is in the public interest to have guilt or innocence determined by a proper trial. Accordingly, the 1995 Act s 56(7) provides that, where a finding has been made that the accused did the act or made the omission constituting the offence and that person is subsequently charged with an offence arising out of the same act or omission, any order made under s 57(2) shall cease to have effect.

Pleas in bar of trial: res judicata

Res judicata refers to the principle that no-one can be required to face a court for a second time on a matter which has been disposed of already by either conviction or acquittal. Accordingly, if a court has held a charge to be irrelevant, or incompetent, the prosecutor cannot place the accused before the court again on a charge or (in relation to competency) in circumstances not materially different. So in *HM Advocate v McNab*[108] an attempt to reindict in circumstances which had already been held to be incompetent was the foundation of a successful plea in bar of trial (applying a much older case, *Longmuir v Baxter*[109]).

HM Advocate v M[110] is an example of a case in which, the first indictment having been dismissed as irrelevant, the Crown served a fresh indictment in which changes had been made sufficient to defeat the plea of *res judicata*.

Where the accused has stood trial on, or pled guilty to, the matter already, he is said to have "tholed his assize". The parameters for this are, however, quite strict.

104 Section 57A(2).
105 Section 57A(7).
106 Section 53(8).
107 Section 58(1A).
108 1994 SCCR 633.
109 (1858) 3 Irv 287.
110 1986 SCCR 624.

In *Hilson v Easson*[111] Lord Ormidale said that "the essence of the plea is that the person tendering it has already been brought to trial by the prosecutor and has then stood his trial for, or pleaded guilty of a specific offence duly set out in an indictment or other competent form of complaint". In *HM Advocate v Dunlop*[112] Lord Cameron summarised the position by saying:

> "[I]n order that the plea of *res judicata* will lie the former proceedings must have been orderly and regularly conducted to a conclusion and in the case of solemn procedure this involves the return of a verdict by a properly constituted jury … where no verdict has been received or returned … the whole proceedings are vitiated and in the absence of a verdict the plea of 'tholed assize' cannot lie."

It was a matter of concession in that case that the first prosecution does not have to have proceeded to sentence.

It is of the essence of the plea that the first proceedings were competent. In *Hilson* the Lord Justice-General described as "downright nonsense" the proposition that the accused had tholed his assize because an English court had, in apparent ignorance of the fundamental principles of criminal jurisdiction and the provisions of the Treaty of Union which address the separate identity of Scots law, purported to take untried Scottish offences into account in sentencing him for English offences. This is a mistake which English courts still make from time to time.

At the time of writing, the Scottish government was considering what legislation to introduce on the basis of the Scottish Law Commission Report, *Double Jeopardy*. The rule proposed by the Commission was that a second prosecution should be prohibited where a person has previously been convicted or acquitted of an offence and:

(a) the second indictment or complaint charges an offence of which it would have been competent to convict the accused on the first indictment or complaint (so, for instance, an earlier verdict on a trial for murder will bar subsequent prosecution for attempted murder, culpable homicide, assault etc); or

(b) the second indictment or complaint charges an offence which is an aggravated form of the offence charged on the first occasion (so, for instance, a previous conviction or acquittal of assault will bar a subsequent prosecution for assault to severe injury).

That was intended by the Commission to amount to a clarification and restatement of existing law; but certain ministerial statements suggested that legislation might go further and relax the prohibition.

Pleas in bar of trial: mora/a hearing within a reasonable time

Mora is concerned with delay. The court has an inherent jurisdiction to refuse to deal with a prosecution, whether under solemn procedure or summary procedure, which has become oppressive as a result of delay. The law was reviewed by a full bench in *McFadyen v Annan*,[113] in which the Lord Justice-Clerk (Ross) said that:

111 1914 SC (J) 99.
112 1974 SLT 242.
113 1992 SCCR 186.

"What the Court has to ask itself is if the delay, whether caused by the Crown or not, has been such as to prejudice the prospects of a fair trial ... the real question which the Court has to consider in all cases where delay is alleged is whether the delay has prejudiced the prospects of a fair trial. This involves the Court asking itself whether the risk of prejudice from the delay is so grave that no direction by the trial judge could be expected to remove it. In the case of summary procedure the question must be whether the risk of prejudice from the delay is so grave that the sheriff or justice could not be expected to put that prejudice out of his mind and reach a fair verdict."

The Appeal Court considered the issue further in *Normand v Rooney*[114] and observed that the question of "putting the prejudice out of one's mind" required some explanation. The Lord Justice-General (Hope) formulated the test, in a summary prosecution, as being "whether the prejudice is so grave that no Sheriff or Justice could be expected to reach a fair verdict in all the circumstances". This, it is suggested, recognises the particular nature of the prejudice rather better, especially when the Lord Justice-General went on to say:

"I see no reason to doubt on this information that the Sheriff who hears the evidence at the trial will be able to arrive at a fair verdict, after making such allowance as may be appropriate for any disadvantage which the respondent may suffer due to the lapse of time which has occurred."

This has now to be seen in light of Article 6.1 ECHR. Article 6.1 requires that, in the determination of a criminal charge against him, everyone is entitled to a hearing within a reasonable time. For several years after the entry into force of the Scotland Act 1998 s 57 there was substantial activity around this issue but in *Spiers v Ruddy*[115] the Judicial Committee of the Privy Council held that an indictment should only be dismissed on this ground where the delay has created a situation which makes fair trial impossible. In other cases, the delay can be cured by expedition, a reduction in sentence or by compensation. The frequency with which the point is taken has, therefore, been reduced dramatically. Where it does arise, the following principles apply:

- The period to be taken into consideration does not necessarily commence on the first occasion on which the suspect (and eventual accused) learns that he is under investigation. In Convention law, the period commences when the accused has been charged, which means, for Convention purposes, the date when official notification is given to him by a competent authority that it is alleged that he has committed an offence, or the date from which his situation is substantially affected as a result of the suspicion against him.[116] The Court of Appeal has held that the computation of time in England and Wales will normally start with either a defendant being charged or being served with a summons as a result of information being laid before the justices. The court recognised, however, that in some cases a defendant will be so substantially affected before that as to be, as a matter of substance, in no different position from a person who has been charged.[117] The High Court of Justiciary has drawn a distinction between investigation and

114 1992 SCCR 336.
115 2009 SC (PC) 1.
116 *Eckle v Germany* (1983) 5 EHRR 1.
117 *Attorney General's Reference No 2 of 2001.*

notification.[118] In a police complaint case, the taking by the investigator of the notebook of the police officer under investigation does not amount to "notification".[119] In a case involving child abuse the taking of steps by those responsible for the welfare of the victim, without reference to the police or to the procurator fiscal, does not start the clock.[120]

- The correct approach is for the court to consider whether the period involved is *prima facie* unreasonable. Only if it so considers does the onus pass to the prosecutor to explain the delay.[121]

- There is no generally "appropriate" time required, either for the police to report a matter to the procurator fiscal, or thereafter for any of the stages which lead to eventual indictment. Every case has to be examined on its own facts.[122] It is, however, the period as a whole that is important[123] and it is not correct to adopt a piecemeal approach either by the defence criticising individual periods of inactivity in a case which as a whole proceeds within a reasonable time[124] or by the Crown seeking to justify each individual chapter of the time taken in a case which, overall, has taken too long.[125] The period to be taken into account lasts until the determination of the charge and that includes any appeal.[126]

- What will amount to a reasonable time will be determined in light of existing Scots law standards and not by reference to the particular periods of time which the Strasbourg court has in the past regarded as unreasonable.[127] Notwithstanding the Lord Justice-General's recognition in *HM Advocate v McGlinchey and Renicks*[128] that the Convention applies an international standard and that exclusive concentration on national standards would result in the application of Article 6.1 differing as between the States Parties to ECHR, this has meant in practice that the threshold of unreasonableness has been set rather lower in Scotland than elsewhere.

- An assertion that there has been, even *prima facie*, some unreasonableness will be justified only if some factual basis for inferring such unreasonableness can be identified and averred.[129]

- "It will be easy, but ... quite wrong, to describe the timescales achieved by, say, a busy Procurator Fiscal's department as demonstrating some kind of 'failure', merely because greater resources would have made it possible to deal with more cases faster. Correspondingly, it is inappropriate to describe the improvements which could thus theoretically be achieved with greater resources as a 'remedy' for such a 'failure', which it is somehow the duty of the funding authorities to fulfil."[130]

---

118 *Robb v HM Advocate* 2000 JC 368 at 374 and 377; *Reilly v HM Advocate* 2000 SCCR 879.
119 *Dyer v Watson and Burrows* 2002 SC (PC) 89.
120 *McLean v HM Advocate* 2000 JC 140.
121 *McNab v HM Advocate* 1999 SCCR 930.
122 *Gibson v HM Advocate* 2001 SCCR 51.
123 *Smith v HM Advocate* 2000 SCCR 926; *Dyer v Watson and Burrows*.
124 *HM Advocate v McGlinchey and Renicks* 2000 SCCR 593.
125 *Kane v HM Advocate* 4 May 2001.
126 *Neumeister v Austria* (1979–80) 1 EHRR 91; *Monnell and Morris v United Kingdom* (1987) 10 EHRR 205.
127 *McNab*; *McGlinchey and Renicks*.
128 2000 SCCR 593.
129 *Gibson*.
130 *Gibson, per* Lord Prosser.

- The right to a hearing within a reasonable time does not, in a case in which there is an insufficiency of evidence, preclude the prosecution authorities from keeping a file open against the possibility of a change in circumstances making it possible to proceed. In *Robb v HM Advocate*,[131] Lord Prosser said that:

> "If at the beginning of the relevant period there is a clear insufficiency of evidence, or if the competent authorities reasonably consider that to be the position, the passage of time thereafter, with no further proceedings being taken will be unsurprising. In some cases, it will be possible to say that further investigations should have been undertaken or that arrangements should be made to review the case. A failure to take proper investigative steps may well constitute unreasonable conduct ... [but] ... it does not seem to us to be unreasonable to keep the file open for review, when serious allegations have been made. A lapse of time in unchanging circumstances may not be attributable to the State or entail unreasonable delay on the part of the State."

- It is legitimate for the prosecutor to prioritise cases and that process is recognised to be imprecise. In deciding upon priorities, a wide discretion is inevitable.[132] However, (a) particular characteristics of the individual affected by the delay can be a relevant factor, in so far as they render the delay particularly prejudicial. This is especially true of cases involving child accused;[133] and (b) if a backlog of work, which causes delays, is not addressed by prompt remedial action it may become what the High Court of Justiciary has called "systemic", "inherent" and "uncured" and hence an unreasonable failure.[134]

- Lord Bingham of Cornhill summarised the correct approach in practice thus in *Dyer v Watson and Burrows*:

> "In any case in which it is said that the reasonable time requirement ... has been or will be violated, the first step is to consider the period of time which has elapsed. Unless that period is one which, on its face and without more, gives grounds for real concern it is almost certainly unnecessary to go further, since the convention is directed not to departures from the ideal but to infringements of basic human rights. The threshold of proving a breach of the reasonable time requirement is a high one, not easily crossed. But if the period which has elapsed is one which, on its face and without more, gives ground for real concern, two consequences follow. First, it is necessary for the court to look into the detailed facts and circumstances of the particular case. The Strasbourg case law shows very clearly that the outcome is closely dependent on the facts of each case. Secondly, it is necessary for the contracting state to explain and justify any lapse of time which appears to be excessive."

Separation or conjunction of charges or trials

It is fundamental that the trial must be fair and it is arguable that if some combinations of unrelated charges appear on the indictment the mere presentation of the combination to the court will be so prejudicial that the Crown should not be permitted to proceed to trial upon all of them at once.

---

131 2000 SCCR 354.
132 *Gibson.*
133 *HM Advocate v DP and SM* 16 February 2001.
134 *O'Brien and Ryan v HM Advocate* 7 June 2001.

This is the theory but it is rare that such an argument succeeds. An example of a case in which it did is *HM Advocate v McGuinness*,[135] in which the Crown combined charges of assault on one date with an unrelated charge of murder on another date. However, the Lord Justice-Clerk in that case explained that the test is "whether it is fair to the person or persons accused to put a particular accumulation of charges in one indictment" and stressed that the decision is one for the discretion of the court.

In *Brown v HM Advocate*[136] Lord Justice-General Hope had to deal with a case in which the accused was charged with "a catalogue of different crimes alleged to have been committed in different places and under different circumstances". He said that:

> "It is well settled that the combination in a single indictment of charges relating to different kinds of crime committed at different times in different places and circumstances does not of itself give rise to a material risk of prejudice to the accused, and it would not be appropriate on this ground alone for the charges to be separated. ... It is common ground that it is only where a material risk of real prejudice can be demonstrated that the granting of a motion to separate charges can be justified."

In *Brown* the fact that the accused would need to attack the character of Crown witnesses on some of the charges (thus exposing himself to the risk that his own criminal record would be in issue) was held not to be a sufficient ground for separating charges, since the trial judge would have a discretion whether or not to allow his record to be put in issue. That judge could take the risk of prejudice into account in so deciding.

Separation of trials is a related matter and arises where there are multiple accused. The starting-point is that it has been recognised since at least *HM Advocate v Parker and Barrie*[137] that related offences committed by two or more persons should in general be tried together. Separation is possible, but Lord Moncrieff said in *Robt Turner and Others*[138] that "[i]t generally requires some specification of peculiar circumstances to render it necessary or desirable". Slightly more recently, in *Gemmell and McFadyen v MacNiven*,[139] the Lord Justice-General said:

> "Persons accused of the joint commission of a crime have no right to insist on a separation of trials; and there is nothing oppressive in refusing a separation, unless it is asked for on some ground which goes to the conditions of a fair trial."

The conjoining of charges or trials is rare in the extreme but it is possible that by proceeding separately against accused persons for an offence which they are alleged to have committed in concert the Crown may bring about unfairness and in such circumstances such a motion may be made.

Preliminary objections under specified sections of the Act (special capacities)

Section 27(4A)(a) provides that the fact that an offence was committed whilst on bail is to be held as admitted unless challenged by preliminary objection. Other sections referred to by s 79(2)(b)(ii) make similar sorts of provision. The most

---

135 1937 JC 37.
136 1992 SCCR 59.
137 (1888) 2 White 79.
138 (1881) 18 SLR 491.
139 1928 JC 5.

important in practice is probably s 255, which deals with the fact that certain crimes can only be committed by a person who possesses a particular qualification, such as being the holder of a licence, the master of a vessel or the occupier of a house. In terms of s 255 such "special capacities" are held to be admitted unless challenged. In *White v Allan*[140] the special capacity (that of being a prostitute in relation to a charge of importuning under the Civic Government (Scotland) Act 1982 s 46(1)) was challenged and, since the Crown failed to lead any evidence to prove that capacity, the accused was acquitted. By contrast, in *Allan v McGraw*[141] the court affirmed that being a female prostitute is a special capacity in relation to s 46(1) and that, since it had not been challenged at the appropriate time, it was to be held as admitted.

As a general rule, a special capacity exists in any statutory offence where the prosecutor would otherwise have to prove the capacity as part of the proof of the case. As the Appeal Court put it in *Smith v Allan*:[142]

> "We are of opinion that 'any special capacity' ... applies to all persons who are specifically charged in a particular capacity with committing an offence which can only be committed by persons in that special capacity."

Special capacities do not apply to common law crimes, for the simple reason that such crimes can be committed by anyone at all and not only by those possessing particular qualifications.

Perhaps the commonest special capacity is that of being disqualified for holding or obtaining a driving licence, and this is relevant to a charge of driving whilst disqualified. In *Paton v Lees*[143] the High Court held on appeal that to be disqualified by order of the court is to possess a special capacity and in *Smith v Allan* it was held that to be disqualified by reason of age is also to possess such a capacity. In *Aitchison v Tudhope*[144] it was held that to be subject to a bail order is a special capacity; and in *Newlands v MacPhail*[145] the provision was held to apply to contraventions of the Civic Government (Scotland) Act 1982 s 58(1), which can only be committed by persons who have two or more unspent convictions for theft.

Applications for part of the transcript of judicial examination not to be read

Section 278(2) makes it possible to apply for part (or, indeed, all) of the transcript of judicial examination not to be read. The grounds upon which such applications should be granted are not specified in the Act but the obvious one is that a passage in the transcript is inadmissible (perhaps because the procurator fiscal overstepped the limits on questioning) or prejudicial (for example, because the accused disclosed something which is irrelevant to the charge but goes to his character). In practice, the issue is usually dealt with by agreement between the Crown and the defence.

Objections to admissibility of evidence

One party or the other—usually the defence—will often be able to identify in advance some element in the evidence which it regards as inadmissible. The most

---

140 1985 SCCR 85.
141 1986 SCCR 257.
142 1985 SCCR 190.
143 1992 SCCR 212.
144 1981 SCCR 1.
145 1991 SCCR 88.

common example is the record of any interview conducted by the police with the accused. It is helpful to try to resolve such objections in advance of the trial and so one often finds that the court will fix a hearing to do so, sometimes with evidence being led. We noted above that, in *Thompson v Crowe*,[146] it was established that, where the fairness of an interview is challenged, it is for the Crown to satisfy the judge that the interview was fair. That will usually be done (or at least attempted) at such a hearing. In other cases it may be possible to deal in advance of the trial with any objection to the admissibility of the results of a search or of surveillance.

Admissions as to documents and other matters

Section 79(2)(b)(v) provides for an assertion by a party that there are documents the truth of the contents of which ought to be admitted, or that there is any other matter which ought to be agreed. The Crown has occasionally used this provision, with varying success, to try to force the hand of the defence in relation to apparently non-contentious evidence in fraud trials.

Other points which could be resolved with advantage

This is a catch-all.

Other matters usually dealt with at preliminary hearings or first diets

When we come to consider the trial, and the law relating to witnesses, we shall see that special provision is made for special measures when children and other vulnerable witnesses give their evidence. Applications for such measures are most often dealt with by a judge or sheriff in chambers, on the paper application alone, but it is sometimes necessary to deal with them at preliminary hearing or first diet.

There are particular protections accorded to witnesses in sexual offence cases, in terms of the 1995 Act s 274. It is possible to apply, under s 275, for relaxations in those protections so as to allow relevant questions to be asked. Such applications tend to be made and dealt with at this first stage.

Devolution issues

At this point, it is convenient to deal with the law on "devolution issues". This is a concept introduced by the Scotland Act 1998 and defined fully by Sch 6 para 1 to that Act. In a criminal procedure context, the question whether a purported or proposed exercise of a function by a member of the Scottish Government is, or would be, incompatible with any of the Convention rights or with Community law (that is, EC law) is a devolution issue. So is a question whether a failure to act by a member of the Scottish Government is compatible with these things. This runs alongside s 57(2) of the Act, which makes it *ultra vires* for a member of the Scottish Government to do anything which is incompatible with any of the Convention rights or with Community law. The Lord Advocate is a member of the Scottish Government and accordingly a question whether something the Crown is doing or intends to do in the course of a prosecution breaches ECHR or EC law is a devolution issue. That means that the question has to be decided within

146 1999 SCCR 1003.

the framework of the rules provided for deciding devolution issues. Those rules are set out in the Scotland Act Sch 6 and in Chapter 40 of the Act of Adjournal (Criminal Procedure Rules) 1996.

So far as indictment cases are concerned, rule 40.2 provides that, where a party to proceedings on indictment proposes to raise a devolution issue, he shall, not later than seven days after service of the indictment, give written notice of his intention to do so to the clerk of the court in which the trial is to take place. Rule 40.6 requires that the written notice shall

> "specify the facts and circumstances and contentions of law on the basis of which it is alleged that a devolution issue arises ... in sufficient detail to enable the court to determine ... whether a devolution issue arises in the proceedings".

At the same time as it is given to the clerk of court, that written notice must be served on the other parties to the proceedings and on "the relevant authority". For present purposes, "the relevant authority" means the Advocate General and the Lord Advocate;[147] though of course the Lord Advocate will receive intimation as a party to the indictment proceedings. If the relevant authority—in practice, the Advocate General—wishes to become a party to the proceedings, he must give notice within seven days of receiving the notice.

In *HM Advocate v Montgomery*[148] the Lord Justice-General noted that the legislation makes no specific provision for a hearing on the devolution issue but noted distinct parallels between some devolution issues and the plea of oppression in bar of trial. It is understood that the two periods of seven days were selected deliberately so as to allow devolution issues to be dealt with at preliminary diets and that, in practice, is what happens.

In terms of the Scotland Act Sch 6 paras 9 and 11 it is open to a court other than a court consisting of two or more judges of the High Court of Justiciary (ie courts other than the Justiciary Appeal Court) to refer the devolution issue to the Appeal Court and it is open to the High Court sitting as a court of two or more judges to refer the issue to the Supreme Court. Schedule 6 para 13 provides for an appeal from the High Court to the Supreme Court and this is discussed below.[149]

Rule 40.5 precludes the raising of a devolution issue otherwise than in accordance with this procedure except on cause shown. The High Court has taken a reasonably relaxed view of what constitutes such cause, at least where the point which it is sought to take appears to have some *prima facie* merit, but it would be unwise to presume upon such an approach.

ADJOURNMENT AND ALTERATION OF DIETS

The 1995 Act s 75A makes provision for adjournment of trials. Procedurally application is usually made by minute under s 75A(5). Whether or not to grant an adjournment is a matter for the discretion of the judge who deals with such an application. However, the Appeal Court gave some guidance as to the proper approach to such a motion in *Skene v McLaren*,[150] where the Crown sought to have

---

147 Rule 40.1.
148 2000 SLT 122.
149 Page 170.
150 1976 SLT (Notes) 14.

a summary trial adjourned because witnesses were not available. Lord Justice-General Emslie said:

> "When a motion is made by one party or the other to adjourn a diet of this kind on this ground and no question arises as to whether it is well founded in fact, there are two questions to which the sheriff must address his mind if he is to arrive at a proper decision upon the motion. The first question is whether the grant or refusal of the motion will be prejudicial to the accused and if so what is the probable extent of that prejudice. The second question is whether prejudice to the prosecutor would result from the granting or refusal of the motion and once again the degree of probable prejudice must be estimated. … To these two questions we would add a possible third, namely prejudice to the public interest which may arise independently of prejudice to the accused or to the prosecution in the particular case in which the motion is made."

This was reiterated in *Tudhope v Lawrie*.[151]

There are clear examples of the kinds of situation in which an adjournment should be granted in *Normand v West*[152] and *Stewart v Normand*.[153] In *West* it was held that, where the defence sought an adjournment because two essential witnesses were absent and the defence had only recently been instructed in respect of the need to cite these witnesses and could not proceed in their absence, and the Crown sought an adjournment on the ground that an essential Crown witness, duly cited, had failed to appear, the relief stipendiary magistrate should have granted the adjournment rather than refuse on the broad basis that it would be productive of unacceptable delay. In *Stewart* it was held to be oppressive for a sheriff to refuse an adjournment to an accused who produced a doctor's letter stating that a defence witness was unfit to appear. Lord Justice-Clerk Ross said: "unless circumstances are special it will normally be oppressive to refuse an adjournment which is necessary to allow the defence to obtain an essential witness who has been cited". Again, in *McSorley v Normand*,[154] the defence agent mistook the date for trial and so failed to cite defence witnesses and could not attend himself. A substitute agent moved for an adjournment which was refused. It was held that this was oppressive and not cured by offering an adjournment after the trial had been part heard to cite witnesses.

By contrast, in *HM Advocate v Dickie*[155] Lord Hardie commented that, except in the most unusual cases, adjournments should not be granted simply because the accused wanted the services of a particular counsel.

---

151 1979 SLT (Notes) 13.
152 1991 SCCR 76.
153 1991 SCCR 940.
154 1991 SCCR 949.
155 2002 GWD 7-222.

8 Summary Proceedings

Although the 1995 Act defers material relating to summary procedure until after it deals with trials under solemn procedure, a different approach is taken here. Trial procedure under solemn and summary procedure is so similar that it can be dealt with in a single chapter, with a large component dealing with those aspects of the law of evidence not already addressed. We deal now with the commencement of summary proceedings and the rules which apply to summary procedure up until the time of the commencement of the trial. There are in fact many analogies with solemn procedure.

INCIDENTAL APPLICATIONS

There is in summary procedure no direct equivalent to the petition. If the procurator fiscal requires in connection with a case under summary procedure the various warrants which the petition would give him in a case dealt with in that way, he will present to the court an incidental application under the 1995 Act s 134. That procedure is open also to the accused.

Section 134 does little more than refer the reader to "the form prescribed by Act of Adjournal" and that form itself (Form 16.4-A) is skeletal in the extreme. It simply requires the applicant to set out in numbered paragraphs "the reasons for the order sought and the statutory process" and then to set out the orders sought.

Whether an incidental application is competent falls to be decided according to the competency of the order sought.

The Criminal Procedure Rules do not lay down any particular procedure for an incidental application. The most common type of application is for a search warrant.

The remedy of the accused who objects to the granting of an incidental application is to take a bill of suspension. This is dealt with in Chapter 11.

THE COMPLAINT

The document which embodies summary proceedings is the "complaint". Whereas a petition can be regarded for some purposes as a step in investigation, the complaint contains the settled charge against the accused. It equates more easily to the indictment than to the petition. However, unlike the indictment, the complaint is the document upon which the first appearance of the accused is focused, and which commences proceedings. Each time the complaint is called in court the court will fix the date for the next time the complaint is to call. If on any such date it does not call the whole proceedings fall.[1] Whether the procurator fiscal can start the proceedings again with a fresh complaint will be subject to the same rules as to competency as applied to the first complaint.

Petition appearance by definition involves an arrest warrant, even if the accused has come to court voluntarily and is committed for further examination on bail without ever seeing the inside of the cells. By contrast, however, there are two ways in which an accused person can appear on complaint. He may appear from custody, whether that results from arrest without warrant, arrest on a warrant obtained as a result of the presentation of the complaint to the court with a request for such a warrant (usually called a summary warrant) or from his release by the police on undertaking to attend on a particular day (which is custody in theory only). Or alternatively he may be "cited" to attend court.

APPEARANCE FROM CUSTODY

Where the accused is the subject of a summary warrant or is arrested on any other basis he must, by the 1995 Act s 135(3), be brought before a court competent to deal with the case not later than the first day after he is taken into custody (not counting weekends and holidays). It was held in *Robertson v MacDonald*[2] that failure to bring the accused before the court in this way does not vitiate the subsequent proceedings on the complaint, though it might give rise to civil damages.

A copy of the complaint is given to the accused before he appears in court.

CITATION TO APPEAR

In the great majority of cases, however, summary proceedings are commenced by service of the complaint with a citation to come to court on a given date, which must, by the 1995 Act s 140, usually be at least 48 hours after service.

Section 141 of the 1995 Act provides for a variety of ways in which service can be effected.

Service may be to the accused personally; the citation may be left with someone at the accused's residence or place of business; it may be left with someone on a vessel on which the accused is a master or member of the crew; if the accused is a company it may be left at its place of business; if the accused is a body of trustees, the citation may be left with any one of them who is resident in Scotland or with their solicitor in Scotland; it may be sent by recorded delivery post. If the accused is on bail in connection with the charges (which can happen where he has originally appeared on petition but the case has been reduced to summary procedure) the 1995 Act s 25(3) provides for the service of documents at the "domicile of citation", which is an address in the UK included in the bail order as the address at which documents may be served and intimations given.

---

1 *Hull v HM Advocate* 1945 JC 83; *Reynolds v Dyer* 2002 SLT 295.
2 1992 SCCR 916.

TIME BAR

By contrast with petition proceedings, the commencement of summary proceedings is in some cases subject to a statutory time limit in terms of the 1995 Act s 136. That section provides that proceedings in respect of offences to which the section applies can only be commenced within six months after the contravention occurred or, in the case of a continuous contravention, within six months after the last date of such a contravention.

The offences to which this rule applies are, in terms of s 136(2), statutory offences which can only be prosecuted summarily and in respect of which the enactment which creates them does not fix a different time limit. It was confirmed by the sheriff in *Higson v Morrison*[3] that since the offence of driving whilst disqualified can be prosecuted on indictment as well as summarily the s 136 time bar did not apply.

Common law offences are not subject to time bar. Neither are statutory offences which can be prosecuted either on indictment or summarily, even if they are prosecuted summarily in fact.

The case law on the subject arises in the context of s 136(3) which, for time bar purposes, deems proceedings to be commenced on the date the warrant to apprehend or cite the accused is granted, provided that warrant is executed without undue delay.

Undue delay

What will amount to undue delay will depend on the particular circumstances and it may be necessary to lead evidence of the circumstances in order to determine the position. It is clear from *McCartney v Tudhope*[4] that the onus of establishing that there has not been undue delay lies with the Crown. It has also been said in a number of cases such as *McNeillie v Walkingshaw*[5] that the question is one of fact and degree for the sheriff and the Appeal Court will be slow to interfere.

Examples of situations in which it has been held that there was undue delay are *Tudhope v Mathieson*[6] in which there was five months' delay in the execution of a warrant because clerks of court were on strike and courts were being convened only for the most serious cases; and *Carmichael v Sardar & Sons*[7] in which there was an unexplained delay of six days in postal service of a complaint where warrant to cite had been granted just within the six-month period. In *Galloway v Clark*[8] there was undue delay where a warrant granted on 16 June and received by the fiscal on 19 June did not reach the police for execution until 27 June. Pressure on the fiscal's typing facilities which delayed preparation of the covering letter did not impress the High Court as an adequate explanation. However, in *Stagecoach Ltd v Macphail*[9] execution of the warrant to cite through normal channels took seven days and a plea to the competency was rejected, as it was in *Buchan v Macnaughtan*[10] in which the accused was at sea when the

---

3 31 January 2001; 2001 GWD 16-600.
4 1985 SCCR 373.
5 1990 SCCR 428.
6 1981 SCCR 231.
7 1983 SCCR 433.
8 11 July 2001.
9 1986 SCCR 184.
10 1990 SCCR 688.

police attempted to serve the complaint and they waited for him to report to the police station to accept service of the complaint on his return (the actual delay being six days after the expiry of the six-month period). In another case, *Young v McLeod*,[11] a middle-aged first offender charged with a drink driving offence failed to appear when cited. The case was continued for three weeks and when she still failed to appear a warrant was granted. That was passed to the police about six weeks before the time bar with instructions to execute it with discretion (ie to try to get the accused to appear without actually being arrested). They made repeated attempts to get her to answer the warrant but she deliberately failed to co-operate. Eventually the procurator fiscal instructed that she should be arrested without further ado and that was done on the day he gave that instruction but 76 days after the grant of the warrant. This took the case about one month beyond the time bar. She took a plea to the competency, which was repelled, and she appealed. In refusing the appeal, the court observed that for the police to have arrested her when they first made contact with her about the warrant would have been unnecessarily severe and oppressive; that the accused was given ample opportunity to comply with the warrant voluntarily and that it was entirely her own fault that she did not do so; that the Crown could not be criticised for giving her the opportunity; and that the case was quite different from those in which the Crown or the police took no steps or left the accused in ignorance of the warrant for a long time.

THE CONTENT OF THE COMPLAINT

Section 140(2) of the 1995 Act contemplates that the complaint will be accompanied by a "citation", though this is not appropriate where the accused appears from custody. Rule 16.1 provides that the citation and the complaint are to be in the form of Forms 16.1-B and 16.1-A respectively. As Form 16.1-B makes clear, the citation tells the accused on what date and in which court his case will be first called.

Rule 16.1(3) requires the procurator fiscal to send with the citation and complaint a reply form which the accused can use to state whether he pleads guilty or not guilty and a means form which the accused can complete and return to inform a sentencing court about his circumstances.

Section 166(2) of the 1995 Act requires that a notice of any previous convictions should be served with the complaint.

By the 1995 Act s 138 the complaint must be signed by the procurator fiscal (or, in the rare cases in which someone other than the procurator fiscal is the prosecutor, by a solicitor). In *Lowe v Bee*[12] it was held that failure to sign the complaint renders it fundamentally null and that a signature cannot be added by amendment. Rule 16.2(1) requires the prosecutor to sign the citation also.

Section 138 goes on to require that the complaint be in the form set out in Schedule 5 or prescribed by Act of Adjournal, and to give effect to Schedule 3 as regards complaints in the same way as for indictments.

The effect of the application of Schedules 3 and 5 is to confirm that the principles of relevancy and specification which apply to complaints are identical to those which apply to indictments.

11 1993 SCCR 479.
12 1989 SCCR 476.

By rule 16.3, failure by the prosecutor to comply with the requirements as to the reply form and the means form does not invalidate the complaint.

THE FIRST DIET IN SUMMARY PROCEDURE

The complaint having been served, either upon the accused in custody or with a citation to appear on a particular day, the case will call in court.

The accused who has been cited to appear is able to answer the charges by post, pleading guilty or not guilty in writing. He is also able to answer the charges through his solicitor without appearing himself. Often, however, he will appear and, of course, accused persons in custody will always appear in court.

If the accused simply fails to appear in answer to a citation, by the 1995 Act s 150(2) and (3) the court may adjourn the case to another diet or may grant warrant to apprehend him. Such warrants are not usually granted unless there is proof, in the form of a completed execution of citation, that the complaint was either served on the accused personally or served on him at his domicile of citation.

Where the accused does appear (as the overwhelming majority do) procedure at the first diet is governed in the first instance by the 1995 Act s 144(1). By that subsection, where the accused is present at the first calling of the case in a summary prosecution and the complaint has been served on him or read to him or he has legal assistance he is to be asked to plead to the charge unless the court adjourns the case in terms of s 145. That section permits adjournment to allow time for enquiry into the case or for other reasonable cause. Such adjournments are referred to as "continuation without plea".

The accused who is called upon to plead must do one of two things. Either he must plead guilty or not guilty, or he must state any challenge which he makes to the competency or relevancy of the complaint. If he fails to state such a challenge at the first diet, s 144(5) prohibits him from stating any such challenge at any future diet in the case except with the leave of the court which may be granted only on cause shown.

In addition, the accused must, by s 144(4) state any denial that he is the person charged by the police. Section 144(5) operates to bar the stating of any such denial thereafter except with leave on cause shown.

In terms of the 1995 Act s 255 the accused must state any challenge he makes to an alleged special capacity, otherwise that capacity is held as admitted.

In terms of rule 40.3(1), where a party to summary proceedings proposes to raise a devolution issue he must give notice of that intention before any accused is called on to plead.

Pleas to relevancy and competency have been dealt with in relation to indictments, as have special capacities and devolution issues. The principles are exactly the same under summary procedure. However, we require to deal here with denials that the accused is the person charged.

Denial that accused is the person charged

So far as the identity of the accused as the person charged is concerned, it must be understood that the identification of the accused is always an issue at trial. Indeed forgetting to have the accused identified in the dock is the classic prosecutor's mistake. If the accused is not identified as the perpetrator of the crime, usually by being pointed out in the dock, he must be acquitted. In limited circumstances, however, the prosecutor in a summary trial can derive assistance from the 1995 Act s 280(9) under which there is a presumption that the person who appears for trial in answer to the complaint is the person charged by the police. *Smith v Paterson*[13] was decided shortly after the statutory precursor of that provision came into force and concerned a case in which the procurator fiscal depute did not ask the police to point out the accused but did take evidence that they had cautioned and charged the person they had seen committing an offence. It was held that the effect of the statutory presumption was precisely what it said and that the person answering complaint is presumed to be the person charged; and that accordingly the sheriff erred in holding that identification of the accused was essential.

Hamilton v Ross[14] takes this further. At a summary trial the sheriff upheld a submission of no case to answer on the footing that only one officer had formally identified the respondent in court as the driver of the vehicle in question. Neither the respondent's solicitor nor the procurator fiscal depute referred the sheriff to the section and he reached his decision without considering the effect of the statutory presumption. On appeal it was suggested that it was now too late to rely on this method of establishing the respondent as the driver. The Appeal Court disagreed, allowed the appeal and remitted the case to the sheriff to proceed as accords.

DEBATE ON PRELIMINARY PLEAS

Where the accused challenges the relevancy of the complaint and/or the competency of the proceedings or gives notice of a devolution issue, the case will usually be adjourned for debate (or, in the case of a devolution issue, intimation to the appropriate law officer and for debate). There is in law no reason why a debate on competency or relevancy should not take place immediately on the plea being stated and occasionally, where the plea is either obviously well founded or obviously without any basis it may be so dealt with. Usually, however, the prosecutor will have had no notice of the plea and will require an adjournment to consider his position and prepare.

At the debate, which equates to the preliminary pleas aspect of a preliminary hearing in the High Court or of a first diet on a sheriff court indictment, the defence will present their argument and the Crown will answer it. If a preliminary plea to the relevancy succeeds, the affected charge or charges will be dismissed unless the prosecutor is allowed to amend and can do so in such a way as to make the charge relevant. If a preliminary plea to the competency succeeds, the whole complaint will be dismissed.

If the preliminary plea does not result in the dismissal of the complaint as a whole, the accused will be called upon, at the end of the debate, to state his plea to however much of the complaint survives. The procedure is then exactly the same as if he had stated his plea at the first calling of the case but (obviously) without the option of stating a preliminary plea.

Where the accused pleads guilty at the first diet (or after a debate, though a plea of guilty after debate is very rare) the court will proceed to sentence. Sentencing is

13 1982 JC 125.
14 1992 SLT 384.

dealt with in Chapter 10. For the remainder of this chapter we are concerned with the accused who pleads not guilty.

PROCEDURE ON NOT GUILTY PLEA

The starting-point when a plea of not guilty is tendered is the 1995 Act s 146. In terms, the section applies where there is a straightforward plea of not guilty or where there is a plea of guilty to only part of the charge and the prosecutor does not accept the partial plea.

Where there are several charges on the complaint and the accused pleads guilty to some but not to others the practice is to defer sentence on the charges to which he has pled guilty until the end of the trial on the other charges. In such a case, s 146 applies to these charges to which the accused has pled not guilty.

Adjournment for trial

By s 146(2) it is open to the court to proceed to trial at once unless either party moves for an adjournment and the court considers it expedient to grant it. In practice it almost never happens that the trial takes place immediately. Such a course is only taken in cases involving foreign nationals who are scheduled to leave the jurisdiction and whom it is not appropriate to keep in custody. The typical cases are those of the foreign lorry driver who is charged with offences in connection with his hours of work or record keeping, or the skipper of a foreign fishing vessel alleged to have contravened the fisheries legislation and arrested by fisheries protection officers. In other cases, the Crown is unlikely to have witnesses immediately available and the defence will in any event want time to obtain legal aid and to prepare. Accordingly, it is s 146(3) which is usually operated and that section permits the court to adjourn the case for trial to as early a diet as is consistent with the just interest of both parties. Indeed, where the accused is in custody, s 146(4) gives him an absolute right to an adjournment for not less than 48 hours unless a shorter adjournment is necessary in order to obtain the evidence of witnesses who would otherwise not be available.

Intermediate diet

At the same time as it adjourns the case for trial, the court is entitled, by s 148, to fix what is known as an "intermediate diet" between the first diet and the trial. By s 148(5) the accused is required to attend any intermediate diet of which he is given notice unless he is legally represented and the court considers that there are "exceptional" circumstances justifying him not attending.

Bail

Where the accused has been cited to the first diet he will be ordained to appear at the intermediate diet and the trial diet. This means that he is ordered to attend. In terms of s 150(8) an accused who without reasonable excuse fails to attend any diet of which he is given due notice is guilty of an offence.

Where the accused is in custody, ordaining him to appear is an option but it is more likely that if he is released it will be on bail. The principles which apply to the granting (or withholding) of bail in a summary case are identical to those which apply in a petition case at full committal; in other words, the prosecutor can oppose bail on some substantive ground but not on the ground that there are further investigations to be made.

As at full committal on petition, both the prosecutor and the accused can appeal in connection with bail.

PREVENTION OF DELAY IN TRIALS

Where the accused is remanded in custody in connection with a summary prosecution he gets the benefit of the 1995 Act s 147, which provides that a person charged with an offence in summary proceedings shall not be detained in that respect for a total of more than 40 days after the bringing of the complaint in court unless his trial is commenced within that period, failing which he shall be liberated forthwith and thereafter shall be "for ever free from all question or process for that offence". In terms of s 147(2) the sheriff may, on cause shown, extend the period.

It is worth noting two cases. The first of these is *Lockhart v Robb*[15] in which a sheriff held that, whilst the serving of another substantive sentence could interrupt the running of the 40 days, as it can the 110 days where that applies, a remand in custody on deferred sentence on another case could not do so.

The second case is *Grugen v Jessop*[16] in which the fiscal began the trial on the fortieth day, knowing that it could not be completed that day because witnesses were unavailable. One was still suffering from serious injuries inflicted by the accused and two others were police officers who were required to give evidence on that day in the High Court. The trial was adjourned part heard for eight days with the accused being further remanded in custody. The accused proceeded by bill of advocation, arguing that what had been done was an abuse of process. The Appeal Court held that it was not. The Lord Justice-General pointed out that if the procurator fiscal had sought an extension it would almost certainly have been granted. He also pointed out that the accused was only in custody at all because he had failed to turn up at an earlier calling of the case for trial.

INTERMEDIATE DIET

In terms of s 148, the purpose of the intermediate diet under summary procedure is to ascertain, so far as reasonably practicable, whether the case is likely to proceed to trial and, in particular:

- the state of preparation of the prosecutor and the accused;
- whether the accused intends to adhere to his plea of not guilty;
- how many witnesses are required to attend the trial;
- the extent to which the duty to try to agree evidence under s 257(1) has been complied with; and

15 1988 SCCR 381.
16 1988 SCCR 182.

- whether any witnesses are vulnerable (so that special measures should be ordered).

The court may also consider any application under s 275 to lead evidence in a sexual offences case of the sort which would ordinarily be excluded by s 274.[17]

SPECIAL DEFENCES, LISTS OF WITNESSES AND PRODUCTIONS

By contrast with solemn procedure, there is no requirement to lodge lists of witnesses or productions. There is, however, a requirement to give notice of any special defence, of any intention to rely on a defence which involves incriminating a co-accused, of any defence of automatism or coercion and of any defence of consent in a sexual offences case. Notice must be given at or before the intermediate diet or, where there is to be no intermediate diet, not later than 10 clear days before the trial.

17 See pp 142–43 below.

9 The Trial

Trial procedure under solemn and summary procedure is very similar indeed, and it may be said in general that such differences as do exist are substantially attributable to the presence of the jury.

FAILURE OF ACCUSED TO APPEAR

Since the general rule is that it is not competent to proceed in the absence of the accused (and the 1995 Act s 92 makes this explicit in relation to proceedings on indictment), his presence becomes the first essential for a trial except in the limited case of summary proceedings where the prosecutor has moved successfully for an order for trial in absence, in terms of the 1995 Act s 150(3C). Otherwise, the usual response to the failure of the accused to appear will be a warrant for his arrest. Under summary procedure, the issue of such a warrant is specifically authorised by s 150(3). Under solemn procedure, the warrant is said by Stoddart to be "issued at common law".[1] The basis of the issue of such warrants under solemn procedure does not seem to have been articulated clearly by the courts; but failure to appear would be a clear breach of bail and would justify arrest even without warrant.[2]

Under both solemn and summary procedure, a warrant will only be granted if it is shown that the accused had received intimation of the diet either in fact or by intimation at his domicile of citation (if he has one).

Under solemn procedure that warrant takes the accused straight to prison on his arrest and the custody time limits start to run though he can submit a bail application. In due course a new indictment will be served and that indictment is very likely to contain a charge under the 1995 Act s 27(1)(a) of failing to appear at the time and place appointed for a diet of which he has been given due notice.

Under summary procedure the accused will be brought before the court when he is arrested and may find himself remanded in custody for his trial (the situation in *Grugen v Jessop*).[3] If he has been on bail he might well find himself served with an additional complaint containing a s 27(1)(a) charge, or with a new complaint combining the original charges and such an additional charge. If he has been ordained to appear he is likely to find himself facing a charge under s 150(8) which makes it an offence for an accused person to fail without reasonable excuse to attend any diet of which he has been given due notice. Even if the procurator fiscal does not institute proceedings for such an additional charge, the sheriff or

---

1 Charles N Stoddart, *Criminal Warrants* (2nd edn, 1999) p 36.
2 Criminal Procedure (Scotland) Act 1995 s 8(1).
3 1988 SCCR 182.

justice might decide to treat the failure to appear as contempt of court and deal with the accused in respect of that.

Section 65(2) of the 1995 Act provides that the 12-month time bar does not bar the trial of an accused for whose arrest a warrant has been granted in respect of failure to appear. *Cairns v Scott*[4] makes it clear that summary proceedings can continue beyond 12 months in such circumstances.

SOLEMN PROCEDURE: SELECTION OF JURY

In preparation for the trial, the clerk of court cites members of the public, from whom the jury is to be chosen, to attend on the first morning of the trial. The clerk has power to excuse attendance, either in advance or on the morning of the trial where a potential juror explains that he or she has a difficulty in serving. The legislation does not give any guidance about the number of potential jurors who must be available but in *Brown v HM Advocate*[5] it was held that having only 22 people available (out of 60 originally cited) lacked the appearance of fairness, and the conviction returned at trial was quashed.

Assuming the accused turns up and pleads not guilty, the trial under solemn procedure begins with the selection by ballot of the jury of 15 persons as provided for in the 1995 Act s 88 and the Act of Adjournal (Criminal Procedure Rules) 1996 rule 14.2. The name and address of each potential juror is written on a separate piece of paper. Each piece is folded and placed into a container (which looks exactly like a large goldfish bowl). There they are mixed and from there the clerk of court draws out the names one at a time. Each juror thus selected takes his or her place in the jury box unless challenged on cause shown under the 1995 Act s 86(2) until all 15 places are filled.

Once 15 jurors have been selected, the 1995 Act s 88(5) requires that the indictment be read to them. Where the indictment is long or complex, the section contemplates that a summary approved by the judge may be read instead (though doing so is rare). Copies of the indictment, without lists of witnesses or productions, are provided for the jury. Where the accused has lodged a special defence, that is read to the jury after the indictment, as required by the 1995 Act s 89 and a copy of that is given to the jury as well.

After the indictment and any special defence are read, the jury takes their oath. At this point, it is said that the indictment has been "remitted to an assize" and it is proper to refer to the accused as "the pannel".

By the 1995 Act s 90, where a juror dies or, for some other reason (illness is the obvious example) cannot appropriately continue to serve, the court may direct that the trial shall proceed before the remaining jurors, though their number may not fall below 12.

SOLEMN AND SUMMARY PROCEDURE: THE FRAMEWORK OF THE TRIAL

Most of this chapter will be concerned with an examination, in some detail, of aspects of the law of evidence which applies at trial. First, though, it is worth providing an overview of the procedure which will apply.

4 1997 SCCR 287.
5 2006 SCCR 80.

Witnesses

The trial under both solemn and summary procedure begins with the prosecutor calling the first witness in support of the charges. There is no opening statement of any kind. Each witness is examined in chief by the prosecutor and may then be cross-examined by the defence and re-examined by the prosecutor.

Joint minutes of agreement

Section 257 imposes a duty to take reasonable steps to secure the agreement of facts by all parties to a trial. If that is achieved it is dealt with by a joint minute under s 256(2). Where such a joint minute has been signed, the prosecutor will tender it to the judge and (under solemn procedure) read it to the jury (or have the clerk of court do so) at whatever point in the Crown case he or she thinks appropriate. In practice, that will often be early in the case because it is likely that material such as books of photographs, which have to be proved as a foundation for later evidence, will be contained in the joint minute. Taking books of photographs as an example, what that means is that, instead of the prosecutor calling the photographer to give evidence, the prosecutor and defence counsel or solicitor agree in writing that the book of photographs was taken at a particular time and place and contains photographs depicting the things specified in the joint minute. Once the joint minute is tendered or read to the jury, its contents become evidence in the case. Technically, unless the photographer is called to give evidence or a joint minute is read, any reference to the photographs is incompetent because they are hearsay.

Books of photographs are only one example. There is no limit to the evidence which can be dealt with in a joint minute. Other things which are commonly so dealt with are the analysis of controlled drugs, the taking of scientific samples such as swabs for DNA comparison and the time and date when the accused was detained or arrested. More substantial matters are also sometimes dealt with in joint minutes. For example, in a homicide case the cause of death might be agreed and in a rape case, where the defence is consent, the fact that sexual intercourse took place is sometimes agreed.

Good practice in drafting joint minutes is to agree *facts*, not evidence, ie not what a witness said when interviewed. What a witness said still requires to be evaluated for credibility and reliability, which is difficult if the court does not hear the evidence of the witness; but if parties agree a fact, it is settled. So one would agree that on a particular date at a particular date a named constable detained the accused. One would not agree that "in a statement dated [date], constable X reported that he detained the accused" (unless the actual making of the statement has to be proved for some other reason).

Statement of uncontroversial evidence

Section 258 makes provision for statements of uncontroversial evidence, in terms of which a party may serve on the other party a statement of facts thought to be unlikely to be disputed. If the statement is not challenged within seven days of service, the facts specified are deemed to be conclusively proved. The Crown is in the habit of serving such statements with the indictment. A statement which is not challenged is dealt with at trial in the same way as a joint minute.

Defence case

After all the prosecution witnesses have been called the defence are entitled to argue that there is no case to answer. If that submission is successful, the accused is acquitted. If there is no submission, or if any submission is unsuccessful, the defence are entitled to call evidence. If the accused is to be a witness he should give evidence before any other defence witnesses.[6] Where there is more than one accused, they lead their evidence in turn. So the first accused will give evidence, followed by any witnesses he wishes to call; then the second accused will give evidence, followed by any witnesses he wishes to call; and so on, until all of the accused have given or led evidence.

Further evidence

Sections 268 and 269 of the 1995 Act make provision for the leading of further evidence under both solemn and summary procedure even though witnesses might have to be recalled for that purpose and even though (under solemn procedure) the witnesses and productions which it is sought to use have not been listed in terms of ss 66 to 68 of the Act. Section 268 deals with additional evidence and is available to both prosecution and defence. Section 269 deals with "evidence in replication", which is evidence led by the prosecutor either to contradict defence evidence or to establish that a witness has previously made a statement which is inconsistent with the evidence which he has given.

Additional evidence to which s 268 applies is, by subsection (2), evidence which the judge considers is *prima facie* material and in respect of which he accepts that at the commencement of the trial either the additional evidence was not available and could not reasonably have been made available or the materiality of the additional evidence could not reasonably have been foreseen by the party. In *Wotherspoon v HM Advocate*[7] the Crown led evidence of a statement made by a witness to a police officer which contained the evidence the witness gave in court (the procedure described at p 134). The Crown also told the defence that the witness had, at precognition, denied making that statement. The defence sought to lead additional evidence of that denial but the High Court held that this evidence would not have been material because it would merely have confirmed something which the Crown did not dispute.

By s 268(1) an application to lead such additional evidence may be made at any time before the commencement of the speeches to the jury (in a trial on indictment) or the prosecutor's address to the judge on the evidence (in a summary case).

The leading of evidence in replication in terms of s 269 is open only to the prosecutor, who may apply to do so after the close of the defence evidence and before the commencement of the speeches to the jury or his own address to the judge on the evidence. The test in relation to evidence to contradict defence evidence is whether the evidence of the defence witness could reasonably have been anticipated by the prosecutor and, as was made clear in *MacGillivray v Johnston (No 2)*[8] and *Neizer v Johnston*,[9] evidence in replication cannot be used to palliate inadequacies in the Crown preparation or presentation of the prosecution.

6 1995 Act s 66(11).
7 1998 SCCR 615.
8 1994 SLT 1012.
9 1993 SCCR 772.

In the latter case, Lord Sutherland drew a clear distinction between the situation in which the Crown had received clear intimation of a line of defence (as in that case) and that in which a line of defence had been sprung on the Crown during the course of the trial.

Part heard trials

Section 91 of the 1995 Act provides that a trial on indictment is to proceed from day to day, unless the court sees just cause to adjourn over a day or days—in other words, for some longer period. Such a longer adjournment occurred in *Kyle v HM Advocate*,[10] where the trial judge began his charge to the jury (at the end of the trial) on a Friday afternoon, it being a holiday weekend. He had not completed it by 5pm and gave the jury the choice of sitting on the Saturday or adjourning until the Tuesday; they chose the Tuesday and the case was adjourned over the Monday to the Tuesday. There was an appeal on the ground that there had been a failure to comply with the requirement to proceed from day to day, but the Appeal Court gave that short shrift, Lord Justice-Clerk Ross commenting that the decision was one for the trial judge, who had no obligation to consult either prosecution or defence on the matter, and that it is impossible to define exhaustively what would amount to "just cause".

Trials under summary procedure, if they are not concluded within the first day (and most are) are adjourned part heard to some other convenient day as soon as possible after the first day.

Jury speeches/address on the evidence

After all of the evidence has been led the prosecutor addresses the jury or (in a summary case) the judge. The accused or his legal representative then do so in their turn, in the order in which their names appear on the indictment or complaint if there are multiple accused. Sections 98 and 161 of the 1995 Act specifically preserve the right of the accused to speak last.

In *Duke v Griffiths*[11] the Appeal Court held (following earlier authorities) that a sheriff who convicted the accused without giving the defence solicitor an opportunity to make submissions had erred and that, provided there were material issues (such as credibility of witnesses) about which submissions could be made, failure to give the opportunity is an irregularity of a kind that inevitably means that the trial is not fair (so that any conviction obtained has to be quashed).

If a party, in addressing the court on the evidence, makes points about the evidence when he did not cross-examine the witnesses on those matters, the court is entitled to take that failure into account in deciding whether to give the arguments any weight at all.[12] It might, after all, be that the witness could have answered the point if the party had possessed the courage to ask him about it.

Charge and verdict

Finally, under solemn procedure, the judge will charge the jurors, giving them directions as to the law but making it plain to them that it is for them to decide

10 1987 SCCR 116.
11 2010 SCCR 44.
12 *Mailey v HM Advocate* 1993 JC 138; *Al Megrahi v HM Advocate* 2002 SCCR 509.

what facts they hold to be proved but that they must rely on his directions as to the law. One of those directions, in terms of *Affleck and Quinn v HM Advocate*,[13] must be:

"to explain the verdicts which are open to them, to inform them that they may return a verdict by a majority, and then to emphasis the only matter of importance: that no verdict of guilty can be returned unless eight members of the jury are in favour of that verdict".

The requirement for at least eight members of the jury in favour of a guilty verdict before that verdict can be returned remains even if the size of the jury is reduced below 15 (for example, by illness).

The jury then retires to consider its verdict, returning once the verdict has been reached. Under summary procedure the judge simply announces his verdict after both parties have addressed him (and perhaps after a short adjournment to consider the matter).

There are three verdicts open to a jury or to a judge under summary procedure. These are guilty, not proven and not guilty. The guilty and not guilty verdicts are self-explanatory. Although in *Neil v HM Advocate*[14] the High Court held that it is not necessary to explain the not proven verdict to a jury on the ground that it is well understood in Scotland, it does need to be said that it is a verdict of acquittal. It founds a plea of tholed assize.

Schedule 3 to the 1995 Act provides for a range of alternative verdicts. In terms of paragraph 8 offences of dishonesty are very nearly interchangeable, and in particular on an indictment or complaint charging theft it is open to the jury or judge to convict of reset. In terms of paragraph 10 a person charged with a completed crime may be convicted of attempt at that crime and, indeed, where the charge is one of attempt the accused may be convicted of attempt even if the evidence is enough to establish the completed crime. In *Muldoon v HM Advocate*[15] the crime charged was assault with intent to rape but the evidence established a completed rape. He was convicted of the offence libelled and the conviction was upheld on appeal. Some statutes, such as the Sexual Offences (Scotland) Act 2009, make detailed provision for the alternative verdicts which are available to a court in relation to particular charges.

Within this basic framework, there is much (especially in relation to evidence) which requires elaboration.

THE WITNESSES

Presence in court

It is unusual for a witness to be in court before he himself gives evidence, though the 1995 Act s 267 does make provision for the court to permit this to happen if it appears that the presence of the witness would not be contrary to the interests of justice. Where it happens that a witness is in the court before giving evidence but without such permission, s 267(2) leaves it to the discretion of the court whether to admit the evidence of the witness. The issue, of course, is whether the evidence of

13 1987 SCCR 150.
14 1948 JC 12.
15 1967 SLT 237.

the witness has been coloured by what he has heard and so the subsection limits the exercise of the discretion to cases in which it appears to the court that the presence of the witness was not the result of culpable negligence or criminal intent and that the witness has not been unduly instructed or influenced by what took place in his presence or that injustice will not be done by his examination. *MacDonald v Mackenzie*[16] makes it clear that the onus is on the party tendering the witness's evidence to satisfy the court that the discretion should be exercised in his favour.

It is competent for a solicitor to give evidence on behalf of his or her client, even if he or she has been conducting the trial on the client's behalf. However, solicitors who are tempted to do so have to bear in mind that s 265(2), which permits this, also deprives the accused of the right to object to questions put to that solicitor on the grounds of confidentiality.

Use of aides memoire and statements

The Scottish criminal courts have traditionally relied heavily on oral evidence and, even though there is an increasing use of written material, the oral evidence of witnesses is still of huge importance. Memory, however, can be an unreliable thing, especially in relation to details which do not, at the time of the incident, strike the observer as being of critical significance. On the basis that notes made while an incident is fresh in the memory are more likely to be reliable than unaided memory months—or years—later, the courts allow witnesses to refer to such notes in the course of giving their evidence, provided that they are original notes (not transcriptions) made by the witness himself (otherwise they fall foul of the rule against hearsay) and made at the time of the incident or so soon after that the incident is still fresh in the memory (otherwise their value as an objective and accurate note of events disappears). Police officers in particular are in the habit of giving evidence under reference to their notebooks in this way. There is, however, no reason at all why other witnesses who possess such notes should not have their assistance. Such notes do not require to be lodged as productions in the case.

Subject to what is said elsewhere in this book about disclosure,[17] it should be noted that in the first instance it is only the Crown which can require that notes made by police officers are referred to. The defence in a criminal case are not entitled to require production of the notes of police officers unless the officers have referred to them in examination in chief. This is on the basis that the notes have been made for the police report and are therefore confidential on public policy grounds. In *Hinshelwood and Another v Auld*[18] two men were charged with contravening the Police Act 1919 by attempting, in speeches which they made at a public meeting, to persuade police officers to go on strike and to assault senior officers. Certain police officers who gave evidence at the trial had made notes during the meeting but did not refer to the notes when being examined in chief. In cross-examination they were asked to produce the notes but the procurator fiscal objected, successfully, on public policy grounds.

In holding that the sheriff had been right to refuse the defence access to these notes, Lord Justice-General Clyde explained that, where the witness has looked at the notes when giving his evidence in chief, considerations of fairness compel their

16 1947 JC 169.
17 See p 65.
18 1926 JC 4.

production to the defence. However, he went on to say that there is a broad general rule that any communication which is made by an inferior official to a superior officer in the same department is, on grounds of public policy, a confidential document, and is not producible in evidence. To decide otherwise, would, he said, render police work impossible. If the actual report made by police witnesses was thus protected, so should notes and drafts be.

The issue was revisited by the Appeal Court in *Deb v Normand*[19] when the accused (who was charged with driving through a red traffic light) argued that the notebook was the best evidence (in that it was more likely to be reliable than the officer's recollection) and that the trial judge had therefore been wrong to refuse to order its production. In refusing the appeal, the Appeal Court made it clear that the notes are subservient to memory:

"The best evidence of the state of the traffic signal and that it was at red was the evidence of Constable Scougall of his recollection. That recollection, he said, was assisted by his having refreshed his memory by reference to the notebook. But the refreshing of a witness's memory by reference to a document does not make that document the best evidence."

Now, in terms of the Criminal Justice and Licensing (Scotland) Act 2010 s 54, before a witness gives evidence the prosecutor may give him or her a copy of any statement which he or she has made. In terms of the 1995 Act s 261A (inserted by the 2010 Act) the court may, in certain circumstances, allow the witness to refer to the statement while giving evidence.

The spouse or civil partner of the accused

At common law one spouse is not a competent witness against the other except where he or she is the victim of the offence in which case the spouse is both competent and compellable for the prosecution. This is modified by the 1995 Act s 264 (as substituted by the Criminal Justice and Licensing (Scotland) Act 2010) which makes the spouse or civil partner of the accused a competent and compellable witness for any party.

Expert or skilled witnesses

In most matters, judges or juries, presented with the facts, can draw their own conclusions. However, there are occasions on which some assistance is required. In such cases, evidence may be led from a "skilled witness"—that is, "a person who, through expertise or education or both, is specially qualified in a recognised branch of knowledge, whether it be art, science or craft".[20]

It is not competent to lead expert evidence as to the content of Scots law and that includes those rules of public international law which are part of Scots law. This is so even if counsel or solicitors are unsure of the law. The proper course is for legal submissions to be made.[21] Foreign law, on the other hand, is a question

---

19 1997 SLT 107.
20 Margaret L Ross and James Chalmers, *Walker and Walker: The Law of Evidence in Scotland* (3rd edn, 2009) para 16.3.1.
21 *Lord Advocate's Reference (No 1 of 2000)* 2001 SLT 507.

of fact and may be ascertained by evidence. An example is to be found in *HM Advocate v Megrahi (No 3)*.[22]

Who is an expert?

Although the expression "expert witness" is in everyday use in the Scottish courts, the expression, "skilled witness" is technically more appropriate. It reflects the fact that such evidence is competent in relation to any area beyond everyday understanding and to the importance of practice as well as of formal qualifications. In *Hewatt v Edinburgh Corporation*[23] the court, in a civil case, accepted that a police constable who had special duties in respect of road safety could give such evidence as to the degree of danger represented by a particular hole in the road. An example of this in a criminal case is *White v HM Advocate*.[24] Police officers had expressed an opinion that the quantity of LSD found in the possession of the accused was greater than could be expected if the drug was for the use of the accused alone; in short, that it was a dealer quantity. Appealing against her conviction, the accused contended that it was incorrect to allow police officers to give opinion evidence on the dosage of drugs a user would consume and that such opinions ought only to be expressed by medically qualified persons.

Lord Justice-Clerk Ross said that this submission was not well founded. He went on to say:

> "[P]olice officers who have served for some time with the Drugs Squad do acquire knowledge of such matters as the quantity of drugs which a drugs user would consume in a day or in a week and so forth. Provided that such a witness's qualifications as a police officer and his experience in the Drugs Squad are first established, such evidence, in our opinion, is clearly competent. Evidence of this nature is not competent only to medically qualified witnesses."

Based on this, police officers routinely give evidence about the significance of quantities of recovered drugs and about the value of drugs on the black market.

It has been said that:

> "An expert witness in a criminal trial can give two types of evidence. He can testify to the facts and he can give opinion evidence. The distinction is one of degree for in a broad sense everything which an expert says within his own field of expertise contains an element of opinion."[25]

The distinction may be one of degree but it is, nevertheless, a useful one and it is helpful in assessing the evidence of a skilled witness to determine whether at a particular point that witness is giving evidence of fact or is giving evidence of opinion.

The factual basis for the expert's opinion

The importance of laying the basis of fact for the opinion evidence of an expert is emphasised by *Forrester v HM Advocate*[26] in which opinion evidence which was intended to link the accused with the crime following a comparison between

22 2000 SLT 1401.
23 1944 SC 30.
24 1986 SCCR 224.
25 R Pattenden, *Expert opinion evidence based on hearsay* [1982] Crim LR 85.
26 1952 JC 28.

material used for the crime and material said to have been found in the accused's pocket turned out to be useless when the Crown failed to establish by sufficient evidence that the material had indeed been found there. That importance was further underlined in *Blagojevic v HM Advocate*,[27] a murder case in which the police subjected the accused to two interviews, each quite short, and separated by a period of about three-quarters of an hour. During the first interview the accused denied his presence at the locus. During the interval a police officer told him that he was not doing himself any favours by that denial. During the resumed interview he admitted his presence at the locus and stabbing a man. The defence did not call the accused, but did seek to call a psychologist to show that the accused was "suggestible" to a degree which could explain the shift in his position. The Crown objected, successfully, to this evidence.

The defence appealed, arguing that the general issue of fairness, relating to the break in the interview and what then transpired, provided a sufficient foundation for the leading of the psychologist's evidence. The Appeal Court identified the issue as being whether a proper basis had been laid for the leading of the evidence. It referred to *HM Advocate v Gilgannon*[28] for an example of a case in which it was clear from the evidence led for the Crown that the accused was mentally incapable of giving an accurate account. It pointed out that in Blagojevic's case, however, the accused was not suffering from either a mental illness or a personality disorder. His only area of vulnerability was that it was said that stress modified his response pattern. It then said:

"In the absence of evidence from the appellant himself that his statement was influenced … or from the police that he was seen to be suffering from emotional stress or was under any pressure … the jury could only speculate as to whether his vulnerability affected him. On this occasion [the psychologist's] evidence lacked therefore any proper basis."

Suggestibility, which (if established) could make an interview unfair, is now usually dealt with as a preliminary issue,[29] so that the question is now much less likely to be one for the jury. The point, however, remains. It is necessary to lay the proper foundation for the evidence of the skilled witness.

The factual basis for the skilled witness's evidence is likely to come from one of two sources. Often, the skilled witness will be presented with facts spoken to by other witnesses. Indeed, in order to facilitate this, the skilled witness is generally allowed to be present in court and hear the evidence of the witnesses to fact unless objection is taken, though he is excluded from court while other witnesses giving opinion evidence are in the witness box.

The other source for the factual basis on which a skilled witness's opinion is based is the examination which may have been made by the skilled witness himself. Where the factual basis is being laid in the first part of the skilled witness's own evidence, he will not be permitted to be in court during the evidence of other witnesses as to fact.

Typically, in such a case, a forensic scientist will speak to an analysis of, say, two or more blood samples and that analysis is a question of fact. Thereafter, he will go on to express an opinion about the possibilities in relation to the source of one or more of these samples. There, his evidence is a matter of opinion. A pathologist will speak first to the findings at post mortem and these will be matters of fact. He will then speak to the conclusions which he draws as to cause of death and this part of his evidence is opinion.

The function of the expert

The classic statement of the function of a skilled witness who gives opinion evidence is to be found in a civil case, *Davie v Magistrates of Edinburgh*[30] where Lord President Cooper said:

> "Expert witnesses, however skilled or eminent, can give no more than evidence. They cannot usurp the functions of the Jury or Judge sitting as a Jury ... their duty is to furnish the Judge or Jury with the necessary scientific criteria for testing the accuracy of their conclusions, so as to enable the Judge or Jury to form their own independent judgment by the application of these criteria to the facts proved in evidence. The scientific opinion evidence, if intelligible, convincing and tested, becomes a factor (and often an important factor) for consideration along with the whole other evidence in the case, but the decision is for the Judge or Jury. In particular the bare *ipse dixit* of a scientist, however eminent, upon the issue in controversy, will normally carry little weight for it cannot be tested by cross-examination nor independently appraised, and the parties have invoked the decision of a judicial tribunal and not an oracular pronouncement by an expert."

It will be apparent from this that there are real limits on the function of the skilled witness. To begin with, the evidence which such a witness gives must relate to matters beyond everyday experience. Matters within everyday experience will be regarded as matters within judicial knowledge and these include such matters as the normal period of human gestation[31] and the elementary principles of dynamics.[32] In *Doyle v Ruxton*[33] the Appeal Court remarked that the argument that judicial knowledge did not include the fact that widely advertised beers were alcoholic was "somewhat unattractive and unrealistic".

The courts are anxious to ensure that the skilled witness does not usurp the function of the tribunal of fact, as the passage from Lord President Cooper's judgment in *Davie* makes clear. If a judge or jury is in a position to draw its own conclusions from the facts then, as Lord Avonside observed in *Assessor for Lothian Region v Wilson*,[34] an expert witness is not essential. In *Walker v HM Advocate*,[35] the High Court noted that, in the circumstances of that case, it would have been open to the jury to conclude that two specimens of handwriting had been written by different people, even without expert assistance. In *Al Megrahi v HM Advocate*[36] it was said by the Appeal Court that it was within the proper competence of a trial court to examine a document which it had before it, provided it did not undertake an exercise where some particular expertise was necessary. Moreover, questions which invite an expert to put himself in the position of expressing a view on the very matter for the determination of the jury will be objectionable. In *Ingram v Macari*[37] it was held that a sheriff had been wrong to hear expert evidence on the

30 1953 SC 34.
31 *Williamson v McClelland* 1913 SC 678; *Preston-Jones v Preston-Jones* [1951] AC 391.
32 *Ballard v North British Railway Co* 1923 SC (HL) 43; *Carruthers v Macgregor* 1927 SC 816.
33 1999 SLT 487.
34 1979 SC 341 at 349.
35 1999 SLT 1388.
36 2002 SCCR 509.
37 1982 SCCR 372.

question whether particular magazines were liable to deprave and corrupt the morals of the lieges. That was the very issue which he had to determine.

Use of literature

One obvious question which arises is the relationship between the evidence of a skilled witness and the literature in the relevant field. Strictly, that literature is hearsay, but this will not result in reference to the literature being excluded. The principle was stated by Pattenden as follows:

> "To some extent all opinion evidence by an expert contains hearsay. Very few experts acquire specialist skills entirely through first-hand experience. Provided the hearsay on which the expert relies is of a sufficiently general nature to be regarded as part of the corpus of knowledge with which an expert in his field can be expected to be acquainted, no objection will be taken to his evidence on this ground."

This was the point at issue in *R v Abadom*[38] in which the appellant argued that an expert on the analysis of fragments of glass could not rely on statistics collated in a research establishment except for those few examples with which he might have been personally concerned. The court, however, was not impressed with this argument and Kerr LJ said:

> "In the context of evidence given by experts it is no more than a statement of the obvious that, in reaching their conclusions, they must be entitled to draw upon material produced by others in the field in which their expertise lies. Indeed, it is part of their duty to consider any material which may be available in their field and not to draw conclusions merely on the basis of their own experience, which is inevitably likely to be more limited than the general body of information which may be available to them ... it is also inherent in the nature of any statistical information that it will result from the work of others in the same field, whether or not the expert in question will himself have contributed to the bank of information available on the particular topic on which he is called upon to express his opinion. Indeed, to exclude reliance upon such information on the ground that it is inadmissible under the hearsay rule might inevitably lead to the distortion or unreliability of the opinion which the expert presents for evaluation by a judge or jury."

It is suggested that this passage accurately reflects Scots law as well as English. In *Davie* the court made it clear that passages from a published work may be adopted by a witness and made part of his evidence or may be put to the witness in cross-examination for his comment; though the court warned against the practice of the judge at first instance scrutinising published work for himself and using passages not referred to in evidence with a view to determining the issue or assessing the testimony of the expert witness.

The availability of the literature for expert evidence is not confined to published work. Some of the literature in *Abadom* was not published and Kerr LJ said:

> "It does not seem to us, in relation to the reliability of opinion evidence given by experts, that they must necessarily limit themselves to drawing from material which has been published in some form. Part of their experience and expertise may well lie in their knowledge of unpublished material and in their evaluation of it."

38 [1983] 1 WLR 126.

However, the court in *Abadom* desiderated explicit reference to the sources upon which the expert has relied.

Vulnerable witnesses

Most witnesses give their evidence in open court but there are special rules which apply to witnesses in trials for sexual offences and to the evidence of those witnesses whom the law regards as vulnerable. That category includes children in particular.

Closed court

In a trial on indictment for "rape or the like" (an expression which is interpreted quite broadly so as to include most sexual offences), the 1995 Act s 92(3) permits the judge to cause all persons other than the accused and counsel and solicitors to be removed from the courtroom. There is no general equivalent under summary procedure. However, in terms of s 50(3) (which applies to both solemn and summary procedure) where a child is called as a witness in a case relating to an offence against decency or morality the court may direct the exclusion of all persons except court members and officers, parties and their lawyers, the press and anyone specially authorised by the court to remain.

There is also, in the 1995 Act ss 274 and 275, protection for complainers in trials relating to sexual offences from certain types of questioning. Those sections are examined in some detail below.[39]

Special measures

Over the last two decades, there has been a substantial move towards the provision of special measures to make it possible for vulnerable witnesses to give their evidence more easily consistent with the overriding need to ensure a fair trial. The starting-point is the relatively informal one of a practice note issued by the Lord Justice-General in 1990 in which he instructed the removal of wigs and gowns while a child is giving evidence. But the main source of the law is the 1995 Act ss 271 to 271M.

Section 271 defines "vulnerable witness" as a person who falls into one of two categories. The first, and simplest, is the child witness—that is, anyone under 16 on the date when the indictment or complaint is served. The second category consists of those persons in respect of whom there is a significant risk that the quality of their evidence will be diminished by reason of mental disorder or by fear or distress in connection with giving evidence at the trial. Section 271(2) requires the court, in making the assessment whether someone is a vulnerable witness, to take into account the nature and circumstances of the alleged offence, the nature of the evidence which the person is likely to give, the relationship between the accused and the person, the person's age and maturity and any behaviour towards the person by the accused, his family or associates or any other person who is likely to be an accused or witness. The court must also take into account such other matters as appear to it to be relevant, including social and cultural background, sexual orientation, domestic and employment circumstances, religious beliefs or political opinions and any physical disability or impairment.

39 See p 142.

The other foundational provision is s 271H, which lists the "special measures" which the court may authorise. They are:

(a) taking evidence by a commissioner;
(b) use of a live television link;
(c) use of a screen;
(d) use of a supporter;
(e) giving evidence in chief in the form of a prior statement; and
(f) "such other measures" as the Scottish Ministers may prescribe.

Live TV links (s 271J) and screens (s 271K) are used very commonly, often in combination with the use of a supporter (s 271L). These are referred to, in terms of s 271A(14) as "standard special measures". Commissioners and using a prior statement as evidence in chief are very uncommon.

A supporter is simply a person who sits in court near the child and provides a reassuring presence—in the words of the statute, the supporter is "present alongside the witness to support the witness while the witness is giving evidence". A supporter is not permitted to communicate with the witness while the evidence is being given, so as to satisfy the requirement of s 271L(3) that "the supporter shall not prompt or otherwise seek to influence the witness in the course of giving evidence".

Where a screen is used, it is positioned so that the witness cannot see the accused but s 271(2) requires that arrangements are made to ensure that the accused is able to watch and hear the vulnerable witness giving evidence. In practice, that is done by a video feed from a camera pointing at the witness to a monitor which can be seen by the accused. Where a live TV link is used, the witness is usually in a special room within the court building. The monitors in the court have integral cameras so that the witness can see the person who is speaking to him or her at any given time (the judge controls the choice of camera).

Applications for special measures are made, in the case of child witnesses, under s 271A and, in the case of other vulnerable witnesses, under s 271C. Applications are usually dealt with in the absence of parties, though an order can be made for a hearing on the application. Children are entitled to special measures as of right. Where the application is for a non-standard special measure, the court has to be satisfied that the measure sought is the most appropriate (by s 271A(9) and 271C(7)).

THE EVIDENCE WHICH THE WITNESSES GIVE

Objections

We have seen that the approach which Scots law takes to the admissibility of evidence is exclusory; that is, there are certain rules the breach of which will render the evidence in question inadmissible. The means by which a party secures compliance with those rules by his opponent, and the exclusion by the court of evidence which breaches them, is by objecting when an attempt is made to lead that evidence. Before we consider the actual rules as to admissibility, we need to look at the procedure upon an objection being made.

Some objections can be predicted from an early stage in the proceedings. For solemn procedure, the 1995 Act s 79(2)(b) provides that an objection by a party to the admissibility of any evidence is a preliminary issue and, in terms of s 79(1), it must be the subject of a notice, failing which it cannot be raised except by leave of the court on cause shown. So, for example, if it is obvious on the face of the transcript of an interview of an accused person by the police that it contains inadmissible material, that objection must be made by notice and dealt with at the first diet (in the sheriff court) or the preliminary hearing (in the High Court).

Other objections only become obvious during the course of trial. In such a case, the party making the objection must do so immediately the evidence is sought to be led and have the objection recorded.[40] If he does not do so, the evidence becomes part of the case to be considered by the court in due course no matter how strong the objection might be. The court will not, except in the most flagrant cases, itself take notice of inadmissibility. For all the judge knows, the parties may have agreed that the evidence can be led, and in an adversarial system—that is, one in which the parties fight the case out and the judge is a kind of referee—it is not for the judge to descend into the arena of controversy.

In *Skeen v Murphy*,[41] a drink driving case, the defence sought, at the end of the case to contend that service of the analyst's certificate as to the accused's alcohol level had not been proved. Such certificates, if served on the accused, are (in terms of the road traffic legislation) evidence in their own right—witnesses are not needed to establish the facts set out in the certificate. However, if the certificate had not been served it was not evidence and the prosecution would have failed to establish an essential of the case (that is, that the accused's alcohol level was over the limit). If the certificate was not evidence it was not admissible and it should not have been put in evidence; but the defence had not objected to it being so put. The Appeal Court held that the end of the trial was too late to raise the question and that the certificate had become evidence in the case. Again, in *Cordiner v HM Advocate*[42] the prosecutor asked a question of the accused which suggested that he had committed a crime not charged, namely subornation of perjury, by attempting to persuade a witness to give false evidence at his trial. On appeal, it was held that there was a technical breach of the law on admissibility of evidence but that, since no objection had been taken at the time, the appellant was to be regarded as having waived compliance with the rule.

A similar (but not identical) point arose in *Higgins and Others v HM Advocate*.[43] In that case, which was one of murder, the Crown led evidence that the dying victim said to a police officer: "They three bastards tore into me. They stabbed me." As we shall see, a statement made by a person who has since died may in some circumstances be admissible evidence but it is not like the evidence of a witness who goes into the witness box. In particular, it cannot be tested by cross-examination. The trial judge should have pointed this out to the jury but did not do so. The accused appealed, arguing that this was a miscarriage of justice. The High Court noted, however, that not only had the judge not pointed out the particular character of the evidence but neither had defence counsel done so in addressing the jury. The court concluded "[t]he value or quality of this evidence was not put

---

40 *Macaulay v Wilson* 1995 SCCR 133.
41 1987 SLT (Notes) 2.
42 1991 SCCR 652.
43 1993 SCCR 542.

in issue by the defence and there is accordingly no reason to think that the failure of the judge to give the correct direction in law led to any miscarriage of justice". The conviction was upheld.

In an Appeal Court context, the 1995 Act s 118(8) provides that, where the accused had legal assistance in his defence, no conviction shall be set aside in respect of any objection to the admission of evidence at trial unless the objection was timeously stated. Applying that, the court said in *McFadden and Spark v HM Advocate*[44] that it will only sustain arguments relating to the admissibility of evidence where no objection was taken at or before the trial in very exceptional circumstances, amounting to a fundamental failure to present the defence. In such a case, the true ground of the appeal would be defective representation rather than the evidential point.

Accordingly, the time to take issue with an attempt to lead evidence which a party to criminal proceedings considers to be inadmissible is the time when that attempt is made and before the witness has had a chance to answer the offending question.

Once an objection is made, the judge will want to know its content. It will often be undesirable to allow the witness to hear what the objection is, much less to hear the arguments presented, because to do so might colour his evidence and perhaps defeat the whole point of objecting. If, for example, the objection is to a leading question (by which is meant a question which merely asks the witness to confirm information provided by the questioner), the party objecting will not want the witness to hear the whole of that information, still less any explanation which might be put forward as to why the evidence is of particular significance. In such circumstances, the judge will direct the witness to leave the courtroom while the matter is being argued.

The need to exclude those who should not hear the detail of the objection becomes most acute in a jury trial. Very often the judge will have to be told the nature of the evidence likely to be elicited by the question objected to, and that information will often be capable of being agreed between the parties (though without its truth being agreed). Manifestly, it would be unsatisfactory that the jury, which will eventually decide the facts of the case, hear such information. Accordingly, except where the point is very short, obvious and cannot conceivably colour the jury's deliberations, the jury will be asked to retire while the point is debated.

The party making the objection will state what it is, preferably formulating the objection as a proposition of law, though this will often be implicit rather than explicit. The party who asked the question objected to will then reply and, after hearing the objector further if need be, the judge will rule on the point.

By the 1995 Act s 107B, the prosecutor may, with leave of the trial court, appeal against any decision that evidence is inadmissible. The trial will be adjourned whilst that appeal proceeds.

Trial within a trial

In *Thompson v Crowe*[45] a full bench reviewed the way in which the law dealt with objections to statements alleged to have been made by accused persons where there

---

44 2009 SCCR 902.
45 1999 SCCR 1003.

is a dispute as to the factual circumstances in which the statement is alleged to have been made. It should be understood that this case predates the legislation which introduced the requirement for issues of admissibility to be dealt with before trial; but the principles apply whenever it is dealt with. The court said:

"(1) ... [I]n all cases it is for the trial judge to decide whether any evidence, including evidence of a statement by the accused, is legally competent and can be led.

(2) The judge must decide any issues of fact which are necessary to enable that legal decision to be taken.

(3) Since the trial judge has to determine any issue of fact before ruling on admissibility, if the facts are disputed, the judge must first hear all the relevant evidence, including any evidence which the accused wishes to give on the point.

(4) If the defence ask for the evidence on admissibility to be heard in the absence of the jury, the judge should ordinarily grant that motion.

(5) The Crown cannot use any evidence given by the accused in the trial within a trial as proof of his guilt. There may, however, be circumstances in which the accused can be cross-examined about that evidence if he subsequently gives evidence in the substantive trial which is materially different. ... Other witnesses can, of course, be cross-examined on any differences in their evidence.

(6) Where an issue arises on the evidence, it is for the Crown to satisfy the judge that the statement is admissible. The appropriate standard of proof would appear to be the balance of probabilities, as the defence conceded in this case.

(7) The judge will exclude evidence of a statement if it was taken in circumstances which render it inadmissible under any rule laid down by the law. In other cases the judge will admit the statement if the Crown satisfy the judge that it would be fair to do so, by proving that the statement was made freely and voluntarily and was not extracted by unfair or improper means.

(8) Any ruling on the admissibility of the evidence of a statement should be given, in both solemn and summary proceedings, after the evidence of the circumstances had been led and any submissions on the evidence have been heard. In this way, any defence submission that there is no case to answer will fall to be made on the basis of the legally admissible evidence led by the Crown.

(9) Where the judge admits the evidence of a statement, evidence of the circumstances in which it was taken remains relevant to any determination of the weight which should be attached to it.

(10) If the judge admits the evidence of a statement and fresh circumstances emerge in subsequent evidence which cast doubt on that ruling, the defence may renew their objection and invite the judge to reconsider the ruling. On reconsideration the judge may confirm or reverse the original ruling in the light of the new evidence. If the evidence of the statement has not yet been led, the judge may exclude it. If it has been led, the judge may direct the jury to disregard it or, if, because of its likely impact, the judge considers that the jury could not realistically be expected to put the evidence out of their minds, then, depending on the circumstances, the judge may desert the diet pro loco et tempore. In the case of a summary trial, the judge will disregard the evidence in reaching a verdict; only rarely would it be appropriate for the judge in a summary trial to desert the diet on the ground that it would be impossible to disregard the evidence in reaching a verdict."

In a summary trial, in which the sheriff or justice cannot send the "jury" part of himself out for the trial within a trial, the procedure is still followed but it was held in *Crooks v Russell*[46] that in a summary trial (by contrast with the position in a jury trial) it is not necessary for the prosecution evidence to be repeated following the decision on admissibility.

The admissibility of evidence

We have already noted Dickson's classic statement of the purpose of the law of admissibility of evidence:

> "to exclude valueless and deceptive proofs, to secure regularity in the investigations and to confine within reasonable limits the duration and expense of judicial proceedings".[47]

This falls naturally into three parts and we can consider the admissibility of evidence in those parts.

The exclusion of valueless and deceptive proofs: hearsay

Hearsay is the most obvious, and perhaps the classic, example of a type of evidence which is regarded as inherently unreliable and misleading, and hence objectionable.

Hearsay is simply reported speech or that which is analogous to it. When a witness attempts to give evidence about what someone else has said to him, that is hearsay. It is, however, important to understand that hearsay as a concept and as an objection does not include statements so clearly connected with the action or event in time, place and circumstances as substantially to form part of it. These statements are said to form part of the "*res gestae*"—the "whole thing that happened"—and this is true whether the maker of the statement is the accused or another person, whether or not a participant. Such statements are characterised as "primary hearsay" and are admissible. It is possible to find many examples of this in the cases. One is to be found in *Glover v Tudhope*[48] in which a man solicited a motorist for sex. The motorist was not called as a witness but the arresting officer's account of the conversation between the parties and of the circumstances was admitted as evidence. That conversation, of course, was the whole essence of the soliciting.

Other examples could be multiplied. In a fraud, the words by which the false pretence is made will, if spoken to by a person who heard them said, be primary hearsay and admissible as such. In a breach of the peace, the obscenities shouted by the accused will likewise be admissible as primary hearsay provided that the witness who gives evidence about them actually heard them shouted. And so on. It is, however, important to note *Hamill v HM Advocate*.[49] In that case, during a police surveillance operation at a house from which it was suspected that drugs were being sold, a man arrived and (misunderstanding what was happening) asked an undercover officer whether he was there for "gear" (ie drugs). The man subsequently became a co-accused of the appellant. The trial judge and, on appeal, Lord Philip dissenting, considered that the words formed part of the *res gestae* against the appellant. However, the appellant had not been present when the words were spoken and so the majority of the Appeal Court held that they were not admissible against him unless it could be shown that the men were acting together in pursuance of

47 W G Dickson, *A Treatise on the Law of Evidence in Scotland* (1887) preface.
48 1986 SCCR 49.
49 1999 SLT 963.

a common criminal purpose. Although it was not expressed in these terms, what the High Court was perhaps doing was limiting *res gestae* to those things that the accused does, either himself or art and part with someone else.

It is another matter altogether if someone gives evidence about an event without himself having observed it directly, so that his evidence must be based on what someone else has told him. That evidence is characterised as secondary hearsay and it will be inadmissible. Such hearsay is in its nature not susceptible to meaningful cross-examination and is therefore open to attack as being dangerous to rely upon because it cannot be tested properly. Suppose A is charged with killing B, C being an eye witness and D having been nowhere near the scene of the crime. If, instead of calling C as a witness, the Crown was simply to call D to say what C told him about the crime, the court could not test that account at all. D would be unable to elaborate on the account given to him, unable to clear up ambiguities, unable to help to clear up discrepancies with the evidence of other witnesses and unable to respond (with any certainty) to the accusation that C had a motive to lie. Moreover, through repetition there is a danger of the original sense of what was said being distorted, especially if it has passed through a number of intermediaries before it reaches the court. For these reasons, the law excludes from evidence all forms of assertion other than those made by the witness on the basis of his own direct observation. The traditional explanation for this was articulated by Lord Normand in *Teper v R*,[50] when he said:

> "[hearsay] is not the best evidence and it is not delivered on oath. The truthfulness and accuracy of the person whose words are spoken to by another witness cannot be tested by cross-examination and the light which his demeanour would throw on his testimony is lost".

Typically, the objection will be made to reported speech but the form of the evidence or of the matter reported does not matter and the reported cases tend to concern hearsay in written reports which are submitted as evidence. In *Grant v HM Advocate*,[51] for example, the accused was charged with putting ear lotion containing carbolic into a bottle of milk intended for his wife's illegitimate daughter; the child consumed the milk and became ill as a result. The wife gave evidence that the accused put carbolic in the child's milk and the doctor who had examined the child was also called as a witness. His report was a production and contained the following passage:

> "The child was crying in extreme pain, and on asking the mother what was wrong with the child she told me that it had been poisoned. She said that her husband had done it."

The conviction was quashed on appeal on the ground that this passage had been hearsay and therefore incompetent; and that its being given in evidence was so prejudicial to a fair trial that it was fatal to the conviction. In giving his opinion, Lord Justice-Clerk Aitchison said:

> "[I]t is really too plain for argument that it was incompetent to put to the jury that passage in the medical report. The evidence was hearsay and it did not cease to be hearsay because the wife had been called as a witness and had deponed to the same effect."

50 [1952] AC 480.
51 1938 SLT 113.

Scientific and other reports

Hitherto, difficulties have arisen for the Crown in relation to scientific and other reports where it turns out that the scientist who gives the report delegated some of the analysis upon which it is based to a lab technician or some other person. The reporting by the scientist of the results which had been reported to him by the technician fell to be excluded as hearsay, as the High Court decided in *Normand v Wotherspoon*.[52]

In *O'Brien v McCreadie*,[53] however, the Appeal Court held that *Normand v Wotherspoon* does not apply where statute provides that the report is sufficient evidence of any fact stated in it. That case concerned a certificate as to the analysis of a drug under a provision which now finds its statutory expression in the 1995 Act s 280(1). By that subsection, for the purposes of certain specified offences a certificate as to specified matters purporting to be signed by specified persons is, provided it has been served on the accused not less than 14 days before the trial and not challenged within seven days of service of the copy, sufficient evidence of the matter so certified. In *O'Brien v McCreadie* the Lord Justice-Clerk recognised explicitly that such documents might contain hearsay but held that the wording of the statute was decisive and that *Normand v Wotherspoon* was to be distinguished.

The effect of the 1995 Act s 280(4) seems to be to extend this exception to the rule against hearsay to a great many scientific reports. That subsection provides that for the purposes of any criminal proceedings a report purporting to be signed by two authorised forensic scientists (and served and not timeously challenged) is to be sufficient evidence of any fact or conclusion as to fact contained in the report and of the authority of the signatories. By contrast with subsection (1), no limit is placed on the nature of the matters which may be certified.

By subsection (5), a forensic scientist is authorised if he comes into one of two categories. He may be authorised by the Secretary of State or he may be a constable possessing the qualifications and experience prescribed by the Secretary of State and authorised by the chief constable of the area concerned.

Even where there is a challenge, s 280(8) provides that the evidence of both forensic scientists is to be sufficient evidence of any fact or conclusion as to fact contained in the report. It seems to follow that the reasoning in *O'Brien v McCreadie* must extend to that oral evidence and that the possibility of objecting to hearsay in such a report no longer exists. Not only that, but whereas the Lord Justice-Clerk in *O'Brien v McCreadie* noted that the certificates with which the court had to deal in that case could only be granted in cases under summary procedure, certificates under s 280(1) and reports under s 280(4) are both explicitly capable of being granted in *any* criminal proceedings.

De recenti statements

De recenti statements—that is, statements which are made shortly after the events in question made by one who is called as a witness—may be admitted in evidence for the limited purpose of supporting the credibility of that witness. Indeed, a five-judge bench in *Ahmed v HM Advocate*[54] held that such statements are admissible

52 1993 SCCR 912.
53 1994 SCCR 516.
54 2009 SCCR 861.

even where the person who is said to have made them denies doing so. *De recenti* statements are not, however, substantive evidence of the facts.

The distinction between that which is part of the *res gestae* and statements which are *de recenti* can be a difficult one. It was somewhat blurred by *HM Advocate v Stewart*[55] when evidence was allowed, as *de recenti*, of what a seven-year-old boy had said about 48 hours after seeing a murder and evidence was also allowed as "*de recenti* and in fact ... part of the *res gestae*" of what the accused had said about the victim within 24 hours of the crime, and of what a deceased witness had said about the accused within 48 hours of the crime. It might have been better for the court to proceed on the basis that evidence which has the accused as its source is always admissible (subject to fairness in the manner in which it is obtained) and that the statement of a dead witness was a recognised common law exception to the rule against hearsay.

HM Advocate v Murray[56] also confuses the issue. In that case, the first statement made by a mentally defective girl when she got home after she was alleged to have been raped was admitted in evidence as part of the *res gestae* even though she was not herself a witness (being incapable of understanding the oath and therefore, at that time, disqualified).

Some remarks of the court in *Andersons v McFarlane*[57] suggest that evidence that a servant girl, who had been assaulted by her employers, had reported the matter to her mother at the first opportunity some days later was admissible as *de recenti* but the issue in the case was its effect in relation to sufficiency of evidence. On the admissibility of *de recenti* statements it requires to be treated with some care.

Finally, in *Ahmed*, the Lord Justice-General (Hamilton) seemed to characterise the making of a *de recenti* statement as primary hearsay and part of the *res gestae*.

Perhaps the safest thing that can be said is that in any case where a statement might be *de recenti* the whole circumstances will have to be examined with care to determine exactly what the status of that statement actually is.

Prior inconsistent statements

De recenti statements are concerned with supporting the credibility of the maker of the statement. Section 263(4) of the 1995 Act is, perhaps, the direct opposite. That section authorises the leading of evidence as to a previous statement made by *any* witness for the limited purpose of demonstrating that his story has not been consistent throughout and thus affecting his credibility adversely. Typically, this relates to what a witness has told the police at an early stage.

The statements which can be put to witnesses in terms of such a provision as relevant to their credibility were considered in *Coll, Petitioner*.[58] In that case, the court distinguished three categories. Statements made in the course of the initial investigation can be put and this will include most statements made to the police. Precognitions, which are defined as statements taken by those engaged in preparing the case for one of the parties, cannot be put because of the risk that their content is affected by the partisan interest of the precognoscer. Into this category fall virtually

---

55 (1855) 2 Irvine 160 at 179.
56 (1866) 5 Irvine 232.
57 (1899) 2 Adam 644.
58 1977 SLT 58.

all statements taken by procurators fiscal and defence solicitors and also statements taken from defence witnesses by the police on the instructions of the procurator fiscal in response to the intimation of a list of witnesses to be called by the defence at trial. The category does not, however, include a transcript of evidence given before a foreign magistrate pursuant to a letter of request. Such a transcript can be used.[59] The final category consists of precognitions on oath, where the procurator fiscal (or, rarely, the defence solicitor) interrogates a witness in the presence of the sheriff, the questions and answers being recorded by shorthand writer, transcribed and signed by the witness. In this case the court considered that the presence of the sheriff was a safeguard against the content being affected as might happen in an ordinary precognition.

In *HM Advocate v McGachy*[60] Lord Sutherland held in the course of a trial that statements taken by the police on their own initiative the day after they charged the accused did not fall to be regarded as precognitions simply because the police had passed the stage of charging. With this we may compare *Low v HM Advocate*[61] in which it was held that it was open to the jury to take the view that a statement taken by a police officer 24 hours after the crime when only three out of eight accused had been arrested was not a precognition. The formulation of this decision suggests that the issue is one of fact for the jury to decide, rather than of law for the court, but this might be influenced by the fact that this case was a substantive prosecution of the maker of the statement for perjury by denying making the statement in the original trial.

We must contrast *Kerr v HM Advocate*[62] in which it was held that a statement obtained on a question and answer basis after the accused had appeared on petition was a precognition and hence could not be put to the witness.

Exceptions to the rule against hearsay

Muldoon v Herron[63] has been regarded by some as an exception to the rule against hearsay though it is important to realise that the High Court in deciding the case did not regard it as such. In *Muldoon* police officers said that shortly after a breach of the peace two witnesses had pointed out the accused as the perpetrators. At court, neither witness could identify them. One of them was not sure if the accused were those he had pointed out and the other denied that they were those she had pointed out. The High Court held on appeal that the evidence of the police was available to link the accused with the crime and upheld the conviction. This approach was developed in *Frew v Jessop*[64] in which two witnesses gave evidence that they had provided police officers with a description of the driver of a vehicle (who was alleged to be guilty of offences) but that they could neither recall that description nor identify the accused. The police officers gave evidence of what the witnesses had told them, which included the registration mark of the vehicle. On appeal, it was argued that this evidence was hearsay and ought not to have been admitted but Lord Justice-Clerk Ross, under reference to *Muldoon v Herron*, said:

---

59 *HM Advocate v Al Megrahi (No 2)* 2000 SLT 1399.
60 1991 SLT 921.
61 1987 SCCR 541.
62 1958 SLT 82.
63 1970 SLT 229.
64 1989 SCCR 530.

"We do not see why any different principle should be applied to evidence of this kind than is frequently applied to evidence of positive identification which the witness has been able to make shortly after the offence has been committed but which he is unable to recall by the time he gives his evidence in court. ... No doubt [such] evidence is hearsay evidence but it is hearsay evidence which forms an exception to the general rule that hearsay evidence is inadmissible."

Evidence of this sort can only be given if the witness who viewed the identification parade or pointed out the accused attends court and gives evidence. In *McNair v HM Advocate*[65] a police officer was asked whether a man listed as a defence witness but not present to give evidence had been asked whether he saw a particular person on the identification parade and whether he had been able to identify anyone. It was held that both questions sought to elicit inadmissible hearsay.

Jamieson v HM Advocate (No 2)[66] is a development of the *Muldoon v Herron* principle. In that case, a witness gave evidence that she had given a true statement to the police at the time but that she could not now remember the details of what she had said. Evidence was led from the police officer as to the content of her statement and this was held by the trial judge to have had the effect of incorporating her statement to the police into her own evidence. The argument that the police officer's evidence had been inadmissible hearsay was rejected on appeal. In terms of *Jamieson*, provided the contents of a statement are put properly before the witness while he is giving evidence, a witness who has made a statement on a previous occasion on matters which he is no longer able to recall at trial, but who says in the course of his or her evidence that that was a true statement, may be held to have adopted the statement as part of his or her evidence. Where evidence is then given of the content of the statement by the officer to whom it was made, the consistency between the two pieces of evidence provides the link between them and completes the chain. The provision in s 261A, introduced into the 1995 Act by the Criminal Justice and Licensing Act 2010, which permits a witness to refer to his or her statement whilst giving evidence does not relax the requirement for both adoption of the statement by the witness and evidence from the police officer about its content.

Section 260 of the 1995 Act has similar, but not identical, effect to *Jamieson*. Subsection (1) provides that, subject to the other provisions of the section, where a witness gives evidence in criminal proceedings, any prior statement made by the witness shall be admissible as evidence of any matter stated in it of which direct oral evidence by him would be admissible if given in the course of those proceedings. In *Niblock v HM Advocate*,[67] the Appeal Court said that, where this is done, the trial judge must give the jury a specific direction about the purpose of the Crown's reliance on the statement and its evidential significance. Section 262(1) excludes statements in precognition (other than precognitions on oath) from the ambit of this section, no doubt for the reasons contemplated in *Coll, Petitioner*[68] (essentially that a precognition is "filtered through the mind of the precognoscer" and hence of questionable accuracy). Section 261(1) excludes statements made by the accused from the ambit of s 260, except where the evidence is taken from him by a co-accused.

65 25 January 1991, High Ct of Justiciary; unreported.
66 1994 SCCR 610.
67 2010 SCCR 337.
68 1977 SLT 58.

The restriction to those matters as to which the witness could competently give direct oral evidence guards against the risk that otherwise inadmissible evidence could come to be given under cover of this provision, and the particular criteria to which the provision is subjected by subsection (2) (except in the case of precognitions on oath and statements made in other judicial proceedings) are intended to provide further safeguards.

First, such a statement is not admissible unless it is contained in a document, though "document" is defined widely by s 262(3) and s 262(2) provides that a statement is "contained" in a document where the maker makes the statement in the document personally, makes a statement which is embodied in a document by any means, whether he knows it or not, or approves a document as embodying the statement.

Second, such a statement is not admissible unless the witness in the course of evidence indicates that the statement was made by him and that he adopts it as his evidence. Accordingly, a prior statement cannot be substituted for the evidence of the witness.

Third and last, the statement is not admissible unless the maker would have been a competent witness at the time it was made.

In some circumstances, however, what an accused person has said to the police, or in judicial examination, will be evidence even if he does not go into the witness box. The rules about this are, however, quite restrictive and they were considered by a bench of nine judges in *McCutcheon v HM Advocate*,[69] in which the law stated in the earlier case of *Morrison v HM Advocate*[70] was reviewed and refined. The law was considered further in *McGirr v HM Advocate*.[71] The following principles can be extracted from these cases (and, in particular, from *McCutcheon*):

- Previous statements by the accused may be thought of as incriminating, exculpatory or "mixed".
- An incriminating statement made by an accused person is admissible against him.
- If the Crown leads evidence of a mixed statement, it is to be taken as intending to found on the incriminating parts of the statement. Considerations of fairness mean that the accused can found on the exculpatory parts.
- It is for the trial judge, not the jury, to decide whether a statement is "mixed".
- Where the Crown leads evidence of such a statement, the trial judge must direct the jury that its contents are available as evidence for or against the accused, whether or not the accused gives evidence; and that they must determine whether the whole or any part of the statement is to be accepted by them as the truth. He should also specifically direct them that if they believe the exculpatory part or parts of the statement, or if the statement creates in their minds a reasonable doubt as to the guilt of the accused, they must acquit.
- Although the Crown can (and often does) lead evidence of an exculpatory statement made by the accused, the accused can only found on that statement

---

69 2002 SCCR 101.
70 1990 SCCR 235.
71 2007 SCCR 80.

if he has given evidence and for the purpose of demonstrating that his account has been consistent throughout.

- There is no duty on the Crown to lead evidence of any previous statement by the accused.

- If the Crown does not lead evidence of an exculpatory or mixed statement, an attempt by the defence to do so prior to the accused giving evidence himself is objectionable (because at that stage the question of consistency has not arisen and the statement is pure hearsay).

The common law rules about hearsay are modified by the 1995 Act s 259, which gives effect to recommendations of the Scottish Law Commission Report "Evidence: Report on Hearsay Evidence in Criminal Proceedings".[72]

The policy proposed by the Commission was:

> "to confirm the traditional preference for direct oral evidence over hearsay but to provide both for the prosecution and for the defence new categories of exception ... which would allow hearsay evidence of a statement to be admitted if there were truly insurmountable difficulties in the way of obtaining the evidence of the maker of the statement from the maker personally".[73]

The section allows hearsay evidence (other than of the content of precognitions) subject to the satisfaction of several conditions. By s 261, s 259 does not apply to statements made by the accused and so the *McCutcheon* principles are unaffected.

The first, and most important, condition is that the judge is satisfied that one of five limited sets of circumstances exists. It is with this condition that we are here primarily concerned. The second and third conditions seek to avoid giving hearsay a higher status than direct evidence. They are that the evidence must be evidence which would be admissible if given as direct oral evidence and that the maker of the statement must be a competent witness. The fourth condition is that there exists evidence which would entitle a jury or judge to find that the statement was made and, more significantly, that the witness has direct personal knowledge of the making of the statement—in other words, that the witness who gives evidence had the account directly from an eye witness. This excludes "double" hearsay, where A comes to court to say that B told him that C said that he had seen something.

The five situations are set out in subsection (2). In the first three of them, hearsay can only be led if notice has been given before the trial or with leave of the court.

The first situation is that the maker of the statement is dead or is, by reason of his bodily or mental condition, unfit or unable to give evidence in any competent manner. So far as it deals with death and insanity this places recognised common law exceptions on a statutory footing. However, it does represent an extension when it includes unfitness by reason of bodily condition.

The second situation is that in which the maker of the statement is named and otherwise sufficiently identified but is outwith the UK and it is not reasonably practicable to secure his attendance at the trial or to obtain his evidence in any other competent manner. This deals with a somewhat difficult situation, because,

---

72 Scot Law Com No 149.
73 *Evidence: Report on Hearsay*, para 4.48.

although witnesses in foreign jurisdictions can be cited, with the assistance of the foreign authorities, in terms of the Criminal Justice (International Co-operation) Act 1990 s 2, they are not compellable.

The third situation contemplated by s 259 is that in which the maker of the statement cannot be found, and all reasonable steps have been taken to find him.

Section 259(3) would exclude the evidence in such a case if the disappearance had been engineered by the party tendering the statement; though in practice it might be hard to make that connection out.

The fourth situation dealt with is that in which a witness refuses to answer questions on the ground that the answers might incriminate him. This will only apply, of course, where the witness has made such a statement to someone else already. The Law Commission thought that, in such a situation, it:

> "should not be acceptable for a criminal to disclose his criminal activity to a person outside the court and then to claim the privilege in order to prevent the disclosure of his crime to a court which requires information relevant to the guilt or innocence of an accused person".[74]

The fifth and final situation contemplated is that in which a person called as a witness refuses to give evidence. Such a person would, of course, be guilty of contempt of court but this does not assist the party seeking to lead that person's evidence. There is an evident utility in relying on the hearsay. Any evidence may be seen as better than none. It was emphasised in *MacDonald v HM Advocate*[75] that this only applies where the judge has expressly directed the witness to answer. It was not enough in that case that a child witness was too distressed to answer.

Although these statutory exceptions to the hearsay rule have been introduced, it is not open to a party simply to spring hearsay evidence upon his opponent at trial. Section 259(5) of the 1995 Act provides that (except where the evidence is that of someone who has refused to give evidence because it might incriminate him or who has refused to take the oath) hearsay evidence cannot be led under these provisions unless notice in writing has been given of that intention and of the witnesses and productions to be adduced in connection with the hearsay evidence. Rule 21.3 and Form 21.3 make more detailed provision, and in particular, Form 21.3 requires that the notice be accompanied by an affidavit of the person who will give the evidence stating what that witness will say.

It is also important to note that, although the trial judge has no discretion to refuse to admit hearsay, once he or she is satisfied that one of the conditions is met, it is open to the accused to challenge the admitting of hearsay evidence in any particular case on the ground that to do so would deprive him of a fair trial, in breach of his Convention rights. In *N v HM Advocate*[76] the Appeal Court observed that there is a continuing duty on the trial judge to consider carefully the fairness of having admitted hearsay evidence as the trial progresses and, if need be, to uphold a submission of no case to answer, to desert the diet, to direct the jury to ignore the evidence or to direct the jury to acquit.

---

74 *Evidence: Report on Hearsay*, para 5.61.
75 1999 SLT 533.
76 2003 SLT 761.

Excluding valueless and deceptive proofs: irrelevant evidence

The first paragraph of *Dickson* begins thus:

> "The first and most general of the primary rules of evidence is this—that the evidence led be confined to matters which are in dispute or under investigation."

Facts which are not relevant are referred to as "collateral" and the reasons for excluding evidence of such facts were noted by Lord Justice-Clerk Ross in *Brady v HM Advocate*:[77]

> "The general rule is that it is not admissible to lead evidence on collateral matters in a criminal trial. Various justifications have been put forward for this rule. The existence of a collateral fact does not render more probable the existence of the fact in issue; at best a collateral matter can only have an indirect bearing on the matter in issue; a jury may become confused by having to consider collateral matters and may have their attention diverted from the true matter in issue. Whatever the justification for it the general rule is clear."

In short, evidence which is not relevant has the potential to be "valueless and deceptive". It may also be said that the leading of irrelevant evidence does nothing to help to "confine within reasonable limits the duration and expense of judicial proceedings" as desiderated by Dickson.

In practice, however, it is not always easy to know exactly when a particular fact will be regarded as collateral. This difficulty becomes especially acute in relation to circumstantial evidence. The concept of relevance can, therefore, become extremely complex. Moreover, the facts which the law will regard as irrelevant will not necessarily be so perceived by the layman. For example, evidence that there are more housebreakings in a particular area when a particular person is out of prison than when he is locked up might be regarded as a piece of circumstantial evidence which would tend to support (though fall far short of proving) the proposition that the person in question is a housebreaker. However, even if it would tend to support the general proposition that the person is a housebreaker, that is all it would support. It does not offer any assistance whatever with the determination of whether that person committed the particular housebreaking with which he is charged. For that reason, it is irrelevant. It is also regarded by the law as prejudicial and is an example of the most obvious category of collateral material, namely evidence of a crime not charged against the accused on the indictment or complaint upon which he is standing trial. An attempt to lead such evidence is, subject to what was said in the full bench decision in *Nelson v HM Advocate*,[78] objectionable.

Evidence of a crime not charged

In *Nelson*, the appellant was charged with drug trafficking offences. Evidence was led that he had, when being detained, obstructed the police. It was objected that the indictment did not contain a charge of obstruction and argued that, this being evidence of a crime not charged it should be excluded as irrelevant. However, the High Court held that the Crown could lead the evidence because what the accused did when approached by police officers was relevant to the proof of the crime which

---

77 1986 SCCR 191.
78 1994 SCCR 192.

was charged. The fact that the behaviour of the accused fell within the definition of another crime, not charged, was not enough to exclude the evidence unless fair notice requires that the other crime be expressly referred to in the indictment. This would be the situation if, for example, the other crime was significantly different in time, place and character from the crime charged. This does not, however, permit the Crown to narrate in the indictment or lead evidence of a crime which has nothing to do with the substantive charge. In *Slack v HM Advocate*[79] it was held to be unfair, on a charge of disqualified driving, to narrate that the accused had taken the car unlawfully.

Character of victim or other witnesses

Evidence of the character of the victim or other witnesses is generally inadmissible. It has no relevance to the merits of the case before the court. However, proof may be led in relation to offences of violence that the injured party was quarrelsome. Alison justifies this by suggesting that, where provocation is claimed as a defence, the relevancy of enquiry into the generally quarrelsome nature of the victim lies in the fact that "it is much more likely that a person of bad temper and quarrelsome habits has been betrayed into some of his usual excesses on the occasion libelled, than one who has always been remarkable for his meekness and serenity of disposition".[80]

Alison also suggests that, where such evidence is to be led "without doubt it will be held indispensable that due notice of the intention to bring forward such proof should have been given by the pannel, that the prosecutor may be on his guard to support his own witness's temper by his own witnesses".[81]

It is not made clear how such notice is to be given but in practice anything will do provided the prosecutor is put on notice that the temperament of the victim will be an issue. The most usual, simplest, approach is to adapt the type of notice which is given of a special defence and, in Alison's example, one can imagine that a notice of a special defence of self-defence could readily be adapted.

It may, of course, be that the prosecutor will wish to take the initiative and lead evidence in chief of the sanguine character of the victim and this seems to be permissible,[82] though the authorities are silent on the matter of notice.

In general, evidence may not be led of specific acts of violence, though Macphail has cited two cases in which this was allowed,[83] these being *HM Advocate v Kay*[84] and *HM Advocate v Cunningham*.[85] The prohibition against proof of specific acts of violence must in general make it very difficult to prove the proposition that the victim was quarrelsome. It must make cross-examination even harder because the obvious question to ask a witness who alleges that a particular person was bad-tempered is what examples he can give (with a view to suggesting that anger was, on the particular occasions, fully justified, or alternatively, that the assessment of his temper is exaggerated). This is, however, precisely the question which the rule forbids.

79 1995 SCCR 809.
80 Alison ii 532.
81 Alison ii 532.
82 *Porteous* (1841) Bell's Notes 293.
83 I D Macphail, *Evidence* (1987) para 16.07.
84 1970 JC 68.
85 14 February 1974, High Court, Glasgow; unreported.

Prior sexual conduct of the victim

The other issue which has confronted the courts is that of the character of a woman who has been sexually abused.

In terms of the 1995 Act s 274, which applies to both solemn and summary procedure and to prosecutions for the sexual offences specified in s 288C (it is difficult to think of a sexual offence that is not specified), unless the defence can bring the case within the exceptions provided by s 275 the court must not admit or allow questioning designed, *inter alia*, to elicit evidence that the alleged victim is not of good character (in relation to sexual matters or otherwise) or has at any time engaged in sexual behaviour not forming part of the charge. The exceptions in s 275 depend on the satisfaction of three criteria, the third (and most important) of which is that the probative value of the evidence sought to be admitted is significant and is likely to outweigh any risk of prejudice to the proper administration of justice arising from its being admitted. The reference to the proper administration of justice is defined so as to include appropriate protection of a complainer's dignity and privacy. Where an application is made successfully under s 275, s 275A comes into play. It contains a requirement for the prosecutor to lay any relevant previous convictions (essentially, for sexual offences) before the court and a presumption that the convictions will be disclosed to the jury.

Section 275 applications are very common in practice. Unfortunately, as Lord Johnston pointed out in *MM v HM Advocate*,[86] "the legislation is unhappily drafted and raises a number of questions of interpretation". In *MM*, the court gave some assistance.

The first and most fundamental thing to be noted is that the court regarded the appeal as turning on the terms of ss 274 and 275, and not on the terms of s 275 alone. That might seem obvious, standing the fact that s 275 applies, in terms, to evidence or questions referred to in s 274. Experience suggests, however, that many s 275 applications do not, in their drafting, have s 274 very clearly in view. In *MM*, Lord Johnston (who gave the leading opinion) found it necessary to consider the legislative policy (as stated in the Policy Memorandum submitted by the Scottish Ministers with the amending legislation) and to say that:

> "having regard to the professed aims of the legislation any interpretation or construction of it must not expand the existing common law position at the time of its enactment and it is more likely that its intention was to limit its effect".

In other words, s 274 operates so as to introduce restrictions on admissibility which were not, or were not necessarily, present in the existing law. Section 275 operates only in relation to those matters dealt with by s 274. It cannot operate so as to give a court power to admit evidence which is rendered inadmissible by some rule apart from s 274. So, said Lord Johnston:

> "[W]hen consideration is given to a detailed application, at least conventionally, the starting-point should be whether it would have been permissible to maintain such a line of questioning at common law before the enactment of the legislation. I consider that, if it was not admissible under the common law at the material time, s 274 should not arise whatever its phraseology."

Lord Johnston referred, for the existing state of common law, to Chapter 7 of the second edition of *Walkers on Evidence*, from which he derived two propositions.

"Firstly ... issues collateral to the issue at the trial were not to be admissible. ... Secondly, general character attacks were not admissible on, for example, the assertion that the complainer is an habitual liar but character attack in sexual matters in relation to bad moral character was permitted."

Lord Johnston added that he did not regard it as permissible at common law to lead evidence of false allegations of sexual assaults on other occasions and said that he considered that position to be consistent with the approach taken by the court in *Cassels v HM Advocate.*[87]

This appears to have at least two consequences. For one thing, the fact that it might be possible to argue that an allegation is within the definitions in ss 274 and 275 will avail an applicant nothing if the allegation is collateral (or, better, has no reasonably direct relationship with the fact to be proved—see Lord Osborne in *Strathmore Group v Credit Lyonnais*[88]) or otherwise inadmissible at common law. For another, what Lord Johnston said about the inadmissibility at common law of evidence of false allegations of sexual assaults on other occasions might make it harder for accused persons to succeed in applications for recovery of documents such as social work and police records which are thought to contain evidence of such false allegations.

It appears, then, that the correct process of reasoning in any s 275 application will be to consider first whether the evidence sought to be admitted is evidence which is rendered inadmissible specifically and only by s 274. If proposed evidence is inadmissible on some other ground, and especially if it is inadmissible at common law, the s 275 application must be refused. Lord Eassie said in *MM* that:

"Section 275 of the legislation was not, in my view, intended to relax the general law of evidence and any application under s 275 must proceed upon the basis that the evidence with which it is concerned would otherwise be admissible under the general law of evidence in criminal trials."

The character of the accused

Evidence as to the criminal record and character of the accused is dealt with by the 1995 Act ss 266 and 270.

Section 266 contains, at subsection (4), a prohibition on the asking of questions of the accused which tend to show that he has committed, or been convicted of, or been charged with, any offence other than that with which he is then charged, or is of bad character, unless—

(a) the proof that he has committed or been convicted of such other offence is admissible evidence to show that he is guilty of the offence with which he is then charged; or

(b) the accused or his counsel or solicitor has asked questions of the witnesses for the prosecution with a view to establish the accused's good character, or the accused has given evidence of his own good character, or the nature and conduct of the defence is such as to involve imputations on the character of the prosecutor or of the witnesses for the prosecution; or

(c) the accused has given evidence against any other person charged in the same proceedings.

87 2006 SCCR 327.
88 1994 SLT 1023.

It is clear, then, to begin with, that where the witness is the accused the asking of questions about crimes not charged is not only objectionable as irrelevant upon the principle that where the question is whether a person did something on one occasion it is not relevant to show that he did a similar thing on another. It is also specifically prohibited by statute. Presumably the prohibition is now to be understood subject to *Nelson*.[89] To this is added a prohibition on asking the accused questions "tending to show" that he has been charged or convicted of any offence not on the indictment or complaint and also on asking questions tending to show that he is of bad character.

The simplest situation relates to previous convictions. Section 266 has to be read with the 1995 Act ss 101(1) and 166(3). Section 101(1) provides for solemn procedure that previous convictions shall not be laid before the jury and that reference must not be made to them in the jury's presence before the verdict is returned. Section 166(3) prohibits in summary cases the laying of previous convictions before the judge until he is satisfied that the charge is proved. Accordingly, the prosecutor must be assiduous not to make any reference to previous convictions before the accused is convicted, especially in a jury trial. The consequences of the prosecution making such a reference can be fatal to the prosecution, though this will not always be the case where the disclosure of previous convictions is at the hand of someone other than the prosecution. *McCuaig v HM Advocate*[90] was a case in which the presiding sheriff asked a police officer to read out the precise terms of the charge which the police had put to the accused, who was being dealt with for attempting to pervert the course of justice by giving a false name. The charge read out by the officer, in the hearing of the jury, contained the allegation that the accused's motive was to avoid production of a schedule of previous convictions relative to him. The prosecutor did not seek a conviction on this charge but not, presumably, because of a fear that the accused had been prejudiced, because convictions were sought in respect of other charges on the indictment and obtained in respect of 16 of them. It was held that there was no miscarriage of justice and the convictions were sustained.

Such laying of convictions does not always happen in the most obvious way. *Cordiner and Another v HM Advocate*,[91] for example, concerned an accused charged with offences said to have been committed at a time when he was in fact in prison. He lodged a special defence of alibi to that effect and his previous convictions were thus disclosed. This was held to be a contravention of the section. The Crown could, of course, have checked this and avoided the problem and so was entitled to little sympathy for its difficulty.

By contrast, we may note *Johnston v Allan*,[92] in which a DVLA printout showing previous convictions and endorsement was accidentally seen by the sheriff in the course of trial. It was held that there had been no contravention of the Act as it could not be said that the document had been laid before the court by the prosecutor. A further variation was *O'Neill v Tudhope*[93] in which the service copy notice of previous convictions was returned to the fiscal by the accused with his letter pleading guilty and was handed to the sheriff at court. However, the

89 See p 140.
90 1982 JC 59.
91 1978 JC 64.
92 1983 SCCR 500.
93 1984 SCCR 424.

guilty plea was not accepted and a trial diet was fixed. Unfortunately the notice of previous convictions remained with the court papers, where it was seen by the trial sheriff. On appeal, it was held that there was nothing to suggest that the previous convictions came to the notice of the sheriff as a result of any decision of the prosecution nor was there any constructive "laying" of convictions by the prosecutor. Accordingly, the section was not breached.

It will be recognised that this sort of approach depends upon the proposition that a sheriff can act properly and put things out of his mind, a principle elaborated in *Kerr v Jessop*,[94] where the prosecutor elicited from a witness that the appellant had been previously convicted of driving while disqualified. The Appeal Court held that the prosecutor had been careless in framing the question and pressing that line and that there had been a breach of the section; but nevertheless found that a sheriff ought to be able to disregard such evidence and in this case that there had been no miscarriage of justice. The same principle applies to juries in terms of *Binks v HM Advocate*.[95]

Again, where a witness erroneously reveals the existence and nature of a warrant outstanding against an accused that is not *per se* a breach of the section. This was the situation and result in *Carmichael v Monaghan*.[96] *Andrew v HM Advocate*[97] establishes that such disclosure by a witness does not automatically breach Article 6 ECHR.

Exceptions

The prohibition in s 266 is subject to four exceptions. If one of them applies, the accused who gives evidence can be asked questions on the matters which the section would otherwise prohibit.

The first exception relates to the situation where the proof of the commission of or conviction for another offence is admissible to show that the accused is guilty of the offence with which he is presently charged. The most obvious example of this is the offence of driving whilst disqualified by order of the court (rather than by reason of age). In such a case, proof of the disqualification inevitably involves proof of the conviction which resulted in the disqualification. However, this does not give the prosecutor complete *carte blanche* as to that conviction. Rather, he will require to restrict what he proves to what is essential to proof of the new charge.

It may well be, for example, that the conviction was imposed in respect of a complaint which contained a number of offences, only some of which resulted in disqualification. In such a situation an extract of the earlier conviction may be produced but only the charge which founded the disqualification may be referred to. In *Boustead & Another v McLeod*[98] the extract conviction produced to prove disqualification contained a charge in addition to the charge required to prove the disqualification and the conviction was quashed. In another case, *Mitchell v Dean*,[99] the extract conviction produced by the prosecutor to prove the disqualification disclosed that "the accused admitted six previous convictions". This was enough to vitiate the proceedings.

94 1990, High Court of Justiciary; unreported.
95 1984 JC 108.
96 1986 SCCR 598.
97 2000 SLT 402.
98 1979 JC 70.
99 1979 JC 62.

The practice is to charge the disqualified driving on a separate complaint or indictment from any other charges arising out of the same incident so as to confine the exposure of the previous conviction to that charge in respect of which it is strictly necessary and this is done in any other similar case also. The one exception to this is where the second charge follows inevitably from the first, as where a charge of driving without insurance appears on the same complaint as driving whilst disqualified. If a man is disqualified from driving he cannot possibly have insurance and is not prejudiced by the two charges appearing together. This was the position in *Moffat v Smith*.[100]

Graham v HM Advocate[101] was a case in which one of the accused's replies when charged by the police with a series of offences which included assault on his wife was "that cow's got me the jail again". The prosecutor led evidence of that reply. The sheriff held this to be a breach of the Act and directed the jury to ignore it. The High Court, however, took the view that the breach was "deliberately engineered quite unnecessarily and without any justification by the procurator fiscal" and in the circumstances was so grave a breach that the conviction must be quashed. By contrast, *Deeney v HM Advocate*[102] was a case in which a Crown witness, unprompted, gave evidence that the accused "was on licence". This was held not to be an infringement of the section. It may well be that one factor which influenced the court in *Graham* was the fact that the reply had no evidential value at all. It neither assisted the Crown on the merits (because it did not constitute any kind of admission) nor the defence (because it was neither a denial nor an explanation). It was, in short, pure prejudice.

The second exception has two alternatives. It applies either where the defence has, by evidence from prosecution witnesses or the accused himself, attempted to set up the accused's good character or where the nature or conduct of the defence has involved imputations on the character of the prosecutor or of prosecution witnesses.

The reference to imputations upon the character of the prosecutor is of virtually no practical significance in the Scottish system under which almost all prosecutions are conducted by a public prosecutor. Evidence directed to the prosecutor's character will almost inevitably be inadmissible as irrelevant and so the situation will not arise. The presence of this element in the subsection is thought to be a product of the fact that the provision is ultimately derived from one which applied in both Scotland and England. Clearly, under a system such as the English one where private prosecution has a significant part to play, attacks on the character of the prosecutor can assume a greater significance, because the prosecutor will often also be the victim of the crime. The provision might be of some significance in those rare Scottish cases which do involve private prosecution but even here, it is suggested, the hurdle of relevancy will have to be overcome by demonstrating that the imputations on the prosecutor's character actually have some bearing on the merits of the case.

The mounting of an attack upon the character of prosecution witnesses is of more significance. The law on this is to be found in *Leggate v HM Advocate*.[103] In that case the essence of the cross-examination of the police witnesses was

---

100 1983 SCCR 392.
101 1984 SLT 67.
102 1986 SCCR 393.
103 1988 SLT 665.

that they had conspired to fabricate evidence. It was held that this constituted an attack on the character of the prosecution witnesses sufficient to bring the exception into play and that it did not matter whether the attack was necessary to the defence on the merits. It was also held that the trial judge had a discretion whether or not to allow questions addressed to the character of the accused. In general one may expect that discretion to be exercised in favour of the defence where the attack on the prosecution witness is genuinely necessary to the defence on the merits; and in favour of the prosecution where the defence are merely mud-slinging. There is value in looking also at *Templeton v McLeod*[104] in which it was held that an accused is afforded the protection of the section where cross-examination as to the veracity of a prosecution witness is necessary to enable the accused fairly to establish his own defence, albeit it involves an invitation to the judge or jury to disbelieve the witness in so far as he testifies in support of the charge; but where such cross-examination goes further and can be seen to involve imputations upon the general character of a witness the accused may forfeit his right to the statutory protection. *Conner v Lockhart*[105] also decided that where it is essential for an accused to establish that a Crown witness has fabricated evidence against him, this is not an attack on the character of the witness but is necessary to establish the proposed line of defence. In such circumstances the accused should not have lost his statutory protection of the subsection and have been cross-examined on his criminal record.

The exception applies (by s 266(7)) where the reputation attacked is that of a deceased victim.

It is, of course, all very well to permit the Crown to ask questions of the accused as to his criminal record or bad character where he has thrown mud at prosecution witnesses or held himself out as being of good character; but he might not give evidence and, if he does, he might lie. Section 270 therefore permits the Crown to lead evidence of the accused's criminal record or bad character where this second exception applies, even though the witnesses necessary to do so have not been on the list with the indictment.

The third ground upon which questions as to character may be put to the accused is that he has given evidence against a co-accused. The meaning of the expression "given evidence against" was considered in *McCourtney v HM Advocate*[106] and in *Burton v HM Advocate*.[107] In *McCourtney*, counsel for the appellant invited the High Court to adopt the test propounded by Lord Donovan in an English case, *Murdoch v Taylor*,[108] which was that the evidence given supports the Crown case against the co-accused to a material extent or undermines his defence. The court noted that this is a stiff test but found it unnecessary to consider whether any lesser standard was appropriate because even this stiff test was satisfied in the case they were considering. In *Burton*, however, the court came off the fence and said in terms:

"... as a matter of law, evidence against a co-accused within the meaning of the sub-section is evidence which supports the Crown case in a material respect or evidence which undermines that of the co-accused".

---

104 1986 SLT 149.
105 1986 SCCR 360.
106 1977 JC 68.
107 1979 SLT (Notes) 59.
108 [1965] AC 574 at 592.

McCourtney makes it clear that in a case where this test is satisfied the trial judge has no discretion to refuse to the co-accused the right to cross-examine that accused as to his character, whilst *Burton* establishes that the right arises not only where evidence has been given explicitly against the co-accused but also where an accused has by implication given evidence against a co-accused. In that case, the first accused (Jones) had claimed to have been in possession of items used in a crime only because the second accused (Burton) had asked him to get them. When the second accused gave evidence, he denied this and said that the first accused had obtained certain of the items for his own purposes. Counsel for the first accused cross-examined the second accused as to his criminal record.

On appeal, it was conceded by counsel for the second accused that his evidence had been "against" the first accused but argued that this was only so incidentally and by implication. It was maintained that the subsection did not apply in such a case, but the court held that it did, observing that:

> "[n]othing could have been more damaging than the evidence of Burton so far as Jones' position was concerned. By giving the evidence which he did Burton stripped or sought to strip from the testimony of Jones his 'innocent' explanation of the possession of the instruments which were incriminating in the highest degree. By doing this, Burton supported the Crown case against Jones in a material respect by leaving him with possession of the instruments without an innocent explanation. At the same time he in the very clearest way expressly undermined the defence which Jones had put forward."

This approach may be contrasted with that in *Templeton* in which questioning by the Crown was not allowed where the imputations on the characters of the Crown witnesses were merely incidental to the substantive defence which it was sought to advance.

Slane v HM Advocate[109] is an interesting variation on the same theme. In that case, evidence of one accused's criminal record was obtained without justification from a Crown witness by counsel for a co-accused in cross-examination. It was held that this did not mean that the accused whose criminal record was thus revealed was entitled to have the indictment against him dismissed on the ground that he had been prejudiced. It is possible to regard this outcome with a degree of cynicism. Presumably the High Court was conscious of the need to avoid having a properly conducted prosecution founder because of the outrageous conduct of the representative of a co-accused.

The fourth exception to the prohibition on reference to the accused's previous convictions is mandatory in character. It is set out in s 275A of the 1995 Act. That provides that where the court allows evidence of the sort generally excluded by s 274 (broadly, as to the character of the victim of a sexual offence) the prosecutor "*shall* forthwith place before the presiding judge any previous relevant conviction of the accused". Subject to certain specified safeguards, such a conviction must then be laid before the jury or (in summary proceedings) taken into consideration by the judge.

The Privy Council considered this in *HM Advocate v DS*[110] and held that the provision is compatible with Article 6 ECHR and that the purpose of the provision is to demonstrate the accused's propensity to offend sexually.

---

109 1984 SLT 293.
110 2007 SCCR 222.

Securing regularity in the investigations

The second purpose of the exclusory approach to the rules of evidence as identified by Dickson is to secure regularity in investigation, the reasoning being that there is a disincentive to improper conduct at the investigative stage if it is known that the product of irregular investigations is likely to be worthless in terms of proof. We have, of course, given detailed consideration to the regularity of investigations in Chapter 4 and it is not necessary to repeat that here. What does bear reiteration, however, is that although irregularity in investigation is a ground of objection to the admissibility of evidence, irregularities may be excused and accordingly mere irregularity will not inevitably result in an objection being upheld. In *Brown v Stott*,[111] the Privy Council recognised that a breach of ECHR in the obtaining of evidence will not necessarily result in that evidence being held to be inadmissible.

Confining within reasonable limits the duration and expense of judicial proceedings: routine evidence

Dickson's final reason for the exclusory rules of evidence is to confine within reasonable limits the duration and expense of criminal proceedings. Statute now seeks to achieve this end not merely by excluding evidence which is irrelevant but also by the routine evidence provisions of the 1995 Act ss 280 and 281.

Section 280(1) gives effect to Schedule 9 and provides that for the purposes of any proceedings for and under the enactments there specified a certificate purporting to be signed in terms of the Schedule shall be sufficient evidence of the matter and qualifications of the person signing. We have already noticed that in *O'Brien v McCreadie*[112] the High Court took the view that Parliament had meant precisely what it said and the hearsay objection at least is excluded by the words of the section. Whether similar reasoning will apply to other objections remains to be seen.

The enactments specified in Schedule 9 cover a wide variety of offences. Those which are of particular practical significance include the Misuse of Drugs Act 1971 (as to which the type, classification, purity, weight and description of a substance may be certified) and the Road Traffic Regulation Act 1988 (as to which the accuracy of speed-measuring equipment may be certified).

Before such certificates are evidence they must, in terms of s 280(6), be served on the other party (usually the accused) not less than 14 days before the trial. The recipient then has seven days within which to challenge the certificate. If such a challenge is made, the evidence of the forensic scientists has to be led to establish the fact or conclusion as to fact.

SUBMISSION OF NO CASE TO ANSWER

Once all the evidence has been led for the Crown, it is open to the defence to submit in terms of the 1995 Act ss 97 and 160 that there is no case to answer. The submission must be that there is no case to answer both on the offence charged and on any other offence of which the accused could be convicted, so that if it would

---

111 2001 SCCR 62.
112 1994 SCCR 516.

be open to the jury to convict of an amended or alternative charge a submission of this sort will be repelled. The submission may be in relation to the charge as a whole or to any part of the charge said not to have been established in evidence. For example, in *HM Advocate v Stewart and Stewart*,[113] the accused were charged that they "did abduct [the complainer] and detain him against his will and assault [him]" in various specified ways, which included the use of a baseball bat and a metal pole. The sheriff upheld a plea to the relevancy of the charge and commented that it would cause difficulties for the accused if they wished to make a submission of no case to answer because "the submission could not effectively be made because it could not strike down the whole charge". On appeal by the Crown, the Lord Justice-Clerk (Gill) explained, under reference to *Cordiner v HM Advocate*[114] that it would always be open to the defence to present an argument in terms of s 97 in relation to all or any part of the charge said not to have been established in evidence. He gave as examples the part of the charge relating to abduction (which constitutes a distinct crime) or "the part of the assault relating to the use of a baseball bat". The jury should be directed to delete any part of the charge on which the submission has been sustained.

Subsection (2) of each section sets out the test which the court must apply to such a submission, which is whether there is insufficient evidence in law to justify the accused being convicted. Considerations of quality of evidence have nothing to do with this, as the High Court made clear in *Williamson v Wither*[115] as follows:

> "[The section] provides that the evidence led by the prosecution is insufficient in law to justify the accused being convicted. It is not whether or not the evidence presented is to be accepted and therefore the only question before the court at that stage is whether there is no evidence which if accepted will entitle the court to proceed to conviction."

What this comes to is that, at the stage of such a submission, evidence in a criminal case is to be taken at its highest for the Crown and looked at to see whether there is enough in law to prove each essential allegation.

If the submission succeeds, then the accused must be acquitted in relation to the charge or charges affected by the submission; and, of course, this may mean all of the charges on the indictment or complaint, in which case the trial is over. The trial proceeds only in respect of charges in respect of which there has been no submission or no successful submission. By s 107A, the prosecutor may appeal the outcome of such a submission.

SUBMISSIONS AS TO SUFFICIENCY OF EVIDENCE

Section 97A permits the accused to make submissions either after the close of the whole evidence or after the prosecutor has addressed the jury. Those submissions are:

(a) that the evidence is insufficient in law to justify the accused's being convicted of the indicted offence or any other offence of which the accused could be convicted under the indictment (a "related offence"), or

---

113 2010 SCCR 341.
114 1991 SCCR 652; see also *Young v HM Advocate* 1997 SCCR 647.
115 1981 SCCR 216.

(b) that there is no evidence to support some part of the circumstances set out in the indictment.

If the submission is successful the accused is entitled to be acquitted, or to have the indictment amended, as the case may be. By s 107A, the prosecutor may appeal the outcome of such a submission.

SUFFICIENCY OF EVIDENCE

It is at this stage that we need to consider what will amount to a sufficiency of evidence. As noted in Chapter 1, before an essential fact can be held to be proved there must be at least two adminicles of evidence to establish it, though these may be direct evidence or circumstantial evidence.

It is important to understand the purpose and nature of corroboration. Two cases are of particular assistance in this. They are *Smith v Lees*[116] and *Fox v HM Advocate*,[117] both of which dealt with corroboration of direct evidence by circumstantial evidence.

Smith concerned an allegation that the accused had taken advantage of a camping trip to cause his 13-year-old niece to handle his private parts when they were together in a tent and the particular issue was summarised by Lord McCluskey thus:

> "[I]f a girl ... gives evidence which the court is prepared to accept that on a specified occasion the accused committed an offence ... by deliberately taking her hand and placing it on his naked private member (or by some other lewd act which left no physical trace), is the court entitled to hold that it has sufficient corroboration that the accused committed that offence on that occasion if the only other evidence adduced and founded upon by the Crown is evidence that (a) at the material time the girl and the accused were together, unobserved, in some private place, and (b) very shortly after the time when the girl says the incident occurred she was seen by another witness to exhibit emotional distress of a kind that led the witness to conclude that something had happened to upset the girl while she and the accused were together in that place?"

In *Fox*, the allegation was one of clandestine injury to a 16-year-old girl who had gone to bed drunk. She said that she had woken to find the accused already having intercourse with her and immediately told him to stop. She was distressed at being thus abused. The accused, on the other hand, told the police that they had begun having consensual intercourse after she woke up, that he had at first been behind her and that because of that she had not seen his face and that when she had turned over and realised that she had mistaken his identity she had withdrawn consent, whereupon he had desisted. On the accused's version, the complainer's distress was attributable to her mistake as to his identity. The issue was whether distress which was equally consistent with each of the competing accounts could amount to corroboration of the complainer's evidence.

In both cases the court was dealing with a situation in which there was a credible and reliable complainer and in which such corroborative evidence as existed was circumstantial. Citing *Smith v Lees*, the Lord Justice-General (Rodger) articulated the position in *Fox* in the following words:

---

116 1997 SLT 690.
117 1998 SLT 335.

"Corroborative evidence is ... evidence which supports or confirms the direct evidence of a witness ... the starting-point is that the jury have accepted the evidence of the direct witness as credible and reliable. The law requires that, even when they have reached that stage, they must still find confirmation of the direct evidence from other independent direct or circumstantial evidence ... the evidence is properly described as being corroborative because of its relation to the direct evidence: it is corroborative because it confirms or supports the direct evidence. The starting-point is the direct evidence. So long as the circumstantial evidence is independent and confirms or supports the direct evidence on the crucial facts, it provides corroboration and the requirements of legal proof are met."

On such an approach, it was held in *Smith v Lees* that distress can confirm that what happened was against the will of the complainer but it cannot confirm the nature of the act which happened. As Lord McCluskey put it:

"The fact of the woman's distress is of value in proving those facts which, as a matter of ordinary human experience, distress is apt to prove. In the present case, for example, the distress of the girl immediately after she emerged from the tent would certainly support the inference that something had happened to distress her within the tent. But does it in itself tell us anything about precisely what did happen within the tent? I do not see that it can."

In *Fox*, on the other hand, the nature of the act was not in doubt. It was agreed by both the complainer and the accused that intercourse had taken place. The complainer's distress, observed by a witness, was held to be capable of confirming her evidence that what had happened had been without her consent. The fact that it was also consistent with the account given by the accused did not deprive it of its corroborative effect.

In *Fox*, the Lord Justice-General expressly reserved his opinion as to whether there might be cases where the circumstantial evidence is ambiguous, but no reasonable jury could choose the interpretation which would support the direct evidence. This was the situation which the High Court, in *Mackie v HM Advocate*,[118] was to characterise as that of "irredeemably ambiguous circumstantial evidence". In *Mackie* the court did not consider that the evidence which was said to constitute corroboration was irredeemably ambiguous but did entertain an argument that evidence which could be so characterised could not be corroborative in a way which suggests that they regarded the argument as well founded in principle.

It follows that the adminicles need not be of equal weight. It would be possible to cite a battery of cases to demonstrate this but particular notice should be taken of three.

The first is *Proctor v Tudhope*[119] in which a man was convicted of housebreaking with intent to steal; he was identified by the householder and it was held that the fact that a police officer identified him as having run off when pointed out as the perpetrator of the crime was sufficient corroboration. The Lord Justice-General said that "not very much was required in the way of corroboration of the testimony of the credible and reliable eye witness who identified the appellant in the act of committing the crime".

In *Ralston v HM Advocate*[120] it was held that where one eye witness made an unhesitating identification there was corroboration in the evidence of a second that

118 26 July 2001.
119 1985 SCCR 39.
120 1988 SCCR 590.

the accused resembled the perpetrator in that his face was the same shape, and that of a third that the accused was possibly the perpetrator.

Finally, in *Nolan v McLeod*[121] it was held that there was sufficient identification where the first witness was "80% sure" and the second "75%" sure.

Particular difficulties have arisen in connection with sexual assaults, where corroboration of the events themselves, and of the lack of consent, can prove hard to find.

The High Court first addressed this issue in *Moorov v HM Advocate*.[122] The accused was a shopkeeper who had, over a period of years, subjected female shop assistants to unwanted sexual attentions, always singly. In upholding his conviction the court applied a principle stated in *Hume on Crimes* over a century earlier. It is worth noting the way the principle was formulated by the Lord Justice-General:

> "Before the evidence of single credible witnesses to separate acts can provide material for mutual corroboration the connection between the separate acts (indicated by their external relation in time character or circumstance) must be such as to exhibit them as subordinates in some particular and ascertained unity of intent, project, campaign or adventure which lies beyond or behind—but is related to—the separate acts."

In other words, there must be some real connection between the acts other than the identity of the accused as the perpetrator. But it is not the case, as is sometimes thought, that what has become known as the *"Moorov* doctrine" applies only in relation to sexual offences. *Lindsay v HM Advocate*[123] is an example of its application to assault and robbery, and further demonstrates that the evidence identifying the accused need not be that of an eye witness. It is, however, the case that it only applies where the charges are all on the same complaint or indictment.

The law was summarised and restated by Lord Coulsfield in *Wilson v HM Advocate*[124] in these terms:

> "In a case in which the Crown seek to prove a number of charges by relying on the principles set out in *Moorov* ... they are setting out to establish that there has been a course of criminal conduct of which individual incidents, each spoken to by a single witness, are instances. In the common case of a series of sexual offences, the witnesses may be held to corroborate one another even though each of them is the only witness who speaks to the commission of any crime at all on the particular occasion about which he or she gives evidence. It is accepted that the *Moorov* principle is not confined to sexual or other clandestine offences. If it can be applied to theft, I see no reason why witnesses speaking to different incidents should not be held capable of corroborating one another, even if each of them is the only witness to the completed act of theft on the occasion to which his or her evidence relates. Thus, if one shopkeeper speaks to a theft by the accused of a packet of cigarettes: a second speaks to a theft of a bottle of lemonade: and a third to a theft of a packet of sandwiches, then, provided the other conditions for the application of the principle are present, it seems to me that the evidence of the witnesses may be held mutually corroborative and establish the three thefts, even though there is no other evidence of the commission or completion of any of them. To say that is not to say that the nature or identity of the goods stolen does not require corroboration. It is to say that the corroboration required for that essential element in the charge is supplied by the application of the *Moorov* principle.

121 1987 SCCR 558.
122 1930 JC 68.
123 1993 SCCR 868.
124 2001 SCCR 455.

... The *Moorov* principle cannot, of course, apply unless there is sufficient similarity between the circumstances of the individual incidents, including the description of the articles said to have been stolen. It would, therefore, probably not apply where the witnesses spoke to thefts of, respectively, a diamond necklace, a sail board and a bar of chocolate, whatever the other circumstances might be. It follows that the *Moorov* principle can most easily be applied where the articles stolen can be said to fall into a single category, such as items of food or sums of money, or under some similar description. I would, however, be reluctant to try to derive some precise rule or requirement from that broad observation. It seems to me that, as with the other conditions for the application of the *Moorov* principle, that is, a reasonable coincidence in time, character and circumstances, it is necessary to consider the particular facts. It seems to me to be possible that there could be sufficient similarity in regard to time, method of operation and other circumstances to justify application of the principle, even where there is some diversity between the articles stolen."

In *Reynolds v HM Advocate*[125] the accused was charged with a charge of assault, abduction and robbery and a charge of assault and robbery. There were some similarities between them and some dissimilarities. The Lord Justice-General said:

"As was pointed out in *Carpenter v Hamilton*[126] cases of this kind, while they must be approached with care, raise questions of fact and degree. That is especially so where, to use Lord Sand's expression, the case falls into the open country which lies between the two extremes. ... We accept that there was a process of evaluation to be conducted, because there were dissimilarities as well as similarities. On the other hand we do not accept that on no possible view could it be said that there was any connection between the two offences. Where the case lies in the middle ground, the important point is that a jury should be properly directed so that they are aware of the test which requires to be applied. ... When ... regard is had to the fact that there are items in the evidence which may on one view be regarded as similarities and then balanced against the dissimilarities, we consider that this case fell within the province of the jury rather than the judge."

In *Stewart v HM Advocate*,[127] the Lord Justice-Clerk (Gill) made it clear that there is no maximum interval of time beyond which the rule in *Moorov* cannot apply and said that "even a long interval may be acceptable if there are other compelling similarities". In practice, the longer the interval of time the more compelling the other similarities will have to be.

In a case of a single incident, to which *Moorov* by definition cannot apply, it will often be possible to prove from scientific evidence, or even the admission of the accused, that sexual activity has taken place but proof of the absence of consent can be particularly difficult unless there is injury to the victim. However, as a result of *Yates v HM Advocate*[128] the emotional state of the victim after the alleged assault can assist the Crown. That was a rape case, intercourse being admitted, in which it was held that the evidence of a witness who spoke to the victim's distressed condition immediately after the incident was enough to corroborate her own evidence as to force and that a knife had been used to threaten her. The court observed that all that was necessary was to find "evidence in general which

125 1995 SCCR 504.
126 1994 SCCR 108.
127 2007 SCCR 303.
128 1977 SLT (Notes) 42.

supports the broad proposition of force, details of which had been given by the girl". In considering this area of law, Lord McCluskey's analysis in *Smith v Lees*[129] must be kept in mind. Distress supports the proposition that something has happened to cause distress but does not assist with the nature of the distressing event.

In *Moore v HM Advocate*,[130] distress 12 or 13 hours after the incident was too remote in time to afford *Yates* type corroboration but as *Cree v HM Advocate*[131] makes clear, each case will turn on its own circumstances. In that case the allegation was rape; there was an admission of intercourse but a defence of consent. A witness heard screams at the time of the alleged crime and there was evidence from others of distress between five and seven hours later. It was argued, relying on *Moore*, that the interval was too long but held that it was a matter for the jury who were entitled to accept that the victim was only prepared to discuss the offence with a close relative, which she had done as soon as reasonably practicable. The matter was put even more clearly by *Cannon v HM Advocate*[132] in which, again in a "consent defence" rape, the only substantial corroboration available was evidence of distress 12 hours later. There was also evidence that there was no earlier stage at which the victim was in contact with someone who might have been in a position to observe the distress and it was held that, since the jury had been given a clear direction by the trial judge that they could only convict if they were satisfied that the distress resulted from the accident, the conviction should stand. It follows that there is no outside limit beyond which distress cannot provide corroboration in this kind of case, though in practice the longer the interval and the more people the victim has been in contact with during that time the less likely it is that distress will assist.

Clearly, it will assist the Crown if there is something to which they can point beyond "mere" distress. In *Stephen v HM Advocate*[133] there was no evidence of injury to the person or clothing of the complainer. There was evidence of scratch marks on the abdomen of the appellant and of the distress of the complainer immediately after the incident. The Appeal Court held that there was sufficient material for the jury to find corroboration of the complainer's version of the events and refused the appeal.

Corroboration by circumstantial evidence

Distress is an example of circumstantial evidence. In *Mackintosh v HM Advocate*[134] the Appeal Court made useful general observations about the way in which circumstantial evidence can be approached. The context was a rape case in which the issue was whether there was corroboration of the *mens rea*—at the time of that case, whether the accused knew that the complainer was not consenting or was at least reckless about it. (The Sexual Offences (Scotland) Act 2009 makes important changes to the law in that area.) The Crown identified a list of circumstances which, they submitted, constituted corroboration on that point. Lord Osborne, giving the opinion of the court, said:

---

129 1997 SLT 690.
130 1990 SCCR 586.
131 1991, unreported.
132 1992 SCCR 505.
133 1987 SCCR 570.
134 2010 SCCR 168.

"In a context, such as this, where the Crown case was said to depend upon circumstantial evidence, the question must be whether the circumstances relied upon in combination can be seen as capable of giving rise to the necessary inference that the appellant must have known that there was no consent to intercourse on the part of the complainer, or, at least, that he was reckless as to whether such consent existed or not. While circumstantial evidence may give rise to a number of inferences, if at least one inference is indicative of guilt of the crime charged, or proof of the essential element in that crime that is in question, then there would be a case to answer. ...

"During the course of the discussion before us, the approach of the advocate depute was to point to several elements in the case, ten in number, which he contended amounted to sufficient proof of mens rea. Plainly there is a danger in scrutinising each of these elements in isolation; it is necessary to consider their effect in combination. However, in our opinion, it is legitimate to consider each one for such significance as it may be thought to possess, provided that one does not lose sight of the need to consider the evidential effect of the various elements in combination."

Corroboration of confessions

Confusion sometimes arises about confessions and from time to time it is thought by some that when a suspect confesses that is all that is required for a conviction. But it needs to be understood clearly that a confession has only one source and that is the accused. That is true no matter how many people hear it made or how often it is repeated. There needs to be some other source of evidence whether the confession is made to one person or to one hundred, whether it is made once or repeated many times and even if it is repeated in judicial examination. It is only one source of evidence and not by itself sufficient. At the very least what is needed is what is contemplated by Lord Dunpark in *Hartley v HM Advocate*:[135]

"If ... a jury is satisfied that a confession of guilt was freely made and unequivocal in its terms, corroboration of that confession may be found in evidence from another source or sources which point to the truth of that confession."

It must be emphasised that the existence of a confession is the essential starting-point for this process. In *Beattie v HM Advocate*[136] the fact that the accused had special knowledge was not sufficient where it occurred in the context of a denial.

Often a confession will be corroborated by direct evidence (for example the admission to intercourse in *Yates*, corroborated by the victim's evidence on that point). The law recognises, however, that sometimes there will be material in the confession which can be shown to be true and which only someone present at the crime could have known; and that will be enough. The rule starts with Alison[137] where he says:

"If a person is apprehended on a charge of theft and he tells the officer who seized him that if he will go to such a place and look under such a bush he will find the stolen goods; or he is charged with murder or assault and he says that he threw the bloody weapon into such a pool, in such a river and it is there searched for and found, without doubt these are such strong confirmations of the truth of the confession as renders it of itself sufficient if the *corpus* is established *aliunde* to convict the prisoner."

---

135 1979 SLT 26.
136 1995 SLT 275.
137 ii 580.

This was precisely the situation in *Manuel v HM Advocate*[138] in which a murderer confessed and told the police accurately where a body and clothing were to be found, and was hanged on the strength of it.

The situation in contemplation in Alison and in *Manuel* was one where the investigator checked afterwards what was disclosed for the first time in the accused's confession; and the possibility of fabrication is for practical purposes excluded. However, the rule is not confined to cases where the information was previously unknown to the police. In *Wilson v McAughey*[139] police found a mechanical digger submerged in the Clyde with a broken window. The accused subsequently admitted vandalism and described breaking the window and driving it into the river. The sheriff acquitted because the digger had not been found as a result of the confession as contemplated in the authorities discussed above; but the High Court overturned that acquittal, holding that it was enough if the confession contained what has become known as "special knowledge" even if it was known to the police. *Wilson v HM Advocate*,[140] which concerned knowledge of the way in which a murder had been committed and the body position, such knowledge having become public, establishes that, where the relevant facts are known to others than the police it is a jury question whether the confession can be said to contain knowledge which is special enough to amount to corroborative material.

The detail in such a confession need not be very substantial. In *Hutchison v Valentine*[141] the words "I canna really mind where aboot in the hotel I got it. I was drunk. I dumped it" were held to be sufficient where there was evidence that a stolen television had been abandoned in the hotel car park.

It was held in *Andrew v HM Advocate*[142] that the fact that the accused said at judicial examination that the "special knowledge" in his statement was actually material he had overheard in disreputable premises did not deprive that material of its corroborative effect. It was for the jury to decide whether to reject what the accused said to the police. Following *Gilmour v HM Advocate*[143] where a statement contains points of identity with the crime and points of discrepancy, it is for the jury to decide how far they will rely on it. All of this may be seen as consistent with the approach in *Fox v HM Advocate*.

Demeanour of the accused

Although the emotional state of the victim in a rape may afford corroboration of the proposition of force and the reaction of the suspect upon being accused may sufficiently corroborate a householder's identification of him as the housebreaker this should not mean that the demeanour of an accused who admits a crime will corroborate his admission. In *McGougan v HM Advocate*[144] the trial judge was held to have erred when he directed the jury that the accused's demeanour when making an admission and in particular his attempt to throw himself out of the window were capable of amounting to corroboration.

---

138 1958 JC 41.
139 1982 SCCR 398.
140 1987 SCCR 217.
141 1990 SCCR 569.
142 2000 SLT 402.
143 1982 SCCR 590.
144 1991 SCCR 49.

Fingerprints, DNA etc

Fingerprints, handwriting and the like are a trap for the unwary. Although on one view a fingerprint is only one source of evidence, it was held in *Hamilton v HM Advocate*[145] and *HM Advocate v Rolley*[146] that it will be sufficient where each step is corroborated, so that there will be two witnesses to the finding of the print at the locus, two to the taking of a print from the accused and two experts to make the comparison (it being clear from *McKillen v Barclay Curle & Co Ltd*[147] that expert witnesses require corroboration like anyone else when their evidence relates to the essentials of a case). However, s 26(7) of the Criminal Justice (Scotland) Act 1980 is authority for only calling one expert in this and similar situations where notice of that intention has been given to the defence. If any of the stages is spoken to by only one witness, the evidence ceases to be sufficient in itself and requires corroboration from some other source.

In *Maguire v HM Advocate*,[148] the same reasoning was applied to the finding, on a mask used in a robbery, of DNA which matched that of the accused. Lord Hamilton (with whom the Lord Justice-General concurred) noted that the mask was intimately connected with the crime, that the DNA evidence pointed to the appellant having at some point had the internal surface of the mask against his skin and that the accused offered no explanation for that—rather, he denied ever having had any contact with the item. Lord Hamilton held that there was sufficient evidence to allow the case to go to the jury and for them to decide what inference they drew from the DNA evidence. The conviction was upheld.

---

145 1934 JC 1.
146 1945 JC 155.
147 1967 SLT 41.
148 2003 SLT 1307.

10 Sentencing

If the accused pleads guilty to or is found guilty of any charge the proceedings enter the sentencing phase. Sentencing can be dealt with on a common basis for solemn procedure and summary procedure, and the 1995 Act does so in considerable detail in Part IX (ss 195 to 254). Those provisions are attended by a very substantial body of case law.

As well as these general provisions, there are particular sentencing provisions in particular offence-creating statutes. Sometimes, for example, an Act will make provision for a disqualification to be imposed as ancillary to a sentence. Obvious examples include disqualification for holding or obtaining a driving licence, imposed under road traffic legislation, and disqualification from acting as a director of a company, imposed in relation to some offences under the Companies Acts.

It would be correct to conclude from the foregoing that sentencing law can be highly detailed. The intention in this chapter is to give an overview of its principles.

MOTION FOR SENTENCE

Although, by contrast with some jurisdictions, the Scottish prosecutor does not ask for any particular sentence, he does initiate the whole sentencing process, at least under solemn procedure. There, once the guilt of the accused has been established, the prosecutor has a discretion whether or not to move for sentence. If he does not do so, it is not competent for the court to proceed to sentence.[1] The motion for sentence can be made by implication from the prosecutor's actings, as in *Noon v HM Advocate*[2] in which, although the prosecutor forgot to say the words "I move for sentence", he did tender to the court a list of previous convictions—an action consistent only with an intention that the court should proceed to sentence—and the competency of the sentence imposed was upheld on appeal.

Under summary procedure there is no motion for sentence and, although the prosecutor will usually take action such as tendering a notice of previous convictions which under solemn procedure would imply such a motion, Nicholson considers that the court may proceed to sentence even if he does not do so.[3]

Once a motion for sentence is made under solemn procedure, or once the accused has been convicted under summary procedure, the court proceeds to consider sentence. Unless the imposition of sentence is for some reason incompetent, the

---

1 See C G B Nicholson, *Sentencing: Law and Practice in Scotland* (2nd edn, 1992) p 114.
2 1960 JC 52.
3 *Sentencing*, p 114.

court does not have the option of making no order. In *Skeen v Sullivan*[4] the High Court was sharply critical of a sheriff who had declined to do so.

PREVIOUS CONVICTIONS

By the 1995 Act ss 69(2) and 166(2) the notice of previous convictions tendered by the Crown upon the accused being convicted must have been served upon the accused along with the indictment or complaint. Sections 101(1) and 166(3) contain prohibitions on references to previous convictions before conviction except where proof of such convictions is necessary to proof of the substantive charge. The most common example of the need to prove convictions in support of a substantive charge is probably that of driving whilst disqualified by order of the court but even there (as noted under reference to cases such as *Boustead and Another v McLeod*[5]) the reference made to such convictions is the minimum necessary to proof.

Forms 8.3 and 16.1-E annexed to the Act of Adjournal (Criminal Procedure Rules) 1996 provide the form to be used for notices of previous convictions.

It was held as long ago as 1842, in *HM Advocate v John Graham*[6] that previous convictions must predate the offence and not merely the date of service of the complaint or indictment or the date of conviction. This is modified by the 1995 Act ss 101A and 166A (both as inserted by the Criminal Justice and Licensing (Scotland) Act 2010) which provide that, where a person is convicted, the court, in deciding on disposal, may have regard to any conviction or alternative disposal (fixed penalty, compensation offer by the procurator fiscal or a work order under the 1995 Act s 303ZA) which occurred after the date of the offence being dealt with but before conviction.

In 1911, *McCall v Mitchell*[7] established that convictions under appeal could not be referred to. This having been said, social enquiry reports will frequently disclose to the court the existence of such convictions which the prosecutor is prohibited from libelling, and Nicholson[8] suggests that it would be absurd if the court was not told, for example, of a long period of imprisonment imposed on the accused in respect of a conviction which could not be libelled, because otherwise any sentence imposed might be wholly inconsistent with the accused's actual situation.

CROWN NARRATIVE

As well as tendering a notice of previous convictions the prosecutor will, in a case of a plea of guilty, give a narrative of the facts to the court.

FORFEITURE

It is possible that the prosecutor will also seek an order for forfeiture of some article used in course of the commission of the offence. This is dealt with under Part II of the Proceeds of Crime (Scotland) Act 1995.

4 1980 SLT (Notes) 11.
5 1979 JC 70.
6 (1842) 1 Brown 445.
7 (1911) 6 Adam 303.
8 *Sentencing*, p 116.

Where the prosecutor certifies that the article in question is perishable, dangerous or worthless or that the possession of it is unlawful, the Proceeds of Crime (Scotland) Act 1995 s 24 operates to forfeit it at once. In other cases, however, the order made will be a suspended forfeiture order and it will take effect only after the passage of a sufficient period of time to allow third parties claiming an interest in the property to vindicate that interest.

PLEA IN MITIGATION

Once the prosecutor has completed his narrative it is up to the defence to make a plea in mitigation. Occasionally the defence version of the facts will be so far removed from that given by the prosecution as to make it impossible for the court to deal with the case. If the defence version is inconsistent with guilt then the case must be adjourned for trial. More commonly, the defence version will still justify a plea of guilty but will vary so far from the prosecution account that the court lacks a proper basis upon which to deal with the case. Where that happens, Nicholson suggests[9] that the court may hear evidence to resolve the issue. Such "proofs in mitigation" are relatively common.

ADJOURNMENT FOR ENQUIRY

Section 201 of the 1995 Act allows the court to adjourn a case before imposing sentence in order to enable enquiries to be made or of determining the most suitable method of dealing with the case. Such adjournments must not be for any single period exceeding three weeks where the accused is remanded in custody or four weeks (eight on cause shown) where the offender is on bail or ordained to appear.

DEFERRED SENTENCE

In terms of the 1995 Act s 202 the court may defer sentence for a period and on such conditions as it may determine. It is quite common for the court to defer sentence for a period of months for the accused to demonstrate that he can be of good behaviour or for a shorter period for the accused to repay the value of stolen or damaged property. The seriousness of the offence is by no means an absolute bar on the taking of this course, and *McPherson v HM Advocate*[10] is an example of deferral of sentence in a case of attempted murder.

At the end of the period of deferral the accused is sentenced for the offence, taking into account the facts of the offence but also how well he has complied with the condition imposed.

The power to defer is sometimes used where there are other proceedings current against the offender, with a view to dealing with him at the same time in respect of all matters.

9 *Sentencing*, p 114.
10 1986 SCCR 278.

"DISCOUNT" FOR GUILTY PLEA

By the 1995 Act s 196 it is open to a court, in sentencing an offender who has pled guilty to an offence, to take into account the stage in the proceedings at which the offender indicated his intention to plead guilty. The practice is that a discount is usually given for a guilty plea and in *Spence v HM Advocate*[11] some guidance was given about how that discount will be calculated, at least on indictment. The factors which will be relevant include the utilitarian value of the plea in avoiding the expenditure of resources in preparing the case for trial. On a plea in terms of s 76 the discount will be of the order of one third. At the first calling at a preliminary hearing (in the High Court) or a first diet (in the sheriff court) the discount will be in the order of one quarter. The Appeal Court said that a plea at trial should not ordinarily exceed one tenth and in some circumstances may be less than that, or nil. Somewhat enigmatically, the court said that "special circumstances may apply to very short and very long sentences, as they do to fixing punishment parts in indeterminate sentences".

SENTENCING GUIDELINES

In selecting a sentence, the court is obliged by the 1995 Act s 197 to have regard to any relevant opinion pronounced by the High Court under s 118(7) or s 189(7). Those provisions allow the High Court, in the context of determining an appeal against sentence, to pronounce an opinion on the sentence or other disposal order which is appropriate in any similar case; in short, to issue sentencing guidelines. The High Court has been relatively slow to do so but an example (dealing with the use of confidential material in a plea in mitigation) is to be found in *O'Neill v HM Advocate*.[12] However, the Criminal Justice and Licensing (Scotland) Act 2010 has made provision for the creation of a Scottish Sentencing Council to develop guidelines and one may therefore expect to see an increase in their use.

PARTICULAR SENTENCES

The following is an outline of the most commonly imposed sentencing options.

Custodial disposals

As already noted, the High Court of Justiciary can impose a sentence of up to life imprisonment and (by the 1995 Act s 205) must do so in a case of murder. The sheriff sitting with a jury can impose a sentence of up to five years' imprisonment (by the 1995 Act s 3(3)) or (in terms of the 1995 Act s 195), where he holds that any competent sentence which he could impose is inadequate, remit to the High Court for sentence. In *McGhee v HM Advocate*[13] the Appeal Court decided that the five-year limit applies to the sentence finally selected. In that case, the sheriff considered that the sentence which the crime deserved was one of six years'

---

11 2008 JC 174.
12 1998 SCCR 644.
13 2006 SCCR 712.

imprisonment but that a discount should be applied to take account of a plea of guilty. The period of imprisonment selected after the discount was five years. It was argued that this was incompetent and that the sheriff should have remitted the case to the High Court but the Appeal Court rejected that argument.

In terms of the 1995 Act s 5(2), the sheriff sitting summarily can impose a sentence of up to 12 months' imprisonment. By the 1995 Act s 7(5) a JP court constituted by a stipendiary magistrate has the same sentencing powers as a sheriff sitting under summary procedure. In other cases, by s 7(6)(a), the district court may impose up to 60 days' imprisonment.

All of the foregoing general limits may be varied by statute. Accordingly, many offences carry lesser maximum terms than the court could ordinarily impose.

If the court intends to impose a determinate sentence (ie a sentence other than life imprisonment) in a sexual offence or a sentence of more than four years in a violent offence and considers that the period at the end of the sentence for which the offender would be on licence would not be adequate to protect the public, it may pass an extended sentence.[14] Where a person is convicted on indictment of an offence other than a sexual offence and sentenced to less than four years, the court may, if it considers it necessary in order to protect the public, impose a supervised release order (which will involve the offender being under social work supervision for a period of time after the end of the sentence).[15]

In all cases in which a custodial sentence is being imposed the court must, by the 1995 Act s 210(1), have regard, in determining the length of the sentence, to any time spent in custody on remand awaiting trial or extradition.

Although imprisonment is the most obvious custodial disposal, there are others which apply in the case of persons under the age of 21. Section 208 of the 1995 Act provides that where a child is convicted on indictment and the court is of opinion that no other method of dealing with him is appropriate, it may sentence him to be detained in such place and on such conditions as the Secretary of State may direct. "Child" is defined by s 307 by reference to the Children (Scotland) Act 1995 and means, essentially, one who has not attained the age of 16 or one who has attained the age of 16 but not 18 and who is subject to a supervision requirement of a children's hearing under the Children (Scotland) Act 1995.

By s 207 of the 1995 Act it is not competent to impose imprisonment on a person under 21 years of age. Instead, the court may impose detention in a young offenders' institution on a person aged between 16 and 21 but only where, after obtaining a social enquiry report from "an officer of a local authority" (that is, a social worker), the court is of opinion that no other method of dealing with the offender is appropriate.

In the case of a person aged 21 or over who has not previously been sentenced to imprisonment, the 1995 Act s 204(2) prohibits the passing of a sentence of imprisonment unless after considering a social enquiry report it considers that no other method of dealing with him is appropriate.

Section 204(3A)[16] provides that a court must not pass a sentence of imprisonment for a term of three months or less on a person unless the court considers that no other method of dealing with the person is appropriate.

---

14 Criminal Procedure (Scotland) Act 1995 s 10A.
15 1995 Act s 209.
16 Inserted by the Criminal Justice and Licensing (Scotland) Act 2010.

Section 210(1)(b) requires the court to specify the date of commencement of the sentence and subsection (1)(c) requires that where the date specified is "not earlier than the date on which sentence was passed" (it is hard to see how it could be later) the court must state its reason for not selecting an earlier date.

Community payback orders

Section 227A of the 1995 Act, as inserted by the Criminal Justice and Licensing (Scotland) Act 2010 s 14, provides that where a person is convicted of an offence punishable by imprisonment, the court may, instead of imposing a sentence of imprisonment, impose a "community payback order". The community payback order replaces probation, community service orders, and supervised attendance orders, whilst seeking to reproduce some of the previously existing community sentencing options in a package tailored for the particular offender. A restricted version of the community payback order (limited to offender supervision, a "level 1" unpaid work or other activity requirement and a conduct requirement) may be imposed alongside a fine.[17] JP courts may only impose community payback orders in that same restricted form, with the addition of residence and conduct requirements.[18]

It is reiterated that this is an introductory text. The following account of community payback orders is, therefore, an introduction, not an exhaustive analysis.

A community payback order is defined[19] as an order imposing one or more of the following requirements—

    (a) an offender supervision requirement,
    (b) a compensation requirement,
    (c) an unpaid work or other activity requirement,
    (d) a programme requirement,
    (e) a residence requirement,
    (f) a mental health treatment requirement,
    (g) a drug treatment requirement,
    (h) an alcohol treatment requirement, or
    (i) a conduct requirement.

An "offender supervision requirement" is a requirement that, during the specified period (at least six months and not more than three years), the offender must attend appointments with the responsible officer (an officer of the local authority who will supervise the person) at such time and place as may be determined by the responsible officer, for the purpose of promoting the offender's rehabilitation.[20]

A compensation requirement is a requirement that the offender must pay compensation for any personal injury, loss or damage.[21]

An unpaid work or other activity requirement is a requirement that the offender must, during the period specified by the court, for the specified number of hours (at least 20 and not more than 300), undertake unpaid work, or unpaid work and

---

17 1995 Act s 227A(4).
18 1995 Act s 227A(5).
19 1995 Act s 227A(2).
20 1995 Act s 227G.
21 1995 Act s 227H.

another activity. Section 227I of the 1995 Act makes detailed provision for the ranges of hours available in different situations. The number of hours is divided into two levels. Level 1 is a requirement for no more than 100 hours and level 2 is a requirement for more than 100 hours. Section 227K provides that in the case of a "mixed" work requirement, any activity other than work must not exceed 30% of the requirement.

A programme requirement is a requirement that the offender must participate in a specified course or other planned set of activities, taking place over a period of time, and provided to individuals or groups of individuals for the purpose of addressing "offending behavioural needs".[22]

A residence requirement is what it says—a requirement that, during the specified period, the offender must reside at a specified place.[23] The length of the period cannot be more than that of the offender supervision requirement which must be imposed at the same time.

A mental health treatment requirement is a requirement that the offender must submit, during the specified period, to treatment by or under the direction of a registered medical practitioner or a registered psychologist (or both) with a view to improving the offender's mental condition.[24] There are complex rules in ss 227R, 227S and 227T about the conditions which must be satisfied before such a requirement can be imposed, the means by which those conditions can be satisfied and how changes may be made in the treatment.

A drug treatment requirement is a requirement that the offender must submit, during the specified period, to treatment by or under the direction of a specified person with a view to reducing or eliminating the offender's dependency on, or propensity to misuse, drugs;[25] and an alcohol treatment requirement is a similar order with a view to the reduction or elimination of the offender's dependency on alcohol.[26]

Finally, a conduct requirement is a requirement that the offender must, during the specified period (not more than three years), do or refrain from doing specified things.[27]

On imposing a community payback order on an offender, the court may include provision for the order to be reviewed periodically.[28]

In terms of the 1995 Act s 227ZC(7), breach of a community payback order exposes the offender to the risk of a fine not exceeding level 3 on the standard scale, of revocation of the order with the court then dealing with the offender for the original offence, or of imprisonment.

Financial penalties: fines

The fine is probably the most commonly imposed sentence. Section 211 of the 1995 Act contains a general power to fine, subject to particular provisions in Acts of Parliament. Under solemn procedure, there is no limit to the amount of the fine which can be imposed in either the High Court or the sheriff court. Under

22 1995 Act s 227P.
23 1995 Act s 227Q.
24 1995 Act s 227R.
25 1995 Act s 227U.
26 1995 Act s 227V.
27 1995 Act s 227W.
28 1995 Act s 227X.

summary procedure, fines are structured within levels on what is known as the "standard scale", which is set out in s 225(2). At the time of writing, that scale was as follows:

Level on the scale	Amount of fine
1	£200
2	£500
3	£1,000
4	£2,500
5	£5,000

Level 5 on the scale, £5,000, is also known as the "prescribed sum" in terms of s 225(8).

By the 1995 Act s 5(2) a sheriff is empowered, on convicting a person of any common law offence, to impose a fine not exceeding the prescribed sum. Section 7(5) gives a district court stipendiary magistrate the same powers as a sheriff. Otherwise, the district court is empowered, by s 7(6)(b), to impose a fine not exceeding level 4 on the standard scale. Section 7(7) prohibits the district court from imposing any fine greater than level 4 unless statute explicitly empowers the district court to do so. It is thought that no statute does so. However, a number of statutes permit fines on summary conviction of up to £20,000 and such fines can be imposed by the sheriff or a stipendiary magistrate.

It should be noted that in *Wann v Macmillan*[29] it was held that the total financial penalty imposed on a complaint in respect of multiple charges can exceed the maximum for a single offence (by contrast with the position as regards imprisonment).

In determining the amount of a fine the court is required, by s 211(7), to take into account the means of the offender so far as known to the court and s 212 specifically permits money found in the possession of the offender to be applied to payment of the fine. The principle of taking into account the means of the offender was applied in *Andrew Redpath & Son v MacNeill*[30] to the case of a corporate offender.

Time for payment of fines is dealt with in the 1995 Act s 214 and is in general the right of the convicted person. It is also one way of taking account of the means of the accused. The general principle is that the payment of a fine should not take an unreasonably long time but the High Court in *Johnston v Lockhart*[31] disapproved of the proposition that a fine should be capable of being paid within one year.

Where payment is not made timeously, the accused will be at risk of imprisonment in default, the period being calculated according to the 1995 Act s 219.

Financial penalties: compensation

The compensation order is closely analogous to a fine and is provided for by the 1995 Act s 249. Such orders are available for personal injury, loss or damage arising out of an offence, except most road traffic offences, and provided the court has not dealt with the case by deferred sentence, probation or absolute discharge. The

---

29 1956 SLT 369.
30 1990 GWD 25-1423.
31 1987 SCCR 537.

maxima are as for fines and the payments are enforced and collected as if they were fines and remitted to the victim by the clerk of court.

Financial penalties: caution

Caution for good behaviour is another financial "penalty" and is provided for by the 1995 Act s 227. The order is for the offender to lodge a sum of money with the clerk of court as a guarantee of his good behaviour during a period which must not exceed 12 months. If during the specified period of time he stays out of trouble he gets the money back with interest; otherwise, he loses it.

Financial penalties: confiscation order

In terms of the Proceeds of Crime Act 2002 s 92, if the prosecutor moves for a confirmation order and the court is satisfied that the accused has benefited from his criminal conduct, the court must order him to pay "the recoverable amount"— which is everything he has up to the value of the benefit from the crime. The procedure is complex and involves written pleading about the accused's financial circumstances.

Admonition and absolute discharge

Admonition and absolute discharge are provided for by the 1995 Act s 246 and are what they say. No penalty is imposed. Admonition is in effect a formal reprimand and absolute discharge not even that.

11 Appeals

Although the 1995 Act deals separately with appeals under solemn and summary procedure and although some of the modes of appeal are somewhat different, they have many common features. This chapter will therefore approach appeals according to the nature of the decision appealed against, rather than according to type of procedure or type of appeal.

THE *NOBILE OFFICIUM*

In extraordinary and unforeseen circumstances, where there is no other avenue of appeal, application may be made (by either the defence or the Crown) to the *nobile officium* of the High Court, which is the power that court retains to do what is just in circumstances for which the law makes no other provision.[1] It is *not* available to avoid an express or clearly implied statutory intention,[2] even where the court considers the statutory rule to be defective so as to require reconsideration by the legislature (as was the case in *Ryan, Petitioner*).[3] In practice it is unlikely to be granted so as to remedy a failure by an appellant to take the steps in procedure required by statute.[4] In most cases, however, a more orthodox avenue of appeal will be available and it is with such avenues that this chapter is chiefly concerned.

It may be noted that, occasionally, the High Court of Justiciary has been prepared to treat a petition to the *nobile officium* as if it was an appeal under the appropriate procedure, purely to avoid undue expense. This is, however, very much an indulgence and not to be counted on. It is more likely to happen where the petitioner is obviously entitled to the remedy sought. An example is to be found in *Gilchrist, Petitioner*[5] in which the petition was treated as if it was the bail appeal that the petitioner should more properly have pursued.

APPEALS FROM PRELIMINARY DIETS, FROM DECISIONS ON COMPETENCY AND RELEVANCY AND FROM DECISIONS ON DEVOLUTION ISSUES

Under solemn procedure the 1995 Act s 74(1) provides for an appeal to the High Court against a decision at a preliminary diet. The 1995 Act s 174 provides a very

---

1 *Black, Petitioner* 1991 SCCR 1.
2 *Anderson v HM Advocate* 1974 SLT 239; *McBride, Petitioner* 2002 GWD 1-19.
3 2002 GWD 6-181.
4 *McLeod, Petitioner* 1975 SCCR Supp 93; *Fenton, Petitioner* 1981 SCCR 288.
5 1991 SCCR 699.

similar appeal mechanism for summary procedure. Detailed provision is made by the Act of Adjournal (Criminal Procedure Rules) 1996 Chapters 9, 15 and 19 but ss 74 and 174 themselves include two important qualifications to the right of appeal.

The first is that such an appeal is competent only with the leave of the court of first instance, which may be granted upon the motion of the party wishing to appeal or *ex proprio motu*. The sections do not specify when that leave must be sought, but rule 9.11(1) provides that a motion for leave to appeal against a decision at a preliminary diet shall be made "at that diet immediately following the making of the decision in question, and shall either be granted or refused there and then".

Under solemn procedure, a judge who grants leave to appeal is required by rule 9.11(2) to consider postponing the trial. The obvious reason for doing so is to allow time for the appeal. Such a postponement might require to be accompanied by an extension of the time limits applying to the case, so far as that can competently be done by the particular judge. By s 74(3) the High Court itself may postpone the trial diet pending an appeal and, if the High Court does so, the period of the postponement does not count towards any time limit which applies to the case. Section 174(2) gives the High Court a similar power for summary procedure.

The courts have not had to consider what is meant by "immediately" in the context of the making of a motion for leave to appeal but McCluskey and McBride have used the phrase "immediately and on the spot".[6] Certainly, given the wording of the rule, any time after the preliminary diet will be too late, even if it is only a few minutes. There is no statutory warrant for calling the indictment or complaint again to allow such a motion to be made and it is thought that to do so would be incompetent. Moreover, it will be recalled that in terms of the 1995 Act s 73(1) the accused must be asked to state his plea to the indictment "at the conclusion" of the preliminary diet. It seems to follow in theory, as it does in practice, that the stating of that plea marks the end of the preliminary diet. Since the requirement to state that plea is the next thing which happens after the decision on the preliminary plea has been given, it would seem that the only window of opportunity for leave to be sought is after the end of the judge's or sheriff's statement of his or her decision and before the accused is asked how he pleads. In other words, if leave is not sought instantly upon the adverse decision being given, it will be too late.

For summary procedure, rule 19(1) stipulates that leave can only be sought by the accused after he has stated how he pleads to the charge or charges set out in the complaint and by rule 19(2) the application for leave and the determination of that application are, as under solemn procedure, to be made "immediately following the decision in question".

The second qualification in the 1995 Act ss 74 and 174 is that the appeal must actually be "taken" within two days after the decision, though by ss 75 and 194, Saturdays, Sundays and court holidays are not counted. Rules 9.6(1) and 19.1(4) provide that such appeals are to be taken by way of note of appeal which is to be in the form of Form 9.6 or 19.1-A and lodged with the appropriate clerk of court not later than two days after the making of the decision in question.

---

6 Lord McCluskey and Paul McBride, *Criminal Appeals* (2nd edn, 2000) p 33.

These forms are skeletal but their most important aspect is probably the requirement to specify the grounds of the appeal. In *Templeton v HM Advocate*[7] an attempt was made to argue a ground of appeal which had not been specified in the note but the Appeal Court refused to entertain that argument. The particular point had been raised in the original minute of notice which led to the preliminary diet but had not been argued at the preliminary diet. Indeed Lord Clyde noted that the solicitor for the appellant had said at the preliminary diet that "it was not a line he was insisting upon". Lord Justice-Clerk Ross pointed out that such an appeal is an appeal against a decision at a preliminary diet and said that it was only the issue which had actually been decided at the preliminary diet which could be considered in the appeal. There is room for an attempt to distinguish this case where the person who argues the appellant's position at the preliminary diet does not explicitly abandon the line in question, though it is thought that the Appeal Court might not be especially sympathetic to such an attempt. Nor does *Templeton* say explicitly that grounds which were argued and decided at the preliminary diet but, *per incuriam*, omitted from the note of appeal will not be considered. There have been cases in other types of appeal, such as *Moffat v HM Advocate*,[8] in which submissions have been allowed to go beyond the stated grounds but both the High Court of Justiciary Practice Note of 29 March 1985[9] and judges of that court (in cases such as *Moffat* and *McAvoy v HM Advocate*[10]) have stressed the importance of the grounds of appeal not only to the Appeal Court but also to any judge who has to write a report for the Appeal Court.

Once the note of appeal has been lodged the clerk must request, and the judge at first instance provide, a report on the circumstances relating to the decision at the preliminary diet. A copy of the report is then sent to the parties.

Once the appeal has been heard, the Appeal Court may affirm the decision of the court of first instance or remit the case to it with appropriate directions. If the court of first instance has dismissed the indictment, complaint or part of it that decision may be reversed and the court of first instance may be directed to fix a trial diet.

Finally under this heading, it should be noted that all will not inevitably be lost if this procedure is not followed, however, because the opening words of both ss 74 and 174 expressly preserve other rights of appeal. Accordingly, in *Harvey v Lockhart*[11] the Appeal Court was prepared in the context of an appeal against conviction to hear submissions challenging a decision as to competency which had been made at a debate but not appealed at that time. The court did observe, however, that it was "in no doubt that the better method of proceeding in a case of this kind would have been for leave to appeal to have been sought before the plea was acted on".

There is an appeal from the High Court to the Supreme Court in connection with devolution issues. The rules are detailed and beyond the scope of this introductory text. They are set out in the Supreme Court Rules 2009[12] and summarised in Supreme Court Practice Direction 10.[13]

---

7 1987 SCCR 693.
8 1983 SCCR 21.
9 *Appeals in solemn procedure and appeals against sentence in summary procedure.*
10 1982 SCCR 271.
11 1991 SCCR 83.
12 SI 2009/1603 (L 17).
13 http://www.supremecourt.gov.uk/docs/pd10.pdf.

APPEALS AGAINST CONVICTION AND/OR SENTENCE

The Appeal Court's approach to the facts

We are concerned here with appeals by the convicted accused, either against that conviction itself or against the sentence imposed. Of course, a successful appeal against conviction will, by definition, carry with it the quashing of the sentence. What must be remembered at all times, however, is that it is not open to the Appeal Court to take a different view of the facts than was taken by the tribunal of fact—the jury in a case on indictment or the trial judge under summary procedure. In *McQuarrie v Carmichael*[14] the purported ground of appeal was that "police evidence at the time of the trial was untrue". Lord Justice-Clerk Ross explained that this is not a matter which can be brought under review in a stated case because the facts are a matter for the sheriff (and, by implication, for the sheriff alone). Similar reasoning may be applied to appeals from conviction by juries, with the added factor that, whereas a sheriff in a stated case sets out the facts he found proved, the jury never explains the process of reasoning by which it arrived at a verdict of guilty. Accordingly, even where the court is prepared to hear additional evidence, the quashing of a conviction will frequently be accompanied by the granting of authority for a new prosecution (though the Crown does not always in fact commence such a prosecution).

In *Al Megrahi v HM Advocate*[15] the Appeal Court approved of the way Lord Justice-Clerk Alness and Lord Anderson put matters in *Webb v HM Advocate*.[16] Lord Alness said:

> "This is not a court of review. Review, in the ordinary sense of that word, lies outside our province. We have neither a duty nor a right, because we might not have reached the same conclusion as the jury, to upset their verdict."

Lord Anderson expressed the point rather more fully:

> "[T]his Court will not re-try a case of this nature in the sense in which, in a civil process, a court of review deals with the decision of a judge of first instance. It is not the function of this Court, but of the jury, to weigh and balance testimony in an endeavour to ascertain, on quantitative or qualitative grounds, how it ought to preponderate. This Court, it is true, in an appeal on fact, is bound to read the evidence, but only for the purpose of deciding whether or not the verdict is unreasonable, or, to use a term familiar in civil procedure, perverse."

The court went on, in *Megrahi*, to say:

> "We have no doubt that, once evidence has been accepted by the trial court, it is for that court to determine what inference or inferences should be drawn from that evidence. If evidence is capable of giving rise to two or more possible inferences, it is for the trial court to decide whether an inference should be drawn and, if so, which inference. If, of course, the appeal court were satisfied that a particular inference drawn by the trial court was not a possible inference, in the sense that the drawing of such an inference was not open to the trial court on the evidence, that would be indicative of a misdirection and the appeal court would require to assess whether or not it had been material."

14 1989 SCCR 371.
15 2002 SCCR 509.
16 1927 JC 92; 1927 SLT 631.

Miscarriage of justice

It is fundamental that the matter for consideration by the Appeal Court in an appeal is whether or not there has been a miscarriage of justice. That is the expression used in the 1995 Act ss 106(3) and 175(5). Accordingly, it is not sufficient for the quashing of a conviction that there has been an error. As Lord Wheatley put it in *Hunter v HM Advocate*:[17]

> "an error in law by the trial judge in regard to the evidence of a witness does not *eo facto* necessarily lead to a granting of an appeal … the appellant has to show that the error resulted in a miscarriage of justice".

In that case, the court weighed the significance of evidence which had not been given as a result of an incorrect decision by the trial judge against the "virtually watertight" prosecution case and decided that the result would not have been affected. The evidence was said to be mitigatory only and the conviction upheld. Another example is to be found in *Blyth v HM Advocate*,[18] in which the trial judge indisputably erred in the direction he gave to the jury about the *mens rea* of rape but, because the issue was not actually one which had arisen in the evidence at the trial, the Appeal Court found that there was no miscarriage of justice and upheld the conviction.

Section 106(3) of the 1995 Act provides that the expression "any alleged miscarriage of justice" includes a miscarriage of justice based on the existence and significance of fresh evidence and a miscarriage based on the jury's having returned a verdict which no reasonable jury, properly directed, could have returned. We shall consider fresh evidence below. As to the reasonableness of the jury verdict, it is to be noted that this will sometimes require the trial judge to comment on the quality of the evidence, notwithstanding the general rule that credibility and reliability are for the jury alone. The test to be applied was stated in the opinion of the Appeal Court, delivered by the Lord Justice-General, in *Mitchell v HM Advocate*:[19]

> "Although in consideration of such a ground of appeal it may be necessary to consider individual items of evidence, it is important to notice that it is the verdict, that is, the conclusion on the whole evidence, which must be considered. Moreover the ground is only made out if no reasonable jury, properly directed, *could* have returned the verdict in question. … The test is objective. … This court is not entitled to quash the verdict of the jury merely because, on the basis of the record of the evidence, it would have reached a different view from that which the jury plainly reached" (emphasis in original).

Since at least *Anderson v HM Advocate*,[20] it has been open to a convicted person to appeal on the ground that there was such a defect in the way he was represented at trial that the trial was unfair and that there was, accordingly, a miscarriage of justice. The court emphasised in *Anderson* that it is not enough that a different lawyer might have gone about defending the case differently. In *Edwards v HM Advocate*,[21] Lord Nimmo Smith observed that most cases on defective representation are no more

---

17   1984 SCCR 306.
18   2005 SCCR 710.
19   2008 SCCR 469 at 521 (para 111).
20   1996 SCCR 114.
21   2009 SCCR 871.

than the application of the principles in *Anderson* to particular circumstances. In practice, what has to be established is that the defence was conducted in a way that no reasonable defence lawyer would have adopted or in a way that failed to follow the instructions of the client.

Procedure

Under solemn procedure the appeal is by note of appeal. Under summary procedure, the appeal is by stated case.

Under solemn procedure, by the 1995 Act s 106(1) a person who has been convicted on indictment may, with leave granted in accordance with the 1995 Act s 107, appeal to the High Court against:

(a) conviction;
(b) sentence;
(c) absolute discharge, admonition, probation, community service or deferred sentence; or
(d) both conviction and sentence or other disposal.

The direct equivalent of this for summary procedure is s 175(2).

Obviously, the first thing which a person who wishes to appeal will have to do is bring that fact to the attention of the court. Under solemn procedure, this is a two-stage process, the first stage being accomplished, in terms of the 1995 Act s 109, by the lodging with the Clerk of Justiciary of written intimation of intention to appeal. That intimation must be lodged within two weeks of the final determination of the proceedings and a copy must be sent to the Crown Agent. Application should be made at this point for any necessary interim orders (such as suspension of disqualification from driving).

Determination of the proceedings is defined by subsections (4) and (5) as occurring when sentence is pronounced or when sentence is first deferred. In terms of the 1995 Act s 111(2) and s 103(7) that period may be extended by a single judge and this was done in, for example, *Boyle v HM Advocate*.[22] As was made clear in *Clayton, Petitioner*,[23] the provisions allowing extensions of time limits in both solemn and summary appeals are not themselves subject to time limits and an application for an extension can therefore be made at any time.

The second stage under solemn procedure, in terms of the 1995 Act s 110, is the lodging with the Clerk of Justiciary of a written note of appeal. By s 110(1), that must be done within six weeks of the lodging of the intimation of intention to appeal. Sections 111 and 103 allow the extension of this period also. There is a practice whereby this six-week period is split into two periods of three weeks. The second three-week period is counted as starting when the transcript of the trial judge's charge is received (since the formulation of the definitive note of appeal is extremely difficult without that transcript).

The form for the note of appeal is set out in Form 15.2-B and its essence is a "full statement of all grounds of appeal", as s 110(3) requires. The importance of the grounds of appeal has already been mentioned in connection with appeals from preliminary diets and stands reiteration here. Submissions which go beyond

22 1976 SLT 126.
23 1991 SCCR 261.

the grounds specified cannot be heard except by leave of the High Court on cause shown. Moreover, inadequate grounds will at the very least irritate the judges who have to deal with the appeal. The Practice Note criticised in particular the bare assertions that there was "misdirection" or "insufficient evidence" without further specification. In *Smith v HM Advocate*[24] Lord Justice-General Emslie had the following to say:

> "The note of appeal tells us that the ground of appeal is 'Misdirection of jury by judge'. Now that, of course, is an irrelevant ground of appeal because it does not specify what the alleged misdirection is ... we are not disposed to entertain appeals containing an attack upon a judge's charge unless the alleged misdirection is clearly specified. There are several good reasons for that: (1) the Crown must have an opportunity to consider its position, (2) the judge must have an opportunity to explain and deal with the alleged misdirection and (3) this court must, in advance of the hearing, be in a position to examine the charge in light of the specific criticisms which are being made."

Similar comments were made in *Mitchell v HM Advocate*.[25]

There was some slight comfort for the appellants in both *Smith* and *Mitchell* in that the court observed in each case that so far as they could see there was no merit in the appeal anyway. However, if in any case there was a good point which the court refused to allow to be argued on the basis of the inadequacy of the grounds stated the result might well be that a conviction or sentence which should have been quashed would be allowed to stand with all that means. There has also to be borne in mind the fact that the content of the note of appeal will be a major factor in deciding whether or not leave to appeal is to be granted and there is therefore a substantial risk that inadequate grounds will provoke a refusal of leave to appeal.

The two stages in commencing an appeal under solemn procedure are, under summary procedure, combined into one. The provision relevant to appeals against conviction and to appeals against both conviction and sentence is s 176, subsection (1) of which provides for such appeals to be made by application for a stated case and demands that such an application should be made by lodging it with the clerk (of the court which convicted the appellant) within one week of the final determination of the proceedings. A copy is to be sent to the respondent and the application itself is to "contain a full statement of all the matters which the appellant desires to bring under review". The form is set out in Form 19.2-A. It is good practice to specify the matters to be reviewed distinctly and in separate paragraphs. Application should be made at this point for any necessary interim orders (such as suspension of disqualification from driving). It is open to the convicting court to grant bail pending the appeal.[26]

There is under summary procedure no equivalent to s 109(5) which defines the final determination of proceedings as occurring when sentence is first deferred. Rather, in *Walker v Gibb*[27] it was held that an appeal by stated case by a convicted accused upon whom sentence had been deferred was premature and incompetent because there had been no final determination of the prosecution. This principle finds statutory expression in the 1995 Act ss 194(3) and 202. The concept of

24 1983 SCCR 30.
25 1991 SCCR 216.
26 1995 Act s 77(1).
27 1965 SLT 2.

final determination was further refined in *Tudhope v Colbert and Another*[28] and *Tudhope v Campbell*,[29] in both of which it was held, on the basis of the statutory predecessor of the 1995 Act s 167, that the proceedings are not finally determined until particulars of conviction and sentence are entered in record of proceedings.

Smith v Gray[30] made it clear that the application must be in writing, and it was held in *Elliot, Applicant*[31] that the requirement to lodge the application with the clerk within one week means that it must be in his hands within that time and not merely posted. Comments in certain textbooks, based on another part of the decision in *Smith v Gray*, to the effect that posting is enough, were disapproved.

Consistent with practice as to other time limits, the date of the determination of the inferior judge is not counted as one of the days of the week allowed.[32]

Elliot concerned an application which was primarily directed to the obtaining of an extension of the one-week period, which is provided for by the 1995 Act s 181(1) and that extension was granted. Accordingly, it may be seen that, just as extensions may be obtained under solemn procedure, so they may be obtained under summary procedure and that missing a deadline will not inevitably prove fatal. However, it should also be borne in mind that the High Court is not obliged to grant such extensions and that the court might not look kindly on applications for extensions which have become necessary as a result of negligence or a cavalier approach to the requirements of the statute. (The time limits are, after all, there for a purpose.) In *Elliot* the textbook references mentioned above provided a substantial excuse for the failure to meet the deadline as it came to be interpreted by the court.

Just as the grounds of appeal are of great importance under solemn procedure, so the statement of matters desired to be brought under review is crucial in a summary appeal by stated case. The High Court pointed out in *Durant v Lockhart*[33] that the requirement to give a full statement of the matters to be brought under review was introduced:

> "so that the sheriff, when he stated the case, could be in no doubt as to what particular issue it was that the applicant was seeking to bring under review, and so that he could state in his findings in fact the matters which were appropriate to that issue".

From time to time, sheriffs have regarded their task as being made impossible by the inadequacy of the grounds in the application and so, in *Galloway v Hillary*,[34] for example, a sheriff refused to state a case on the basis that "insufficient evidence for conviction" was not a statement of matters but merely a "brute assertion". That the Appeal Court will support sheriffs who take such a position is clear from *Dickson v Valentine*[35] in which the appellant applied for a stated case giving as the ground of appeal "that the Sheriff erred in law", without any specification of how and in what respect he was said to have so erred. In the event, the sheriff stated a case, but the Appeal Court commented that he would have been well founded had he declined to do so and said that:

28 1978 SLT (Notes) 57.
29 1979 JC 24.
30 1925 JC 8.
31 1984 SCCR 125.
32 *Hutton v Garland* (1884) 5 Couper 274.
33 1986 SCCR 23.
34 1983 SCCR 119.
35 1988 SCCR 325.

"[Appellants] should understand in future that if they fail to comply with the provisions [requiring a full statement of all matters to be brought under review] the consequences may well be that either the sheriff will decline to state a case or that this court will decline to entertain the appeal."

The 1995 Act s 182(3) makes it incompetent for an appellant to found on any matter not contained in the application, and it is clear that the Appeal Court will not be endlessly indulgent with inadequately formulated applications. In *Anderson v McClory*[36] an attempt to argue a detailed point on the basis of a ground which simply invited the Appeal Court to consider whether, on the facts stated, the sheriff had been entitled to convict was rejected. The court held that this came "nowhere near" the specification required and refused to entertain the argument.

There is in the 1995 Act s 176(3) provision for the amendment of the application for a stated case, so that an application which is defective when lodged, either because it is unspecific or because it does not refer to a ground which it is hoped to argue, can be corrected. The alternative, following *Singh, Petitioner*,[37] is to lodge a second application within the permitted time, though this may be thought to be an unnecessarily cumbersome way of going about things.

Under both solemn and summary procedure, the application for the appeal will be passed to the trial judge. Under solemn procedure, in terms of the 1995 Act s 113(1) that judge is required, as soon as is reasonably practicable thereafter, to provide a written report giving an opinion on the case generally and on the grounds contained in the note of appeal in particular. The equivalent, under summary procedure, is the 1995 Act s 178 which requires the sheriff (or clerk to the JP court) to issue a draft stated case within three weeks of final determination of the proceedings. Form 19.2-B requires the trial judge to:

"state concisely and without argument the nature of the cause and the facts if any admitted or proved in evidence, any objections to the admission or rejection of evidence taken in the proof, the grounds of the decision and any other matters necessary to be stated for the information of the superior court".

Accordingly, the draft will set out the facts which the trial judge has found to be admitted or proved and not merely the statements of the witnesses[38] nor merely the questions and answers which were the subject of objection.[39] *Gordon v Allan*[40] is a particularly clear example of how a stated case should not be drafted. In that case, the appellant was convicted in a district court of assault. The case prepared was, according to Lord Justice-General Emslie, "woefully deficient in that it contained no findings in fact but merely a narration of evidence without any indication of the extent to which the justice accepted or rejected it". The Appeal Court at first remitted the case to the justice to prepare a proper stated case but his second effort was no better than his first and the court simply quashed the conviction, observing that:

"[I]t is no good writing a stated case and pretending that facts found can be discovered by a recitation of evidence. Findings in fact ought to be crisp, clear and certain, and if discussion of the evidence is relevant for the purposes of an appeal the place for that

---

36 1991 SCCR 571.
37 1986 SCCR 215.
38 *Gordon v Hansen* (1914) 7 Adam 441; *Pert v Robinson* 1955 SLT 23.
39 *Waddell v Kinnaird* 1922 JC 40.
40 1987 SLT 400.

discussion is in the note which follows the findings which, upon the evidence, the justice has found himself able to make."

It was made clear in *Bowman v Jessop*[41] that it is incorrect, in a case in which there has been a conviction, to confine the material in the stated case to that which is derived from the Crown case.

The grounds of the decision should be stated distinctly in the stated case so as to avoid the problem which occurred in *Lyon v Don Brothers Buist & Co*[42] in which the sheriff substitute, after setting forth the facts which were proved, stated merely that upon these facts he found the accused not guilty. In a prosecution under the Factories Acts, as that was, with somewhat complex relevant legislation, the Appeal Court's difficulties may be imagined.

The ground of decision is likely to be particularly important when evidence has been disallowed.[43]

There is provision for adjustment of the stated case, and this is to be found in the 1995 Act s 178. The parties have three weeks from the issue of the draft to propose adjustments or to state that they have no adjustments to propose. If the appellant fails to do either of these things he is deemed to have abandoned his appeal. If he is on bail, the convicting court has power to grant warrant for his apprehension and imprisonment.[44]

Where adjustments are proposed, the procedure is governed by the 1995 Act s 179. There is a hearing at which the parties may make representations to the trial judge. Thereafter, the stated case must be issued in its final form, within two weeks of the date of the hearing. There must be appended to it a note of any adjustment which has been proposed and which the trial judge has rejected, together with a note of any evidence rejected by the trial judge which is alleged to support the adjustment concerned and a note of the trial judge's reasons for rejecting that adjustment and evidence. There is also to be appended a note of the evidence on which the trial judge bases any finding in fact challenged as unsupported by the evidence.

The appellant must then lodge the stated case with the Clerk of Justiciary.

Leave to appeal

Before the appeal can go forward, leave from the appeal court is required. The procedure for obtaining that leave is set out in the 1995 Act ss 107 and 180. Essentially it involves a "sift" by a single judge of the High Court.

In terms of these provisions, a judge of the High Court is to consider the content of certain documents and, if he considers that the documents disclose arguable grounds of appeal, he is to grant leave to appeal. In any other case, he is to refuse leave to appeal, giving his reasons in writing (and granting warrant for arrest if the appellant is on bail pending appeal). A further application for leave may be made to the High Court within 14 days of refusal of leave by a single judge and, in that case, the application is dealt with by three judges.

Applications for leave either to a single judge or to three judges are dealt with in chambers and without the parties being present.

41 1989 SCCR 597.
42 1944 JC 1.
43 *Falconer v Brown* (1893) 1 Adam 96.
44 1995 Act s 77(5).

The documents which are to be considered upon an application for leave are set out in each subsection (2). In an appeal under solemn procedure, they are the note of appeal, a certified copy or the original of the record of proceedings, the trial judge's report and a transcript of the judge's charge to the jury if the notes have been extended. Under summary procedure, they are the stated case as issued and the complaint, productions and "other proceedings".

The test to be applied is whether the documents disclose arguable grounds of appeal and this is not a high hurdle. The legislation does not require the judge considering whether or not to grant leave to form any view on the likelihood that the appeal will succeed. It is enough that it is stateable. If the test is passed, the judge is to grant leave and "make such comments in writing as he considers appropriate". In any other case, he is to refuse leave, giving his reasons in writing, and, where the appellant is on bail and the sentence in the case appealed is one of imprisonment, grant a warrant for arrest. The warrant does not take effect for 14 days to allow for appeal to a bench of three judges.

Additional evidence

In some cases, under both solemn and summary procedure, the defence desires to lay further evidence before the court in support of the appeal. It is competent for the Appeal Court to hear such evidence but the circumstances in which it will choose to do so are rather limited.

The starting-point is the 1995 Act ss 106(3) and 175(5), which make identical provision for solemn and summary procedure respectively. In terms of these sections, a person may bring under review of the Appeal Court any alleged miscarriage of justice, including any such miscarriage based on "the existence and significance of fresh evidence which was not heard at the original proceedings". This is qualified by subsection (3A), which provides that such evidence may only found an appeal where there is a reasonable explanation of why it was not heard in the original proceedings.

The requirement that the evidence must not have been heard at the trial is, on the face of it, obvious, but the court has had to deal with certain refinements. The first of these is the meaning of the word "evidence", and in *White v HM Advocate*[45] the question related to a person referred to in the appellant's defence at the trial who had not been available to be identified by witnesses. The same person was later traced. The Appeal Court held that since what was in issue was not the person's evidence but his presence at the trial there was no question of his evidence having a bearing on the verdict and it was not in the interests of justice to allow his evidence to be led.

Assuming that what is proffered actually is evidence, it was made clear in *Maitland v HM Advocate*[46] that the court will decline to hear it if it merely adds to evidence already given. This rule was derived from *Temple v HM Advocate*[47] in which the court had refused to allow additional evidence to be led to supplement evidence given at trial in support of an alibi.

This whole area of law was the subject of several cases and some confusion during the late 1990s and the Appeal Court took the opportunity in *Kidd v HM*

---

45 1989 SCCR 553.
46 1992 SCCR 759.
47 1971 JC 1.

Advocate[48] to state the essential principles succinctly. Most fundamentally, the "governing question" is whether the fact that the additional evidence was not heard at the trial represented a miscarriage of justice, because that is the test set out in the 1995 Act s 106(3)(a). The question for the Appeal Court, therefore, is whether the additional evidence is of such significance as to lead to the conclusion that a verdict returned in ignorance of it must be regarded as a miscarriage of justice. It is not enough to say that the additional evidence has some significance.

In applying this (somewhat demanding) test, the Appeal Court will pay close attention to the quality of the additional evidence. The court said in *Kidd* that it would require to be satisfied that the evidence must be capable of being regarded by a reasonable jury as credible and reliable.

As summarised by the court in *Al Megrahi v HM Advocate*,[49] the law is as follows:

(1) The court may allow an appeal against conviction on any ground only if it is satisfied that there has been a miscarriage of justice.

(2) In an appeal based on the existence and significance of additional evidence not heard at the trial, the court will quash the conviction if it is satisfied that the original jury, if it had heard the new evidence, would have been bound to acquit.

(3) Where the court cannot be satisfied that the jury would have been bound to acquit, it may nevertheless be satisfied that a miscarriage of justice has occurred.

(4) Since setting aside the verdict of a jury is no light matter, before the court can hold that there has been a miscarriage of justice it will require to be satisfied that the additional evidence is not merely relevant but also of such significance that it will be reasonable to conclude that the verdict of the jury, reached in ignorance of its existence, must be regarded as a miscarriage of justice.

(5) The decision on the issue of the significance of the additional evidence is for the appeal court, which will require to be satisfied that it is important and of such a kind and quality that it was likely that a reasonable jury properly directed would have found it of material assistance in its consideration of a critical issue at the trial.

(6) The appeal court will therefore require to be persuaded that the additional evidence is (a) capable of being regarded as credible and reliable by a reasonable jury, and (b) likely to have had a material bearing on, or a material part to play in, the determination by such a jury of a critical issue at the trial.

Powers of court

The powers of the court in dealing with appeals are dealt with primarily by the 1995 Act ss 118 and 183. The Appeal Court may dispose of an appeal against conviction by affirming the verdict of the trial court (ie refusing the appeal), by setting aside the verdict of the trial court and either quashing the conviction or substituting an amended verdict of guilty, or by setting aside the verdict of the

---

48 2000 SLT 1068.
49 2002 SCCR 509.

trial court and granting authority to bring a new prosecution. In addition, under summary procedure, the Appeal Court may dispose of a stated case by remitting the cause to the inferior court with an opinion and a direction as to how to proceed. So, for example, in *Aitchison v Rizza*,[50] where a sheriff had erred in finding that there was no case to answer, the Appeal Court remitted the case to him with a direction to proceed as accords, by which was meant that he should continue with the trial as if he had held that there *was* a case to answer.

If the Appeal Court substitutes an amended verdict of guilty it must ensure that the amended verdict is one which could have been returned on the indictment or complaint before the trial court.

The setting aside of a conviction will obviously have a bearing on the sentence. Where the whole conviction on the indictment is set aside, the whole sentence will fall with it. However, where a conviction is only partly set aside, either because convictions remain on other charges on the indictment or because an amended verdict of guilty is substituted, the sentence might well become inappropriate. Accordingly, the Appeal Court is empowered, in setting aside a verdict, to quash any sentence imposed on the appellant as respects the indictment or complaint and pass another sentence. That sentence, however, must not be more severe than the original sentence.

Authority for a new prosecution is provided for by the 1995 Act ss 118(1)(c) and 183(1)(d), the procedure being regulated by ss 119 and 185. Where such authority is granted, a new prosecution may be brought charging the accused with the same or any similar offence arising out of the same facts. However, by each subsection (2) the accused cannot be charged with an offence more serious than that of which he was convicted in the earlier proceedings and, by each subsection (3), no sentence may be passed on conviction under the new prosecution which could not have been passed on conviction under the earlier proceedings.

Subsection (4) of each section disapplies any time limit which would ordinarily apply to the case but by each subsection (5) the new prosecution must be commenced within two months of the date on which authority to bring the prosecution was granted, otherwise the setting aside of the conviction by the Appeal Court operates as a complete acquittal.

It is not in every case that the court will grant authority for a new prosecution. In particular, where the Crown has contributed to the error which resulted in the miscarriage of justice, the court may be slow to give the Crown a second bite at the cherry. Where, however, the mistake was solely that of the trial judge there is a greater chance of authority being granted. So in *McGhee v HM Advocate*[51] the Appeal Court said that as the miscarriage of justice arose from comments made by the judge and as there was no suggestion that there was any insufficiency of evidence, authority should be given for a new prosecution.

Greater detail was given of the reasoning which led to the granting of authority to bring a new prosecution in *Wilkinson v HM Advocate*.[52] There, Lord Justice-General Hope said:

> "This was a case where the misdirection arose solely out of a decision taken by the sheriff himself. There was nothing done by the Crown, so far as we have been told, which in any way contributed to his decision. The events which were the subject of the charge

50 1985 SCCR 297.
51 1991 SCCR 510.
52 1991 SCCR 856.

... are of relatively recent happening. There is nothing in the facts or circumstances to suggest that it would be contrary to the public interest that a fresh prosecution should be brought."

This should not, of course, be construed as an exhaustive list of the criteria which the Appeal Court will regard as relevant but it is probably a good working guide.

APPEALS AGAINST SENTENCE ALONE

In an appeal by a convicted person against sentence (but not conviction), the issues are much simpler than those involved in an appeal against conviction and the procedure to some extent reflects that relative simplicity.

Under solemn procedure, by the 1995 Act s 110(1)(a), an appeal against sentence alone commences with the lodging of a written note of appeal with the Clerk of Justiciary within two weeks of the passing of sentence. The preliminary step of lodging intimation of intention to appeal does not apply. Thereafter, the appeal proceeds under the same rules as an appeal against conviction or conviction and sentence.

Under summary procedure, an appeal against sentence alone does not proceed by stated case. Instead, the 1995 Act ss 175(9), 186, 187, 189, 190 and 192 provide for a note of appeal against sentence. The form of the note is set out in Form 19.3-A and the note must, by s 186(2), be lodged with the clerk of the court which passed sentence within one week of the passing of the sentence or of the order deferring sentence which is appealed against. The sentencer then prepares a report for the Appeal Court. Section 187 makes provision as to leave to appeal which is equivalent to that for appeals against conviction.

By the 1995 Act s 118(4) and s 189 the Appeal Court may dispose of an appeal against sentence by affirming the sentence or, if it thinks that, having regard to all the circumstances, a different sentence should have been passed, by quashing the sentence and passing another sentence. However, it is very important to note that the sentence will not necessarily be reduced in such a case. The Appeal Court has the power to increase it (though it does so quite rarely nowadays).

This argues for a certain caution in pursuing appeals against sentence, not least because, where the conviction was on indictment in the sheriff court, the Appeal Court is not bound by the sheriff court sentencing limits. In *O'Neil v HM Advocate*[53] the appellant had been sentenced to the then sheriff court maximum of two years in a young offenders' institution for armed robbery. The Appeal Court, having evidently given the appellant (who was representing himself) fair warning of what was likely to happen if he pressed the appeal, said that two years was "grossly inadequate" and substituted a sentence of five years.

CROWN APPEALS

There are two situations in which the Lord Advocate can bring a matter before the Appeal Court under solemn procedure. Under summary procedure the prosecutor (who is, of course, almost always the procurator fiscal) can appeal by stated case on a point of law against either an acquittal or the sentence passed. These Crown rights of appeal have in the past been used very sparingly but their incidence has increased recently .

Lord Advocate's Reference

The first situation is provided for by the 1995 Act s 123 which permits the Lord Advocate to refer to the High Court a point of law which has arisen in relation to a charge (on indictment) of which the accused has been acquitted or convicted. A copy of the reference is to be sent by the Clerk of Justiciary to the accused and to his solicitor and the accused is entitled to be represented. However, in terms of subsection (5) the opinion on the point of law does not affect any acquittal at the trial.

The procedure has been used to establish, for example, that the law relating to admissibility of alleged confessions by an accused is irrelevant to the matter of admissibility in a perjury trial[54] and that to brandish an imitation firearm and demand money is assault even if meant as a joke.[55] We have already noticed *Lord Advocate's Reference (No 1 of 1992)*[56] when dealing with hearsay and documentary evidence. At the time of writing, the most recent use of the procedure was to clarify the law of rape.[57]

Lord Advocate's appeal against sentence

The second situation concerns the Lord Advocate's appeal against sentence under the 1995 Act ss 108 and 175(4A). In terms of those sections, where a person has been convicted, the Lord Advocate may appeal against the sentence passed on conviction (or against probation etc) if it appears to him that the disposal is unduly lenient or on a point of law. The expression "unduly lenient" means that the sentence fell outside the *range* of sentences which the sentencing judge could reasonably have considered appropriate.[58] It does *not* mean that the sentence is merely more lenient than the Appeal Court would itself have selected.[59]

Stated case

So far as summary procedure is concerned, the procurator fiscal's right to apply for a stated case may be used where the Crown considers that, on the facts established, the sheriff has acquitted incorrectly as a result of misdirecting himself in law. The Crown can also appeal where the sheriff has failed to comply with the requirements of the law in relation to the sentence imposed. Provision is made in the 1995 Act s 175(4) for the Crown to appeal against an unduly lenient sentence but only in relation to classes of case specified by Order in Council. No such classes have been specified at the time of writing and such appeals are, therefore, not further considered in this book.

---

54 *Lord Advocate's Reference (No 1 of 1985)* 1987 SLT 187.
55 *Lord Advocate's Reference (No 2 of 1992)* 1992 SCCR 960.
56 1992 SCCR 724.
57 *Lord Advocate's Reference (No 1 of 2001)* 2002 SLT 466.
58 *HM Advocate v Bell* 1995 SCCR 244.
59 *HM Advocate v Gordon* 1996 SCCR 274.

Many summary appeals by the Crown relate to cases in which it has been held that there is no case to answer, since such a decision is a matter of pure law which has resulted in an acquittal. In such cases, as *Keane v Bathgate*[60] makes clear, the traditional approach to stated cases, described above, by which findings in fact are made, is inappropriate. As the High Court noted in that case, the decision in relation to a submission of no case to answer does not in itself require the sheriff to decide the facts. As will be recalled, the effect of *Williamson v Wither*[61] is that the question for the court is whether there is no evidence which if accepted will entitle the court to proceed to conviction. Reflecting this, the Appeal Court said in *Keane v Bathgate* that:

> "in setting out the case for an appeal where the [no case to answer] procedure has been successfully invoked the proper thing for the court to do is simply to set out the evidence which has been adduced by the prosecution and any inferences drawn therefrom for arriving at the decision".

BILLS OF ADVOCATION AND BILLS OF SUSPENSION

Bills of advocation and bills of suspension are remedies which are directed essentially to procedural disasters, usually of a fairly fundamental kind (though this is a working guide and not a proposition of law). Although often regarded as mirror images of one another, they in fact have differing scope and are available at different stages.

Advocation

The bill of advocation is available to both prosecution and defence[62] and in both solemn and summary proceedings. The prosecutor can use it even in relation to the High Court itself, where it sits as a court of first instance. It is also available at any stage of proceedings. Advocation is the calling up or removal of a cause from an inferior to a superior court but its sphere is limited to the correction of irregularities in the preliminary stages of a case.[63] Although the judicial view in the late 1960s seems to have been that the bill of advocation was falling into disuse as a result of the introduction of the stated case, the remedy has since enjoyed something of a renaissance, with the Crown using it, for example, where a warrant has been wrongfully refused.[64] It has been used by the defence where a sheriff continued a part heard trial for eight days with the accused in custody even though the 40-day time limit for commencing the trial had expired,[65] where a sheriff adjourned a trial part heard by another sheriff who had been taken seriously ill[66] and where it was sought to challenge a sheriff's decision to allow an amendment of the Complaint so as to insert the accused's correct name.[67] In none of these cases was it said that the competency of the procedure was in doubt, though the outcomes cannot be said to be encouraging for defence use of the procedure.

60 1983 SLT 651.
61 1981 SCCR 216.
62 See *Durant v Lockhart* 1985 SCCR 72.
63 *MacLeod v Levitt* 1969 JC 16.
64 *McNeill, Complainer* 1984 SLT 157.
65 *Grugen v Jessop* 1988 SCCR 182.
66 *Platt v Lockhart* 1988 SCCR 308.
67 *Hoyers (UK) Ltd v Houston* 1991 SCCR 919.

Suspension

The classic definition of a bill of suspension is Lord Wheatley's in *McGregor v MacNeill*:[68]

> "Suspension is a competent method of review, available in summary proceedings only[69] when some step in the procedure has gone wrong or some factor has emerged which satisfies the court that a miscarriage of justice has taken place resulting in a failure to do justice to the accused."

Suspension, then, is available only to the accused and, in terms of the 1995 Act s 130, only in summary cases. It is a process whereby a warrant, conviction or judgment issued by an inferior judge may be reviewed. It follows that such a warrant, conviction or judgment must exist and that suspension is incompetent before such a warrant, conviction or judgment actually exists. This was the issue in *Durant v Lockhart*[70] in which an attempt was made to take a bill of suspension against a sheriff's decision to adjourn a trial diet, but was refused as incompetent. This is not to say, however, that it is only available after the final determination of proceedings. It was used in *Stuart v Crowe*[71] to attack search warrants obtained by the police and upon which the Crown intended to found at the forthcoming trial and, although the attack failed on its merits, the appropriateness of the procedure was not disputed.

Procedure

The procedure under bills of suspension and bills of advocation is the same. The bill is lodged at Justiciary Office and then placed before a single judge of the High Court for an order for service. If that judge thinks that the bill discloses no substantial ground of appeal, he is entitled to remit the bill to a quorum of the High Court who may, if it agrees with the single judge, refuse the bill then and there. Where, however, the single judge considers that the bill is not clearly without substance he will grant an order for service and the bill is then served upon the opponent. The clerk will also send a copy to the judge whose decision is being challenged. The opponent will then lodge answers and, as in civil pleadings, the effect of those answers will be to identify the areas of disagreement (if any) as to the facts. Lord Justice-General Emslie said in *Neilands v Leslie*[72] that where there is a conflict between the bill and the answers, the court will usually accept the answers. In this regard it is appropriate to recall that, whilst the Appeal Court is not bound to follow the Lord Advocate's account of the facts of a matter, it does treat it with considerable respect, as appears from the judgment in *Bennet v HM Advocate*.[73]

There is a three-week time limit for the lodging of a bill of advocation or suspension.[74]

---

68 1975 JC 57.
69 The 1995 Act s 130 gives statutory form to this restriction.
70 1986 SCCR 23.
71 1992 SCCR 181.
72 1973 SLT (Notes) 32.
73 1994 SCCR 902.
74 1995 Act s 191A.

Index

DG9 7AA
Lewis Sc.